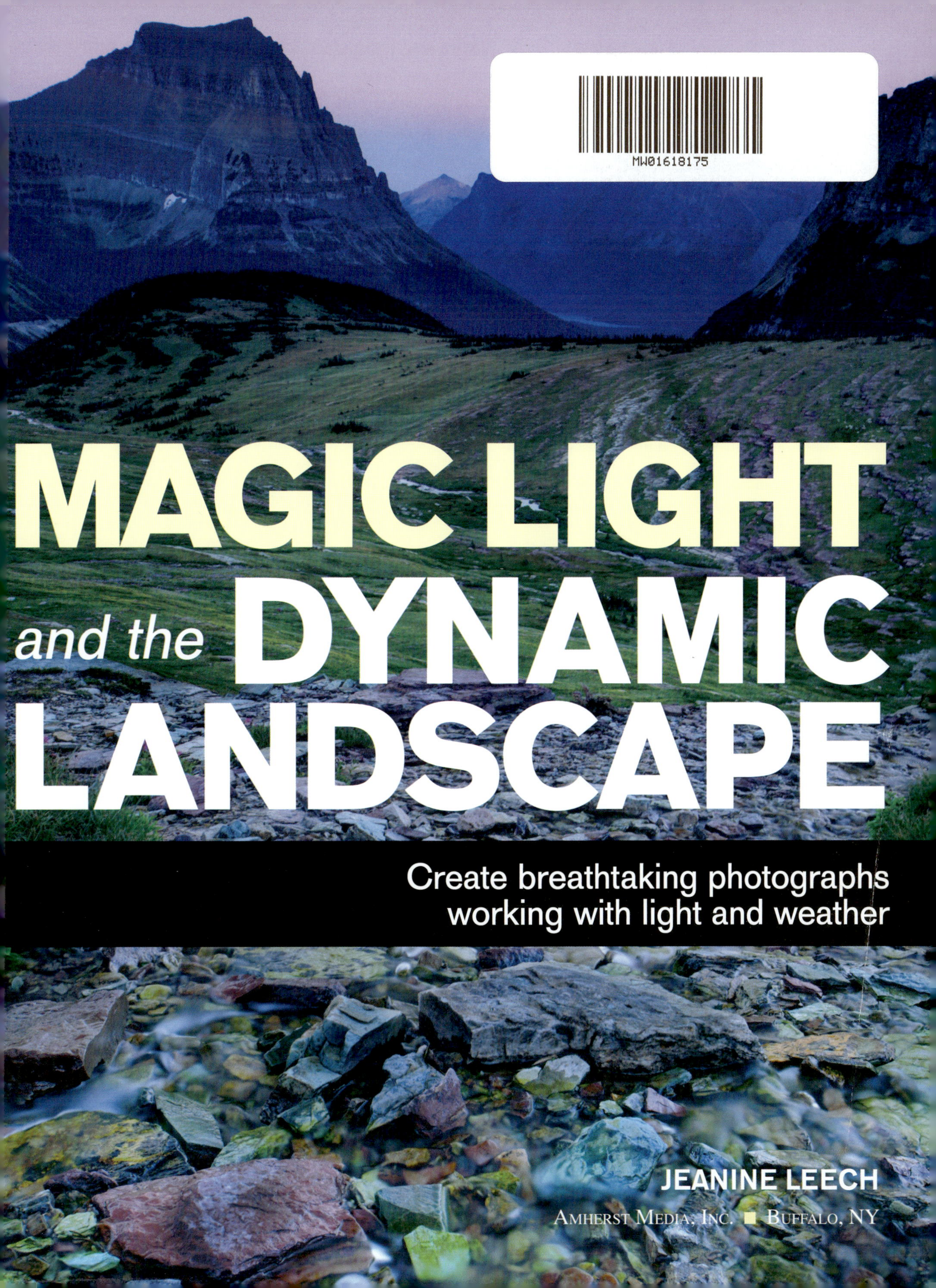

MAGIC LIGHT and the DYNAMIC LANDSCAPE

Create breathtaking photographs working with light and weather

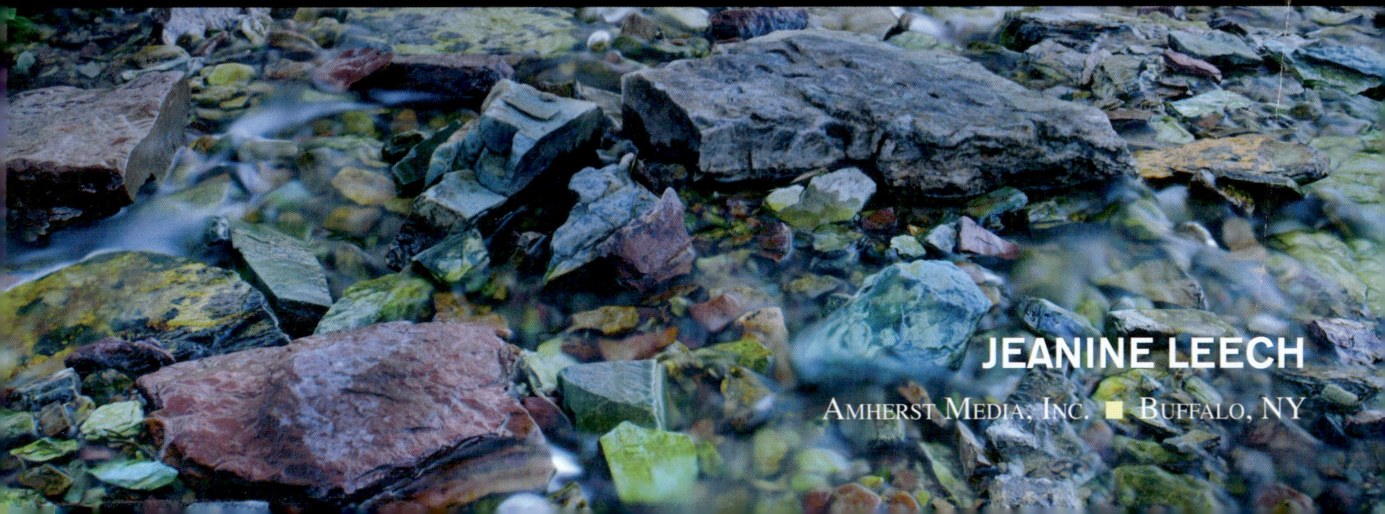

JEANINE LEECH

AMHERST MEDIA, INC. ■ BUFFALO, NY

DEDICATION

I'd like to dedicate this book to the spirit of Nancy Rotenberg, who not only taught me photography but gave me wings to fly and discover my own journey in photography and the creative life. She was an amazing woman, mentor, photographer and, most of all, friend.

Published by:
Amherst Media, Inc.
P.O. Box 586
Buffalo, N.Y. 14226
Fax: 716-874-4508
www.AmherstMedia.com

Publisher: Craig Alesse
Senior Editor/Production Manager: Michelle Perkins
Editors: Barbara A. Lynch-Johnt, Harvey Goldstein, Beth Alesse
Editorial Assistance from: Carey A. Miller, Sally Jarzab, John S. Loder
Associate Publisher: Kate Neaverth
Business Manager: Adam Richards
Warehouse and Fulfillment Manager: Roger Singo

ISBN-13: 978-1-60895-729-3
Library of Congress Control Number: 2013952503
10 9 8 7 6 5 4 3 2 1

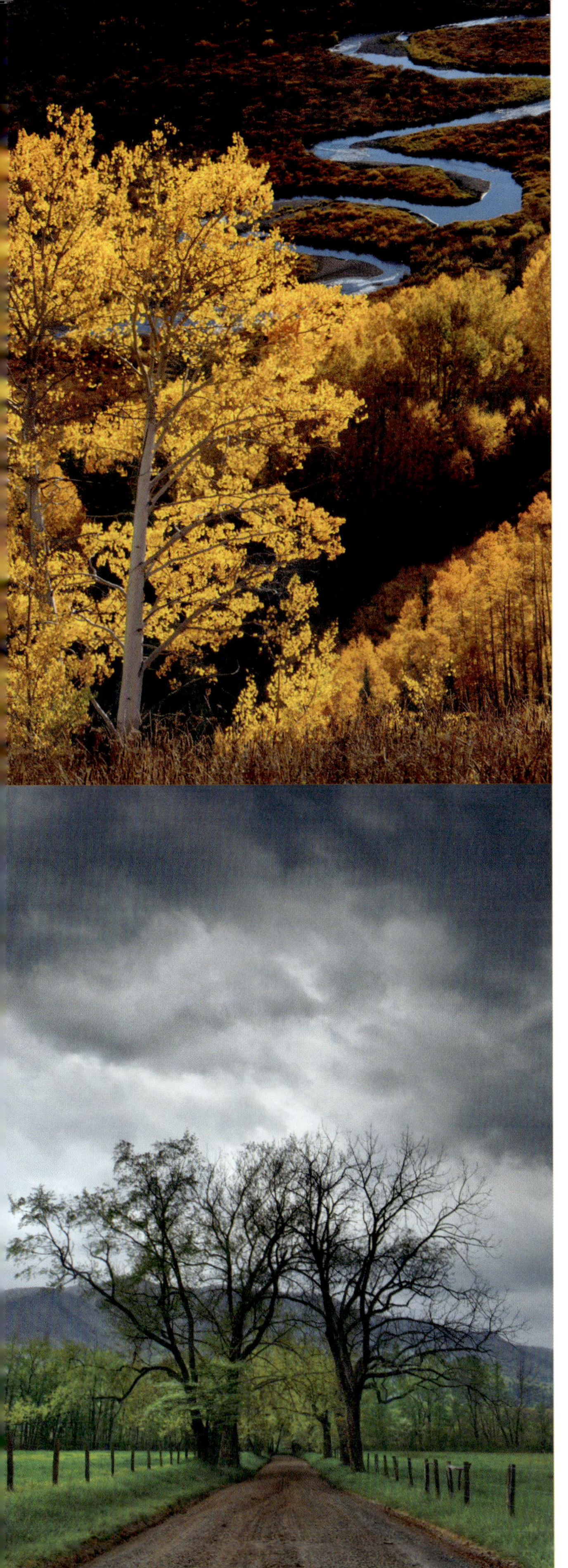

CONTENTS

ABOUT THE AUTHOR

The person we hope to become lives inside each of us. We don't all get there, but we must never stop trying. The hardest part of writing a book has been writing the bio. Talking about magic light is one thing, and talking about myself is another!

As a child, if I wasn't outside playing, I was drawing. My mother, a fine painter and avid photographer, swears that my first-grade teacher raved about my natural sense of composition. My father, a computer repairman, taught me the benefits of hard work and attention to detail. My two older brothers let me tag along through the woods, climbing rock walls and wading hip deep in creeks while keeping lunch dry. I see now that my childhood was basic training for landscape photography. At age fourteen, I saved my money and bought a Pentax K-1000 camera, and photography became my passion.

I graduated from high school knowing that inside of me was a photographer wanting to get out. I earned a degree in Visual Communications from the Art Institute of Pittsburgh in 1987. I soon found myself, the child of a man who worked in the digital world and a woman who worked in the arts, employed as a graphic designer and riding the wave of desktop publishing. Life was good, the camera went digital, I went Nikon, and I never stopped wanting to be a photographer.

It wasn't until 1995 that I stopped wanting to become a photographer and found the courage to *become* that photographer. I owe a tremendous debt to the late photographer Nancy Rotenberg and will forever cherish the years I spent by her side. She taught me how to see light and all the magic that can be squeezed out of it from behind the camera but, more importantly, she also showed me how to ignite my artistic vision and create captivating art. She helped me to realize that it is the uniqueness of the artist that matters, and we all need to follow our own path.

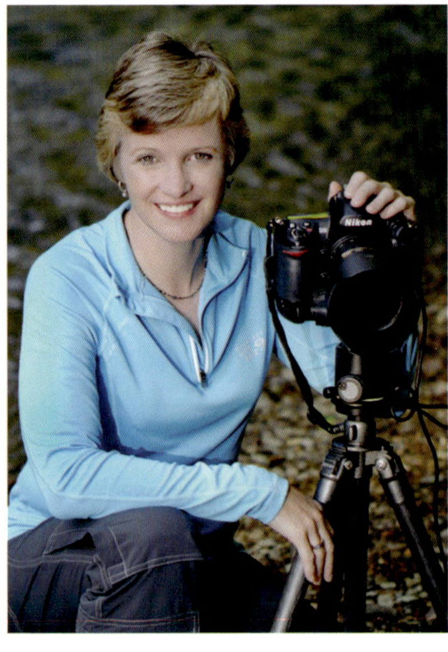

Photo by Chris Keys.

My images have appeared in national and international magazines, they adorn the luxury boxes at the home of the Pittsburgh Penguins Hockey Club, and I have written my own book. I have been honored to win awards in both design and photography, and I am grateful for the support of family, friends, coworkers, and fellow photographers for letting me be me.

For more information and to view my latest work, please visit my web site at photos.jeanineleech.com or 500px.com/JeanineLeech.

ACKNOWLEDGMENTS

I'd like to acknowledge my mom, Mary Lou Smith, for passing along her love of art and photography and encouraging me to pursue my own path.

Thanks go out to my dad and my brothers, Ken and Denny, for all their love, support, and encouragement of my art through the years.

I am also grateful to Michael Lustbader for all his photographic support, help, and advice. He is always ready to lend a hand (or equipment) and share his mobile library. I am forever grateful for his friendship.

Special thanks to Perri (and Tom) Schelat for opening their home to me. Due to their generosity, I was able to experience the trip of a lifetime. Perri and I hiked to new heights to capture the beautiful scenery of Glacier National Park with our cameras. We had great fun, and I thank her for sharing some of her favorite spots with me.

Linda Torbert, my on-the-road roomie, and I laughed and giggled on several trips. Linda has the biggest heart of anyone I know, and I treasure the times we've spent together.

To Matt Polk, thank you for making my dreams to photograph the Pittsburgh Penguins Hockey Club come true.

Thanks go out to Robert Agnew for the guided tours in the Smoky Mountains and Colorado.

My gratitude goes out to Art Becker for recognizing my talent and passing the word along to others. Although we just met, I value his kind words and practical advice.

Thank you, Jim McNutt, for telling me I'm the best photographer, hands down. (I wish that was true!)

I am honored to have had the help of Jennifer Costa, who has edited my previous writing (too many times) without hesitation.

Thanks to you, Chris Ciardi, for encouraging me to pursue my dreams.

And finally, thanks to Amherst Media for allowing me the opportunity to share my knowledge and images so that other photographers can capture magic too.

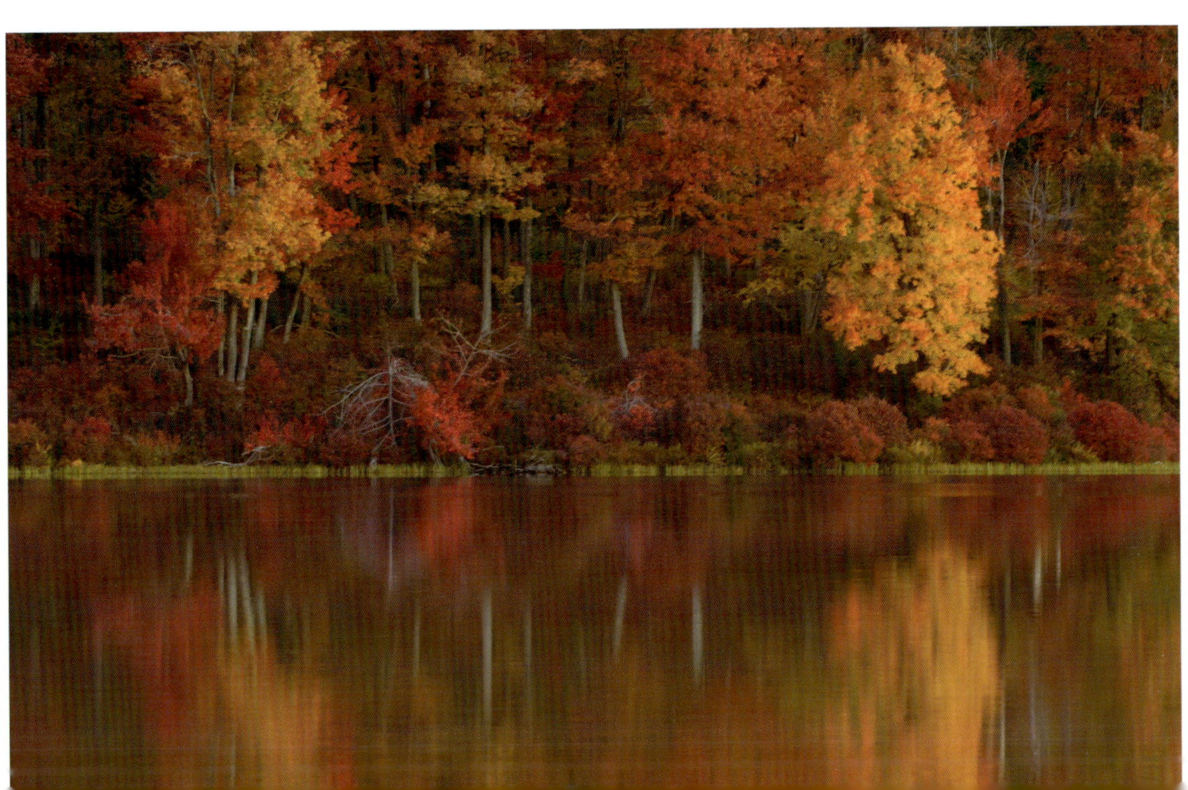

PART ONE: INTRODUCTION

1. MOMENTS OF MAGIC LIGHT

You've probably heard it said many times that photography is painting with light or that photography is all about light. It's true. The artist inside me loves the idea of painting with light. I use it as a brush for color, texture, and dimension to create dynamic and expressive images. Once you learn to see the light and "read" how your camera will record it, you can move beyond the ordinary image to the dynamic.

▼ Sunlight breaks through the clouds for a fleeting moment to light up and isolate a group of trees from the mountainside.

FOCAL LENGTH: 58mm | ISO: 100 | APERTURE: f/20 | SHUTTER SPEED: 1/5 second

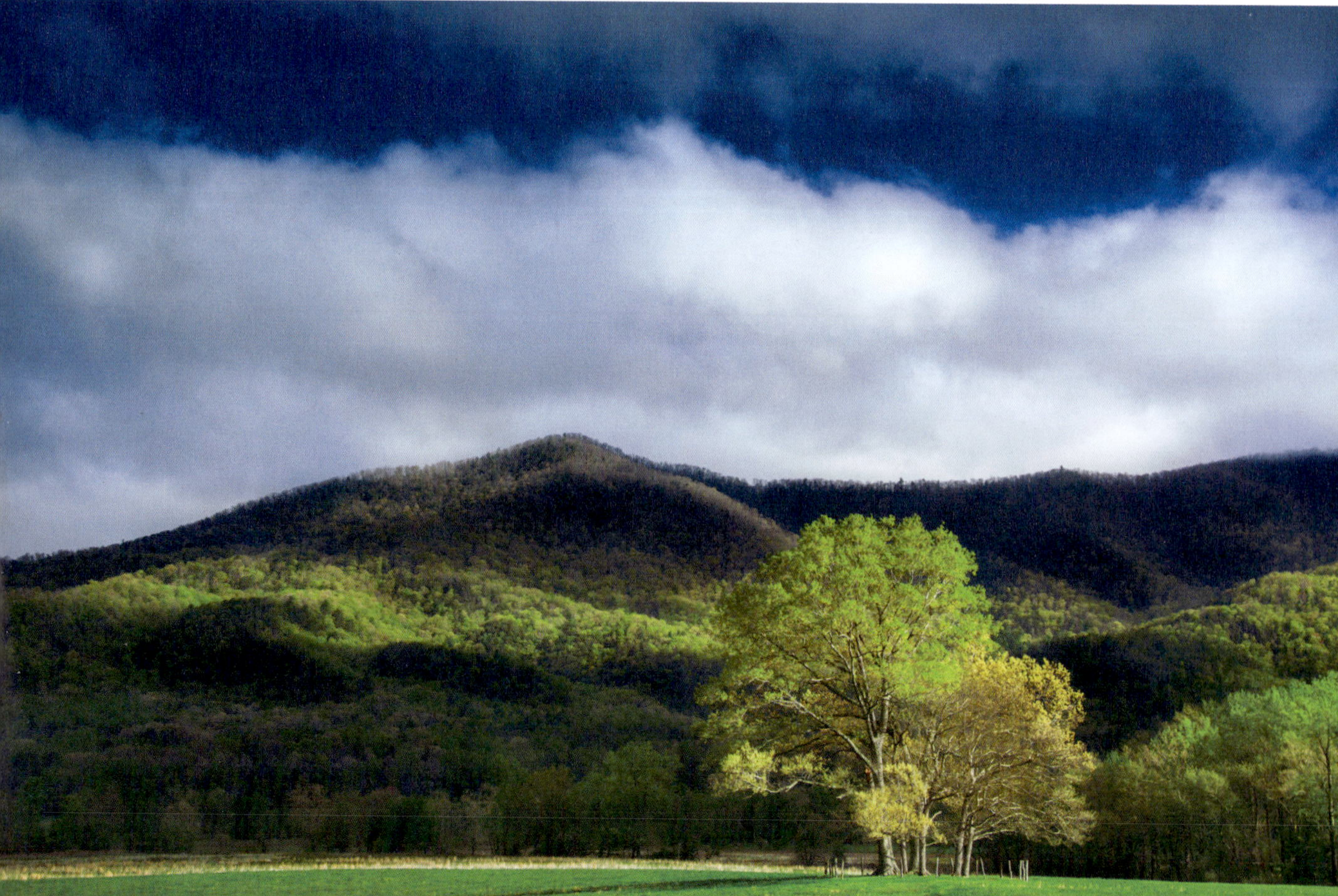

▶ A yellow Adirondack boathouse glows for a few seconds in the warm light of golden hour.

FOCAL LENGTH: 125mm | ISO: 100 | APERTURE: f/22
SHUTTER SPEED: 1.3 second

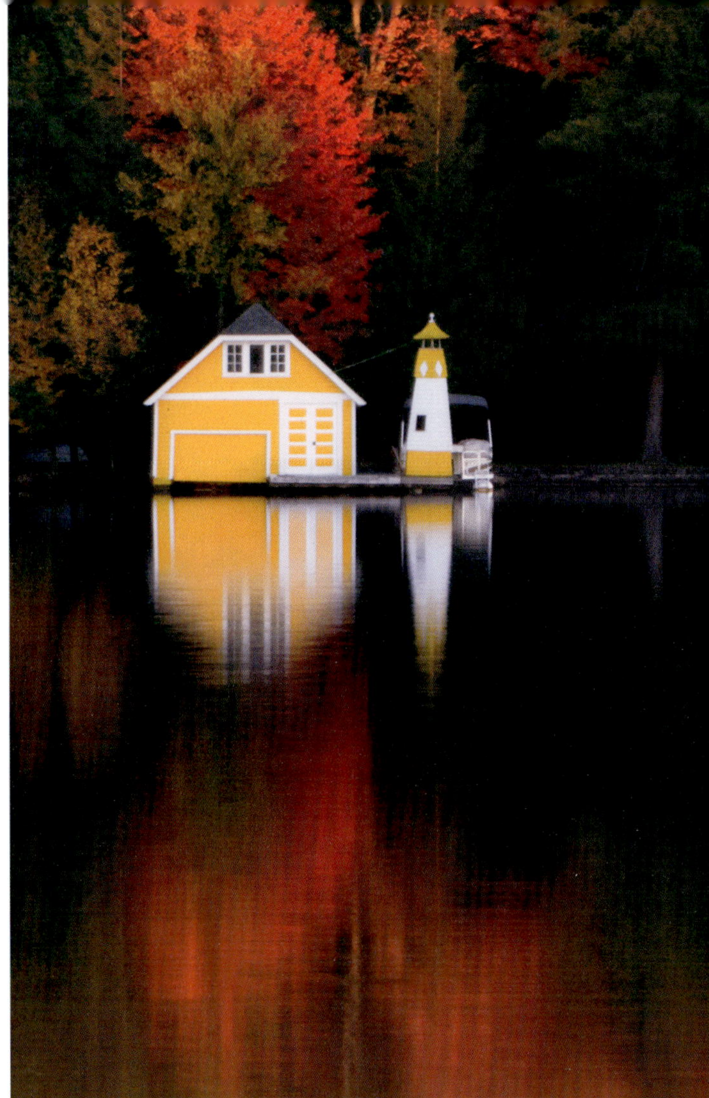

The light at the edges of the day—the time between darkness and the beginning or end of daylight—provides the most opportunities for magic light. The keen photographer will soon see that magic light can be found at other times of the day also. Have you ever noticed how dramatic the sky can be before or after a storm? The deep blues and dark grays of the sky work beautifully with the light on the land. The fleeting light we are after lasts only a few minutes (or seconds), lighting up a single tree, casting a beautiful golden glow on a boathouse, or shimmering through a snow squall over the mountain ridge.

This light creates texture and color so stunning and intense that I have been known to make sudden stops or U-turns to capture the fleeting moment. These moments of extraordinary light get the heart pumping and blood flowing. It makes photography exhilarating. Peak action happens not only in sports (my other favorite type of photography) but also in nature. The light can change within seconds, and the best light may occur only in a single frame amidst multiple captures. All of my photographic training and experience becomes instinctual in this moment. I rely on it to create dramatic images. I've learned to recognize the quality of light, react to it, and successfully record it. You can too, and this book will help.

"Capitaliz[e] on that magical light when and where you find it. But don't get greedy. If you get your hopes up that the perfect light is right around the corner, you're bound to be constantly disappointed. Instead, keep an open mind, polish those off-hour shooting skills, and be ready to work with the tiniest bit of perfect light whenever you might find it."[1]

David Stoecklein
Master photographer of the American West

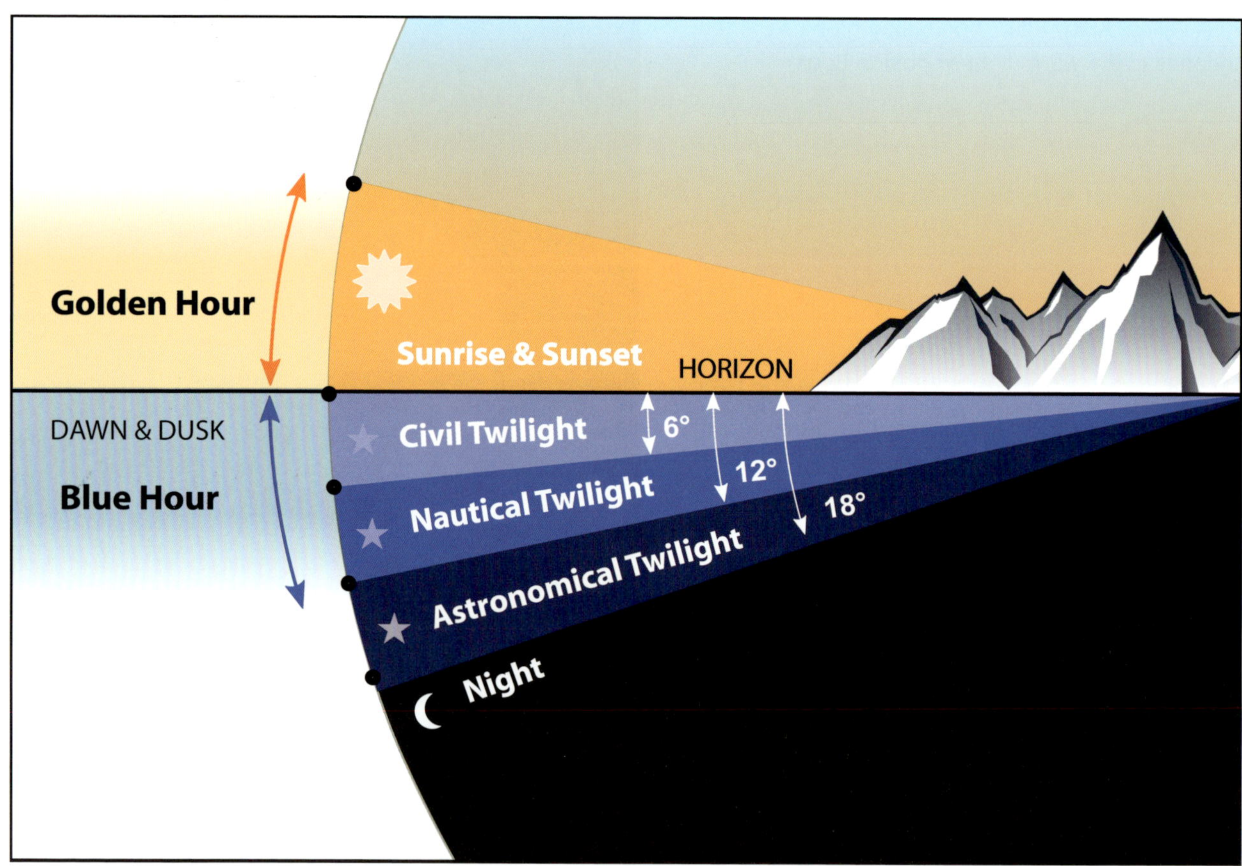

▲ The cycle of light and the terms associated with twilight are the same at sun up or sun down—only the order of the cycle changes.

Capturing the moment requires fast action and a thorough knowledge of your equipment. You need to be able to set up fast. Being able to set up and shoot within seconds can be critical to getting the shot. After years of field experience, my camera's buttons and controls have become an extension of my own hand and eye; this allows me to work quickly.

ALONG THE HORIZON

The edges of the day—when the sun crosses the horizon—is a great time to find magic light. This light is often colorful, moody, and unlike that found at any other time of day. It changes quickly as the first light of the day is revealed or the last remaining rays of light illuminate the sky before the sun drops below the horizon and twilight begins.

There are scientific definitions for the changes in the angle of the sun as it moves along the horizon. These changes affect the quality of light as night turns into day and vice-versa.

THE CHANGING ANGLE OF THE SUN

■ THE GOLDEN HOUR

During the first hour after sunrise and in the last hour before sunset, the sky is full of rich warm golden tones. Photographers call this time period the *golden hour* or *magic hour.* With the low angle of the sun, the quality of light at this time is fantastic. The golden hues and long, soft shadows enhance texture and shapes without harsh shadows or bright highlights. This warm glow is great for landscapes, portraits, and cityscapes.

Sunrise and Sunset

The instant the leading edge of the sun appears on the horizon, *sunrise* begins. *Sunset* is defined as the time when the upper portion of the sun falls below the horizon. During these events, the colors in the sky start to transition from blues and violets to warm yellow, orange, and gold tones. The sun's rays travel longer distances at sunrise and sunset and therefore pass through more airborne particles that cause them to scatter. This scattering affects the color of light and creates brilliant sunrises and sunsets.

■ THE BLUE HOUR

During nautical and civil twilight when the landscape is not completely dark or fully lit and the ambient light is filled with blue tones is often called the "blue hour" by photographers. Although its duration is usually not a full hour the quality of light during this time is quite unique and distinctive from any other time of day or night. It is full of cool blue tones because the sun is below the horizon and the earth is illuminated by *only* the sky.

Civil Twilight

Civil twilight is commonly called dawn, or civil dawn, in the morning. At the end of the day it is called dusk, or civil dusk. It is defined as the time when the center of the sun is 6 degrees below the horizon. This is the brightest phase of twilight as the horizon is clearly seen and the only the brightest stars are visible. This light is soft without direct illumination from the sun and is mostly blue and violet, but can have some warm golden hues.

Nautical Twilight

When the center of the sun is between 12 and 6 degrees below the horizon, nautical twilight occurs. It gets the name from mariners who use the stars for navigation. In the morning, photographers also refer to this time as "first light" as the horizon starts to becomes visible. Each phase of twilight generally lasts about a half hour but it varies based on location and the time of year. The duration is shorter the closer you are to the equator.

Astronomical Twilight

Night turns into astronomical twilight when the center of the sun's angle reaches 18 to 12 degrees below the horizon. Stargazing and moon photography are possible during this time as the sky appears dark with only a very small and almost indistinguishable amount of ambient light visible. Most causal observers consider astronomical twilight to be esentially nighttime.

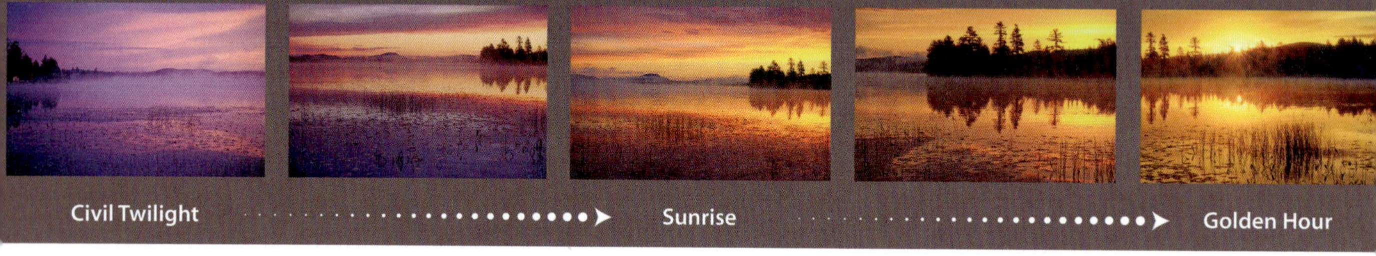

▲ The color palette changes from the blues and violets of twilight to warm yellow and oranges as the sun rises and moves through the golden hour.

A MAGIC MORNING

One magic morning at Raquette Lake in the Adirondack Mountains provided a great example of the light and color transitions from civil twilight through sunrise and the start of the golden hour. A five-frame sequence shows the light and color changes at the edge of the morning. Notice how colors shift and the light becomes more intense as the sun rises.

The light during civil twilight was soft with blue and violet tones as the lake was lit by the upper atmosphere reflecting light downward. A body of water provides a great location to capture the soft illumination of the light in the sky along with its reflection. As the sun continued to rise, soft-yellow warm tones entered the scene.

By sunrise, the color saturation increased while the light became brighter and stronger. Raquette Lake lies within the

▼ Magic light struck with a snow squall over Red Eagle Mountain. All my training and experience came together to capture this stunning moment with a two-frame panoramic image.

FOCAL LENGTH: 35mm | ISO: 160
APERTURE: f/16 | SHUTTER SPEED: 1/3 second

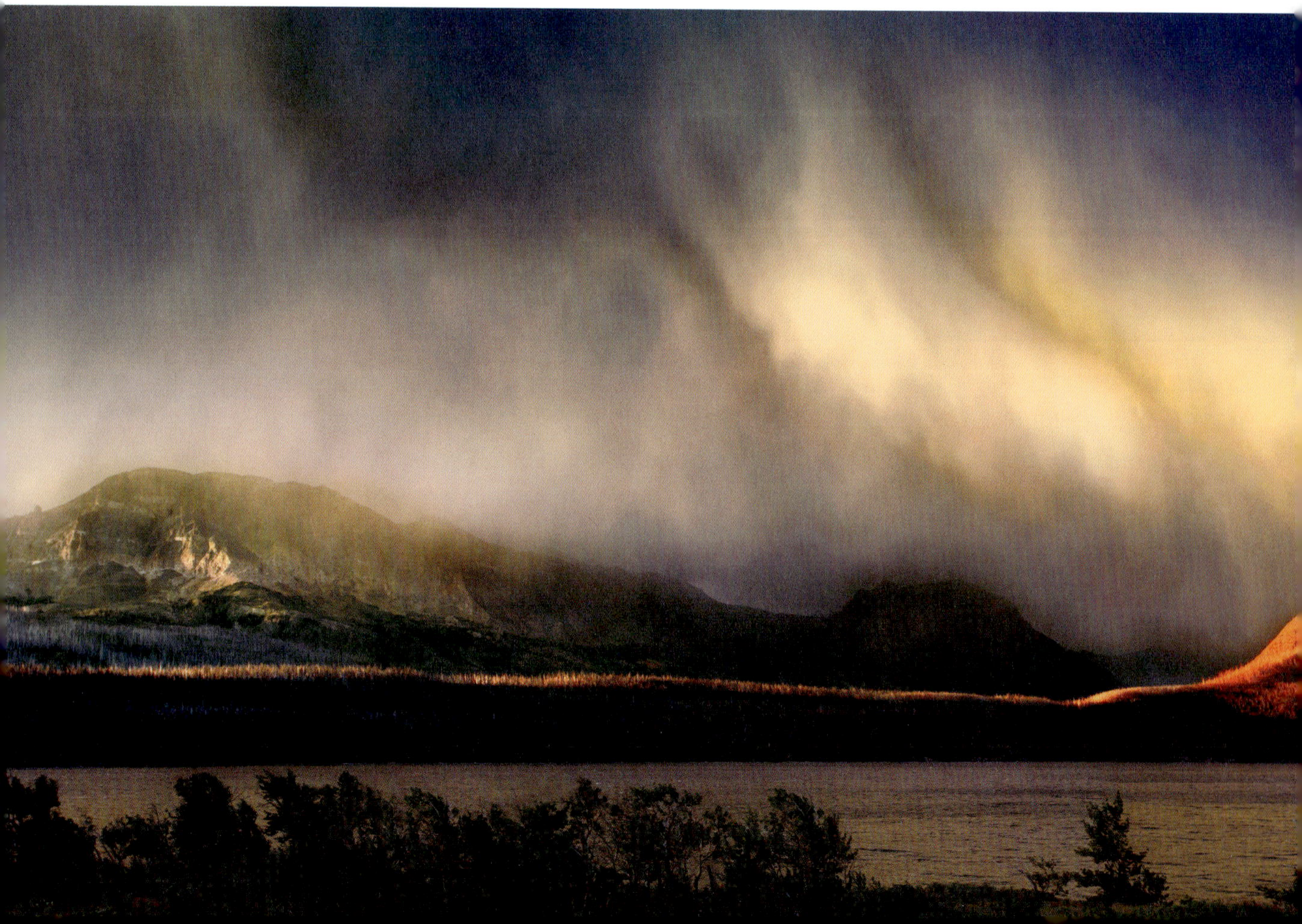

mountains, and those mountains block the sun when it crosses the true horizon at the official sunrise time. The official sunrise and sunset times can be used as a guide, but keep in mind when in the mountains the sight of the actual orb will vary from the official time. The sun's rays begin to show after it rises above the mountain ridge. The light was full of rich yellow tones as the golden hour began.

The easiest way to move beyond ordinary images and capture exceptional photographs is to capture images at the edges of the day. Not only does the early bird get the worm, so does the photographer who arrives early or stays late.

CAPTURING THE MAGIC

After photographing a sunrise at Wild Goose Island in Glacier National Park, it was time for breakfast (or so I thought). Heading toward the small village of St. Mary's along Going to the Sun Road, I was detoured by the amazing light on Red Eagle Mountain.

Stopping suddenly along the side of the road, I grabbed my camera and tripod to capture the magic. With no time to change lenses, I composed the scene with my 17–35mm lens (already on the camera) so that the snow squall and its amazing light filled the top third of the frame. The light was so fantastic that I wanted it to be the focal point of the image.

The storm was moving from my left to the right quickly. The light and texture in the sky were dramatic over the mountain ridge. The top of the lower ridge also lit up and created a leading line up to Red Eagle Mountain. At the time, I thought the light was so fantastic that I would want a panoramic to show *all* of it. I panned my camera to the left to capture its glow for a simple two-frame panoramic.

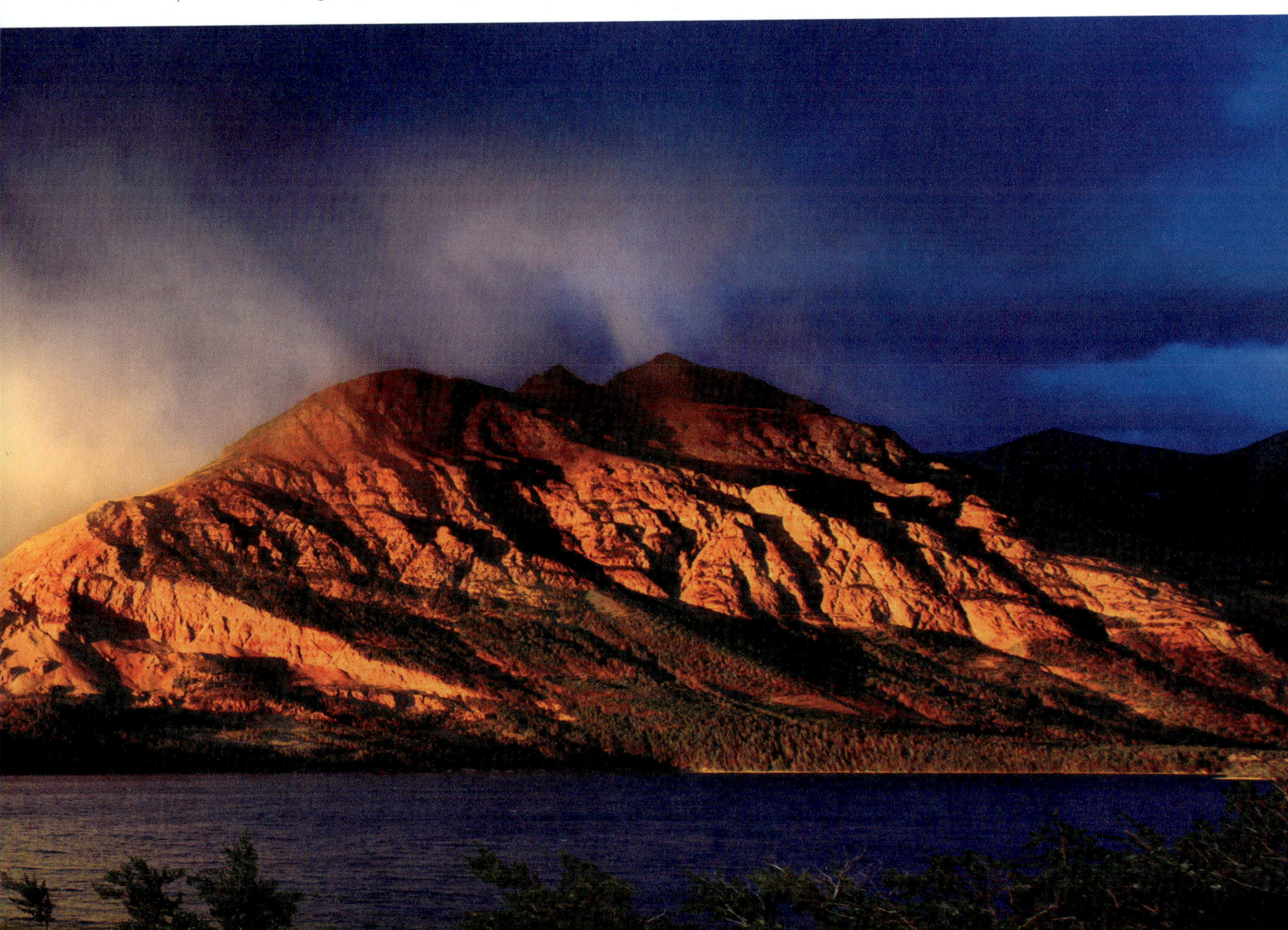

In this moment, with light changing by the second, all my experience and knowledge gets put to good use to successfully capture the magic. It is the culmination of all my training and years in the field coming together. The decision to take two frames for a panoramic came naturally for me. It is easy to get lost in the moment, so relying on the fundamentals was essential.

WHAT MAKES MAGIC LIGHT SO SPECIAL?

True magic light is rare. It happens in a fleeting moment, not to be repeated. Its quality is so unique that it changes the color, appearance, and ultimately the mood of the subjects it falls upon.

Photographer Galen Rowell says, "Most amateur photographers think of landscapes simply as objects to be photographed. They tend to forget that they are never photographing an object, but rather light itself. Where there is no light, they will have no picture; where there is remarkable light, they may have a remarkable picture."[3]

The magic light on Red Eagle Mountain gave it a brilliant reddish-orange glow. It was not named Red Eagle for its amazing color on this day. According to the National Park Service, "James Willard Schultz states that the name was given to the mountain by his Indian wife in 1887, for her uncle, Red Eagle, who had saved their son's life with his prayers to the Sun."[4]

When not under the glow of magic light, the ancient argillite and quartzite rocks have a natural appearance. This is illustrated by the photo taken from the side of Going to the Sun Road about twenty minutes later when the magic light and its unique qualities had disappeared. In this second image, the sky is still dramatic and the light is still "good," but the qualities and color seen earlier are absent. The image captured with

"No painter in their right mind would pay more attention to the brushes than to the paint. No, a painter would study the subtle differences in colours of paint, and how they play on the canvas, how they interact with other colours."[2]

David duChemin
World and humanitarian photographer

▲ This image of Red Eagle Mountain was made with magic light. The overall quality of light emphasizes the color and textures of the mountain.

FOCAL LENGTH: 35mm | ISO: 160
APERTURE: f/16 | SHUTTER SPEED: 1/8 second

► Twenty minutes later, the mountain appeared flat and gray. This image was taken in a slightly different location, but it still illustrates the difference in the quality of light.

FOCAL LENGTH: 35mm | ISO: 160
APERTURE: f/16 | SHUTTER SPEED: 1/3 second

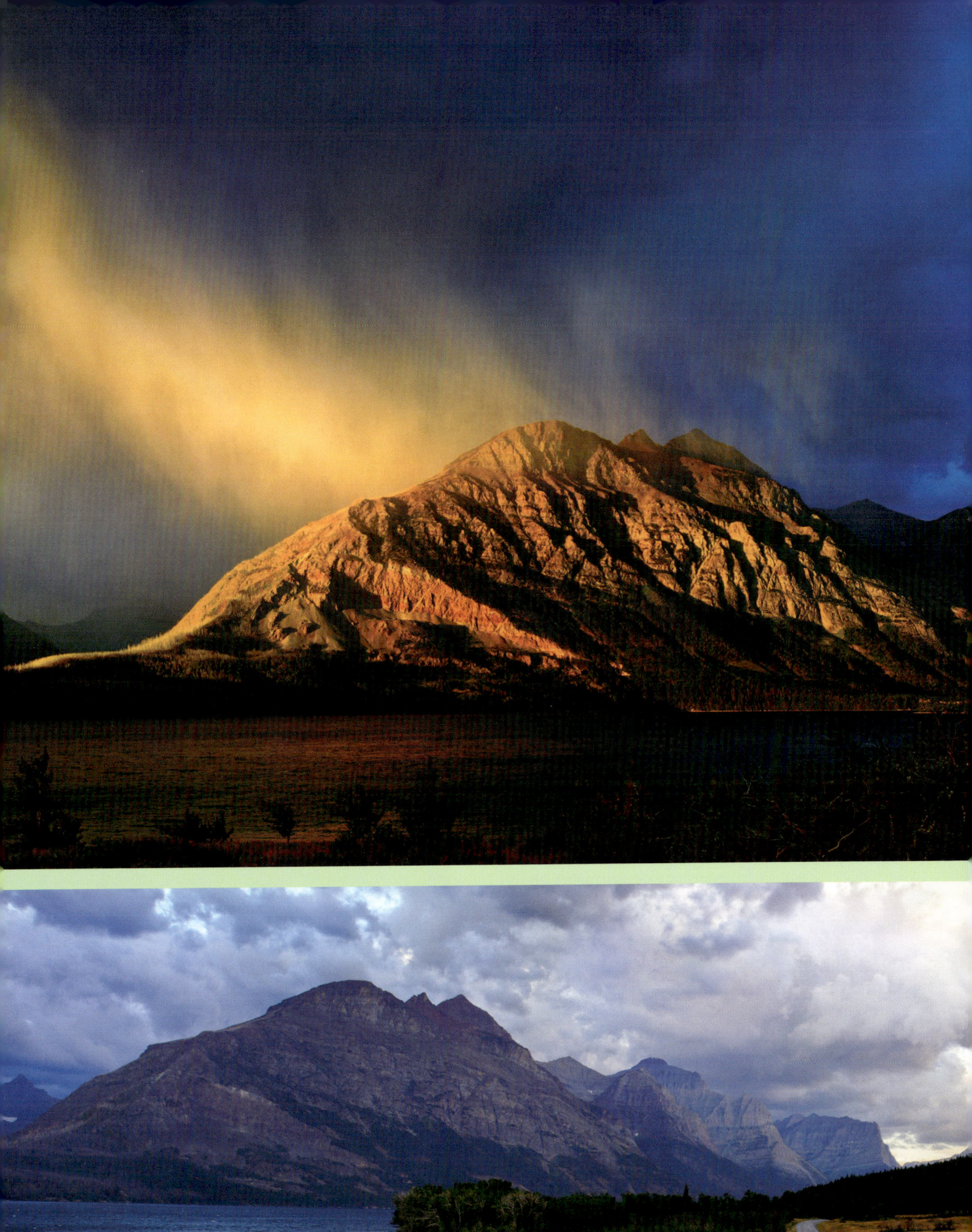

► **Magic light was cast onto the mountainside. The light's vibrant golden tones enhanced the texture.**

FOCAL LENGTH: 35mm | ISO: 160 | APERTURE: f/16 | SHUTTER SPEED: 1/6 second

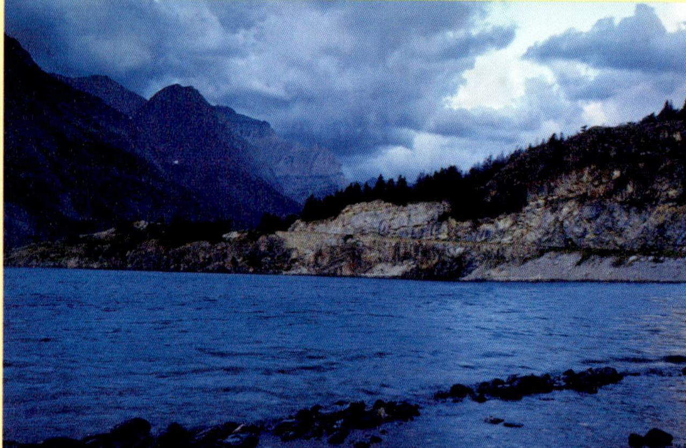

▲ **Within minutes, the special qualities of the magic light disappeared, leaving the mountain pale and gray in comparison.**

FOCAL LENGTH: 35mm | ISO: 160 | APERTURE: f/16 | SHUTTER SPEED: 1/2.5 second

magic light is more expressive and dynamic. It is this quality of light that makes for a one-of-a-kind image.

These moments illustrate some of the many reasons why I love landscape photography.

Less than three minutes later it vanished. Just like that, the magic was gone.

Chasing the light led me up the road to the Rising Sun boat-launch area. The light produced an orange glow on the rocky mountainside that was reflected in the water below. The sky was a cool, deep blue and provided a great contrast against the warm-toned mountainside.

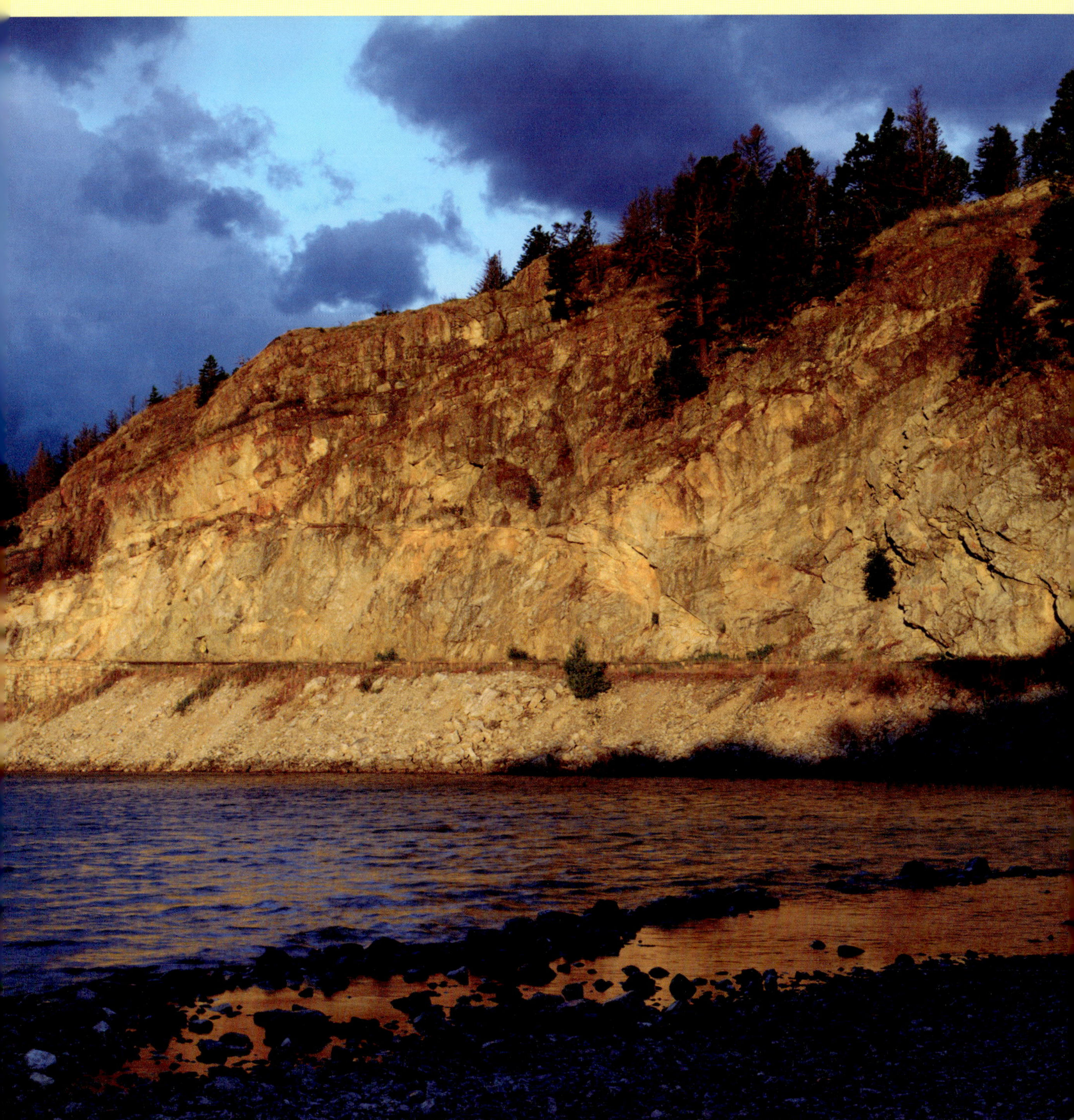

Learning to "read" the light and record these moments comes with experience and knowledge. I quickly set up my camera and tripod to capture the light and vivid colors. I wish there would have been more time to compose a visually compelling image in this beautiful light. Less than three minutes later, it vanished. Just like that, the magic was gone.

2. GETTING THE SHOT

Knowing the basic principles of photography is necessary for capturing magic light successfully. There are many books dedicated to equipment, exposure, and composition, and there are countless more on post-processing. In this chapter, I will simply review the basics of getting the shot. I encourage you to purchase additional books or take a workshop to further your skills and knowledge, and then practice, practice, practice.

THE EXPOSURE TRIANGLE

Proper exposure is critical to producing successful images. If your image is drastically overexposed, chances are you will not successfully convey your artistic vision. Sure, you can set the camera on auto and go about your business, but if you want creative control of your photographs, you must dial in a precise combination of ISO, shutter speed, and aperture settings. These settings make up the exposure triangle.

The three elements of the exposure triangle work in harmony. This means that once you establish your base exposure, should you decide to adjust one of the settings for creative reasons, you will reduce or increase the amount of light used to make the exposure and will need to make a reciprocal adjustment to one of the other two controls.

Let your creative intent be your guide when you determine your exposure settings. If you want to freeze the motion of leaves in the forest on a windy day, you'll want to use

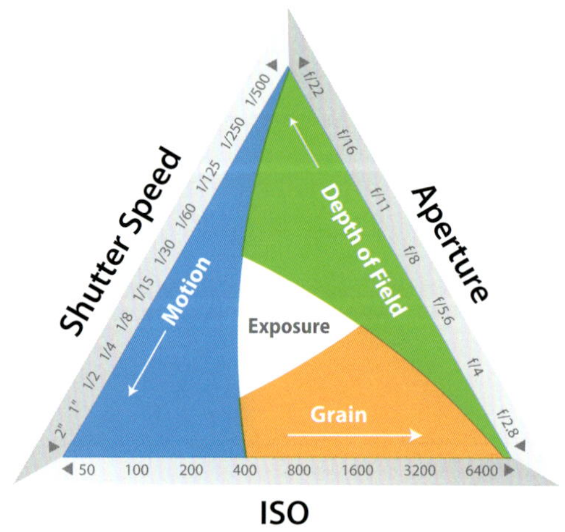

▲ The exposure triangle. Shutter speed, aperture, and ISO work together for ideal exposure.

► Early morning light provided dramatic clouds and blue reflections on Swiftcurrent Lake in Glacier National Park.

FOCAL LENGTH: 24mm | ISO: 100 | APERTURE: f/18 | SHUTTER SPEED: 1/4 second

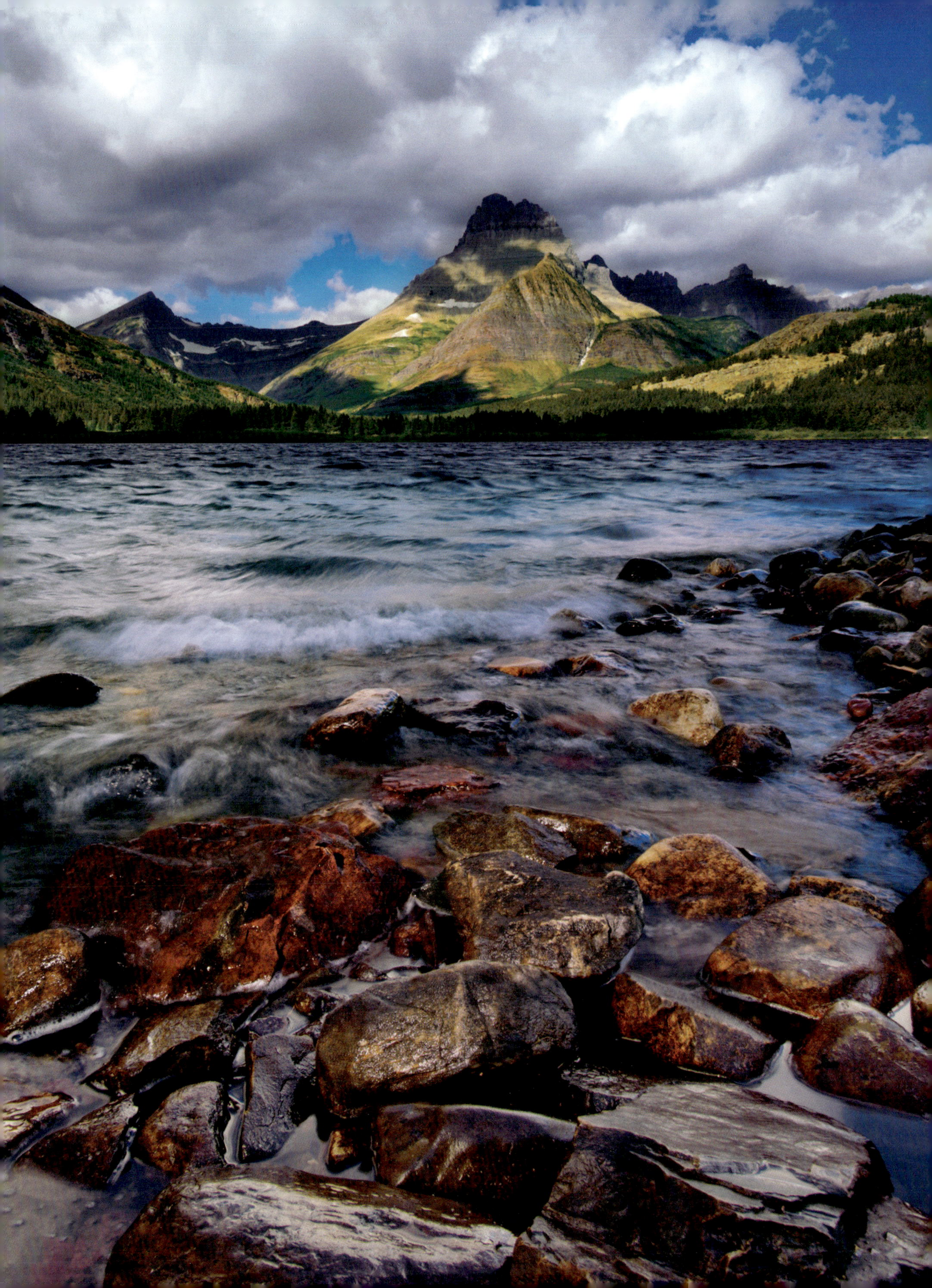

a fast shutter speed. In a situation like this, you probably wouldn't want to choose a wide aperture to allow in more light, as doing so would reduce the depth of field and your forest might not be sharp throughout the frame. Choosing a faster ISO speed to allow your sensor to record more light would make more sense. (See chapter 8 for examples of other creative ways to photograph on windy days.)

Let's look at the creative advantages and effects of making various exposure changes.

Aperture. Setting the aperture is a good place to start when dialing in your exposure, as it controls the amount of light reaching the sensor and determines the depth of field—the area of apparent sharpness throughout the frame. This contributes to the appearance of the two-dimensional image by allowing the photographer to control how much of the scene is sharp. If you want an out-of-focus background, start with the aperture wide open at f/2.8, then adjust the ISO and shutter speed accordingly for the correct exposure.

The relationship between f-stops (a numerical representation of the size of the aperture) and the diameter of the opening is counter-intuitive. A *small* f-stop number like f/2.8 represents a *large* lens opening and a *shallow* depth of field. Conversely, a higher f-stop, say f/22, allows *less* light with a *small* opening and *more* depth of field. To remember how f-stops relate to the depth of field, think of it this way: small = less, big = more.

"Every chosen exposure has potential implications on the look and meaning of our photographs; only we know which combination will create the photograph we see and feel in our mind's eye."[5]

David duChemin
World and humanitarian photographer

THE LAW OF RECIPROCITY

F-Stops. The science of f-stops is steeped in mathematical formulas that we won't get into here. What's important to understand is how f-stops relate to exposure.

The standard f-stop numbers on many lenses are f/2.8, f/4, f/5.6, f/8, f/11, f/16, f/22, and f/32. Memorize them.

When you move up the scale (say you change your aperture from f/8 to f/11), you lose one stop of light. Photographers call this "stopping down." When you move in the other direction, you "open up" the lens to allow one stop more light in. Most digital SLRs can also measure exposure in one-half or one-third-stop increments. These clicks of the dial allow for smaller, more precise exposure adjustments.

Setting the aperture is a good place to start when dialing in your exposure.

A full-stop change in aperture results in a doubling or halving of the quantity of light that will reach the sensor. When reducing the exposure by one full stop (e.g., choosing an f/8 aperture over an f/5.6), the amount of light affecting your exposure is cut in half. When increasing the exposure by a full stop, the amount of light used to make the exposure is doubled.

The other exposure controls—shutter speed and ISO—operate in the same way. This means that if you made a two-stop change in your shutter speed (e.g., changing from 1/125 to 1/500 to freeze motion), you'd need to change your ISO or aperture two stops (selecting a two-stop higher ISO or a two-stop wider aperture) to maintain the light levels and achieve the desired exposure.

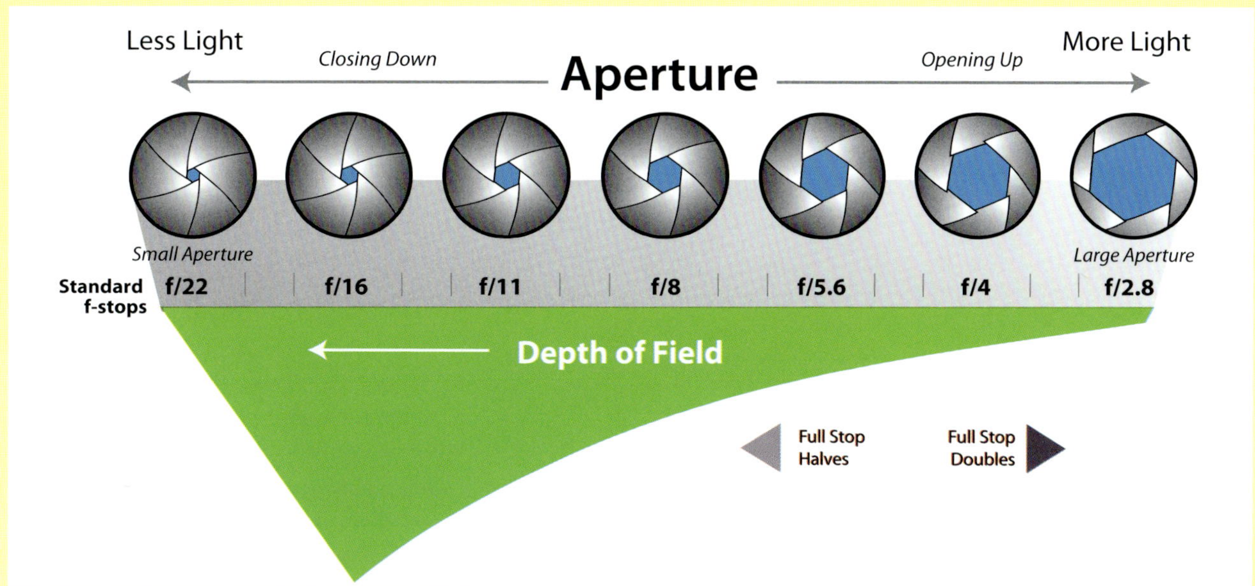

▲► The aperture is the opening in the lens that allows light to strike the image sensor and create an exposure. An f/2.8 aperture is a large opening; it allows much more light to enter in than an f/22 aperture. The larger the opening (smaller the f-stop number), the less depth of field (the area of sharpness from the front to the back of the frame).

Large Aperture

f/2.8 = Bigger opening, more light, less depth of field

Small Aperture

f/22 = Small opening, less light, more depth of field

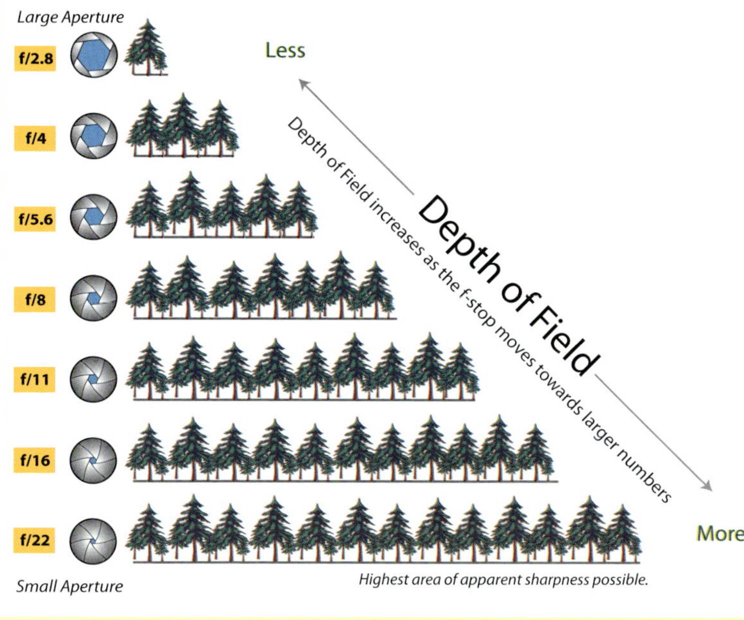

► The aperture setting determines the depth of field within the image. The area of apparent subject/scene sharpness increases with smaller apertures (larger f/stop numbers). A setting of f/22 provides much greater depth of field than an f-stop of f/2.8.

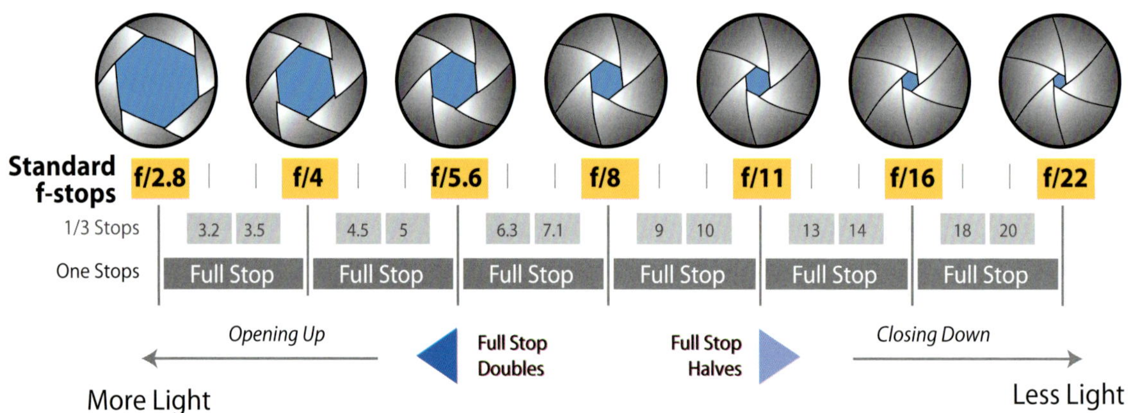

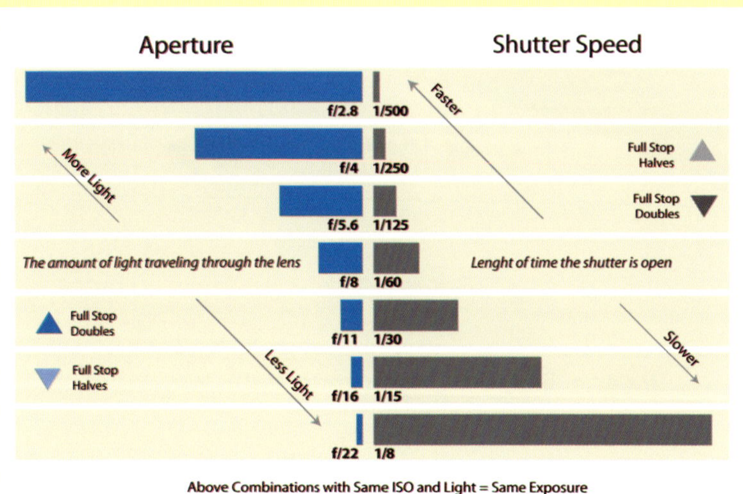

◄▲ The law of reciprocity states that, to maintain a given exposure, you must adjust one exposure setting whenever you change another control. For example, when you stop down from f/8 to f/11, the amount of light allowed to affect the exposure is halved. A corresponding adjustment to the shutter speed (from 1/60 to 1/30) would allow twice as much light in to make the exposure. (*Note:* An ISO change from ISO 100 to 200 would achieve the same balance.) As outlined in the sections on aperture, shutter speed, and ISO, these decisions are made to suit specific artistic needs.

Shutter Speed. The length of time the camera's shutter remains opened is governed by the shutter speed setting that is selected. Slower shutter speeds allow more light to be recorded than do faster settings.

Slower shutter speeds allow more light to be recorded than do faster settings.

Photographers also select a shutter speed in order to blur or freeze motion. Fast shutter speeds freeze subject motion (and can eliminate blur that results from a slightly unsteady hand), while slow shutter speeds can emphasize it. For example, the appearance of soft, velvety water is created when a slow shutter speed is selected that allows the moving water to "flow" and "blur" through the frame.

► Shutter speeds control the amount of time that the shutter stays open to allow light to strike the film/sensor. Fast speeds—fractions of a second—not only limit the amount of light received but are also used to freeze motion. Slow shutter speeds are used when the photographer wants to increase the amount of light used to make an exposure, or to blur motion.

► Moving from an ISO of 50 to ISO 100 would allow twice as much light to affect the exposure. At high speeds, digital noise may result.

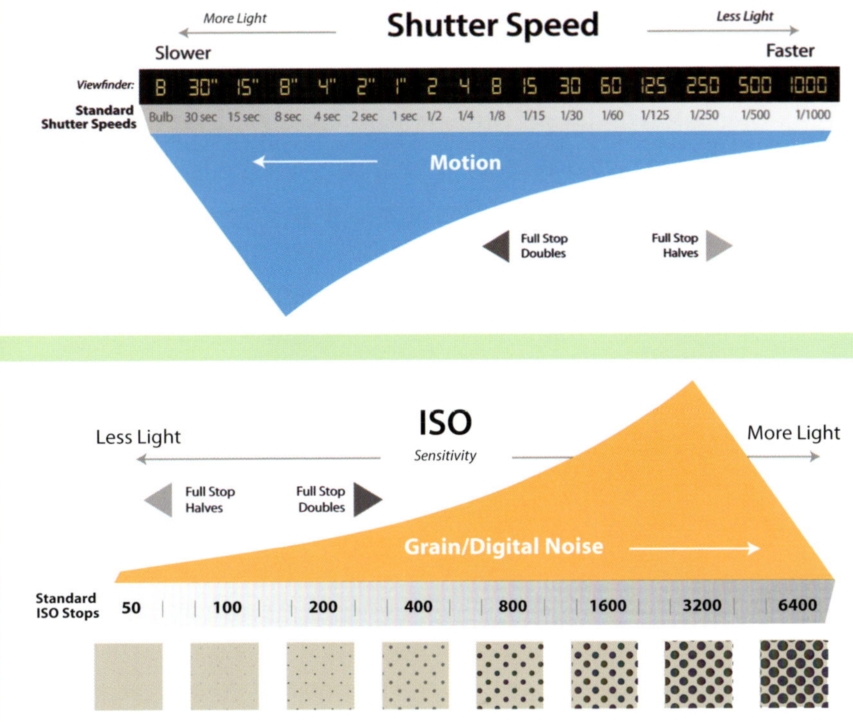

Standard shutter speeds range from about 1 second to 1/1000 second or more. The Bulb setting allows the photographer to keep the shutter open as long the button is pressed. This is useful for exposures over 30 seconds (the longest setting available on most cameras) when capturing scenes during night or twilight when the available light is very low. *Note:* A tripod-mounted camera with a cable release is recommended when using slow shutter speeds, as even the slightest camera movement can result in blur.)

How fast must your shutter speed be in order to freeze motion? That depends on the speed of the subject, direction of the movement, and distance from the camera. A shutter speed that is faster than the speed of the moving subject will freeze the action and be sharp (provided it is in focus!). A subject moving across the frame will require a faster shutter speed than one that is moving toward or away from you. Also, the closer the subject is to the camera, the faster the shutter speed must be to stop the action. Why is this? Picture a motorcycle speeding past you three blocks away. When you raise your lens to photograph it, your subject takes longer to travel across the frame than would that same motorcycle, shot with the same lens focal length, were it much closer to your lens.

The closer the subject is to the camera, the faster the shutter speed must be to stop the action.

ISO Settings. The ISO setting you choose determines your camera's sensitivity to light. Fast settings allow for maximum image-sensor sensitivity to light. This can be useful in a scenario where you want to record an image with a fair amount of detail and want to freeze motion. Let's say you choose an aperture of f/8. You shoot at f/8 and 1/500 and ISO 400, but you see that your scene is a bit too dark (underexposed). You don't want to change the aperture because you want sharpness; you don't want to slow your shutter speed because you want to freeze motion. Adjusting your ISO to 800 or higher might just save your shot. Slow ISO settings, conversely, are often used in situations when there is a lot of light in which to record your images or you want to blur action and changing the shutter speed would negatively impact your shot.

There is more to making an ISO setting decision than simply achieving the right light level for your image, though. Fast ISO speeds result in digital noise (a pattern of speckles or dots that impact the quality of your image). As technology improves, noise is becoming less of an issue. That said, it's best to err on the side of caution and shoot at as low an ISO as your scene will support to increase the odds that you'll have clean, noise-free images.

Mastery of the three elements of the exposure triangle are necessary skills for creating exceptional images. Every artistic endeavor—photography, sculpting, or music—begins with mastering the basics and developing sound technical skills. Learning these basics will help you to expose images correctly, and from there your creativity can soar as you experiment with new techniques and effects.

Mastery of the three elements of the exposure triangle are necessary skills for creating exceptional images.

▼ A slow shutter speed of 1/20 second blurs raindrops and gives the illusion of mist and fog. A shutter speed of at least 1/125 will stop the raindrops in mid-flight and render them as tiny white dots in your image. Selective use of the exposure triangle produces a moody image with depth.

FOCAL LENGTH: 66mm | ISO: 250 | APERTURE: f/10 | SHUTTER SPEED: 1/20 second

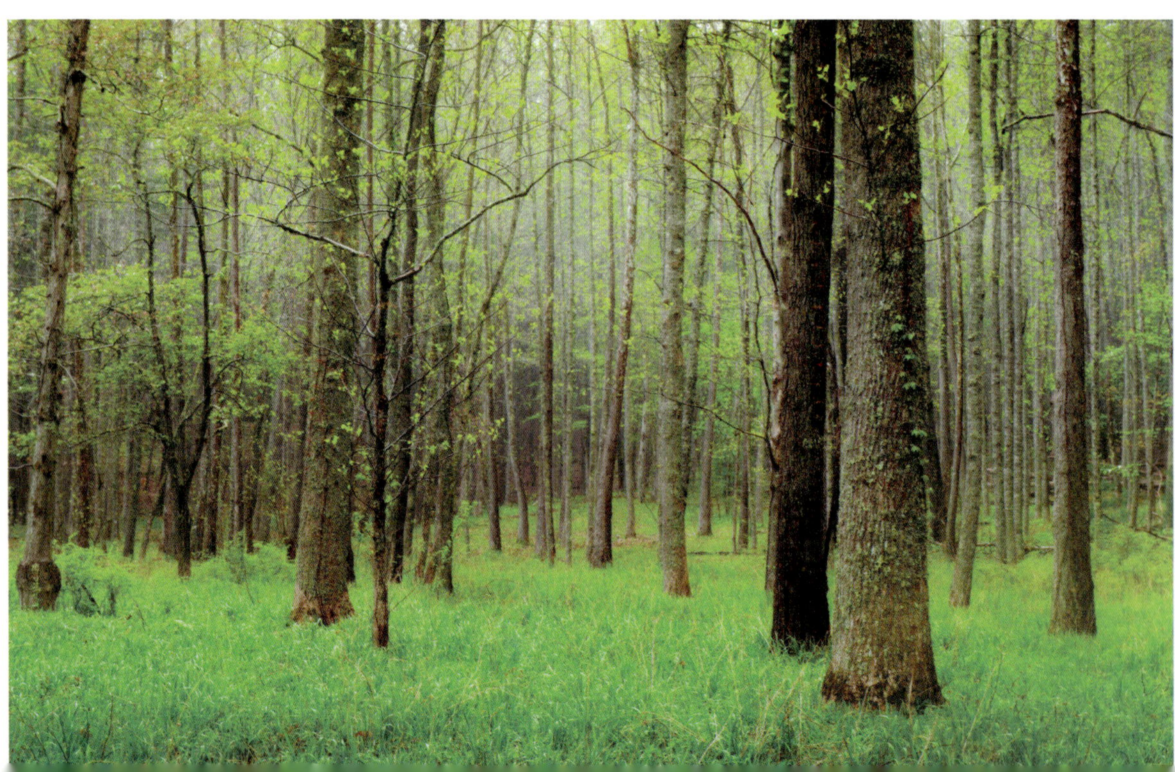

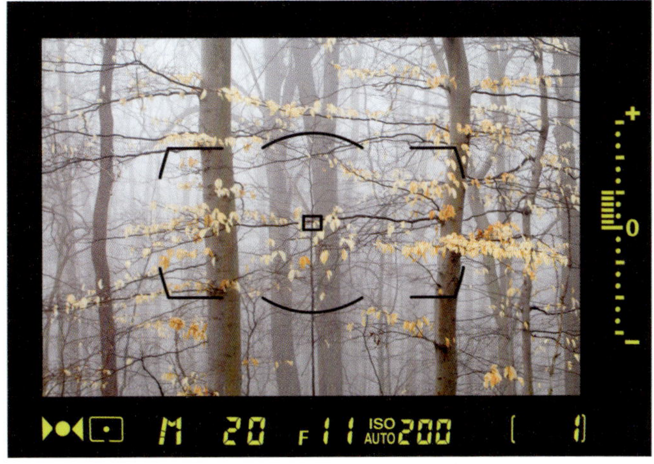

► In my viewfinder, the exposure display on the right side shows the image is one-stop overexposed. Each dot represents a third-stop and the lines equal one stop. This image was taken in manual mode. The exposure was 1/20 second and f/11 at ISO 200.

EXPOSURE MODES

Most DSLRs allow you to shoot in manual mode, program mode, or aperture or shutter priority mode. You can select any of these modes as a starting point of the exposure triangle. Some cameras also offer an auto ISO setting, but I don't recommend using it because seldom is the ISO the basis of your exposure.

The aperture priority mode (Av or A) or shutter priority (Tv or S) mode can be a good starting point for beginners because the only exposure variable that must be selected is the aperture or shutter. The camera automatically selects the settings that will result in a "correct" exposure. If you want to focus a viewer's attention on water droplets on oak leaves on a nearby tree, you might choose a wide aperture like f/2.8 to throw the background out of focus. You could press the shutter button and the resulting image would be properly exposed. If you wanted to freeze a bird in flight, you might choose shutter priority mode, dial in a setting of 1/500, squeeze the shutter button, and get a dead-on exposure.

Manual mode shooting allows for greater control and creativity. In manual mode, all the settings are up to the photographer. Nothing is automatic, and each setting is independent of the others. I prefer this mode as it allows me to make all of the exposure decisions and easily tweak them for pinpoint accuracy. (I use a meter to guide my exposure decisions.)

In program mode, the camera selects the exposure settings, but the photographer can override them.

METERING

Digital cameras have built-in light meters to measure the light. It is this measurement of light that determines the recommended exposure settings.

Camera meters don't think; they are simply programmed to read every scene as "average" . . .

Camera meters don't think; they are simply programmed to read every scene as "average" with 18 percent reflectance of light (i.e., middle gray). If your scene is average, then your light meter will record it accurately. However, there are many times when the scene is not middle-toned; snow is an obvious example. Sunrises and sunsets can be tricky, so we need to compensate for the meter's reading. This can be done by adding or subtracting light or time from the recommended exposure based on your intent for the image. There may also be times when you want an

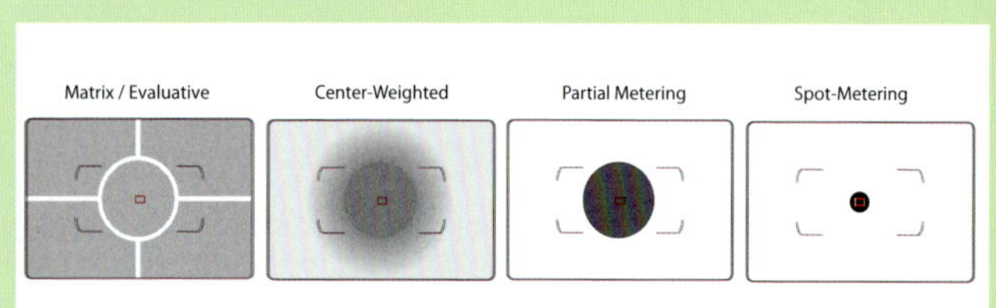

▲ Commonly used icons representing standard metering modes.

image to be slightly overexposed to create a light, airy feel or underexposed for a dark, moody image.

In tricky situations, the key is to have a good starting point. I begin by spot metering a mid-tone area. Green grass tends to be a good mid-tone, but you can also use a gray card—a piece of cardboard that is designed to provide 18 percent reflectance.

Cameras offer several metering modes, the names of which vary from one manufacturer to the next.

- Color Matrix (Nikon) or Evaluative (Canon) metering measures the light in multiple areas and then uses sophisticated mathematical algorithms to calculate the exposure based on the whole scene.
- Center-weighted metering uses a large circle in the middle of the frame for the majority of its evaluation and fades out to the edges.
- Partial metering, common on Canon cameras, measures 8 to 10 percent of the center of the frame.
- Spot metering is very precise; in this mode, the meter measures only 2 to 3 percent of the frame area.

EXPOSURE COMPENSATION

Exposure compensation adjusts the camera's suggested meter reading to make an image brighter or darker. It lets you add (+) or subtract (-) from the exposure by turning the exposure compensation dial. To make your image one stop brighter (overexpose), turn the exposure compensation dial to +1. To underexpose the image by one stop, your turn the dial to -1. Many DSLRs allow you to make adjustments in third-stop or half-stop steps, up to two or three full stops in either direction. Some professional cameras allow for as much as five stops of exposure compensation.

Another reason I shoot in manual mode is the ease at which I can add or subtract brightness from my exposure. In manual mode, there is no need for exposure compensation because I am setting the exposure myself. When I want to overexpose by one stop, I simply make sure the exposure display in the camera is one stop to the plus (+) side. When using program, aperture, or shutter priority modes, the exposure compensation has to be set to +1. This requires the extra step of setting the exposure compensation and *remembering to cancel it* when you are finished to avoid unwanted overexposure later.

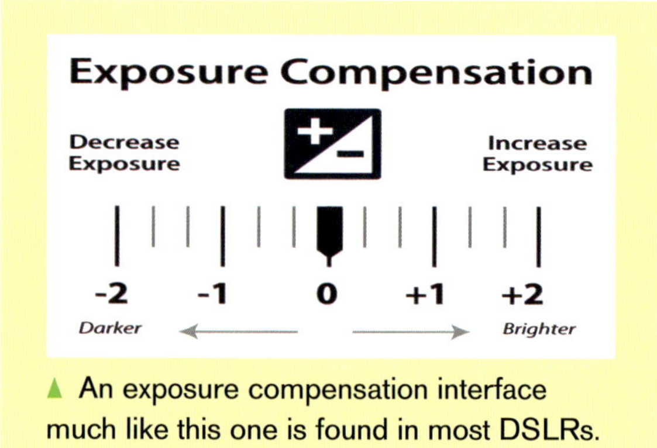

▲ An exposure compensation interface much like this one is found in most DSLRs.

HISTOGRAM

Back in the days of film, it was critical to get a correct exposure, as there was very little exposure latitude (*and* no way to verify it was correct). Fortunately, with digital cameras, that has changed. Now, we can look at the histogram to see the tonal range and verify that we captured an acceptable exposure.

A histogram is a graphic representation of how the tones, from light to dark, are distributed throughout the image. Ideally the data will span from left to right and drop off before reaching the edges. Clipping (i.e., a loss of image data) occurs when the histogram pushes against the edge. If the data runs over the right edge, part of the image will be overexposed or "blown out" with no detail in the highlights. If it spikes at the left edge, the shadows will be "blocked up"—pure black with no detail.

Clipping is most common in high-contrast situations, as the contrast range is greater than the sensor can handle. In these scenarios, it is best to "expose to the right" for the highlight detail. Be careful to avoid clipping and detail loss in bright areas, as missing pixel data cannot be recovered. It is okay if there is a small spike that represents specular highlights (a very small spot of bright light that contains no detail—often from glass, metal, or shiny surfaces), but a large light area of clouds, for example, should stay within the edge and not be clipped. If you have to choose, it is better to have dark shadows without detail than blown-out highlights.

Alternately, you can use a split neutral-density filter to even out the exposure in some scenes or bracket the image to create several different exposures in order to create a high dynamic range (HDR) image. These are techniques I will discuss in detail later on in this book.

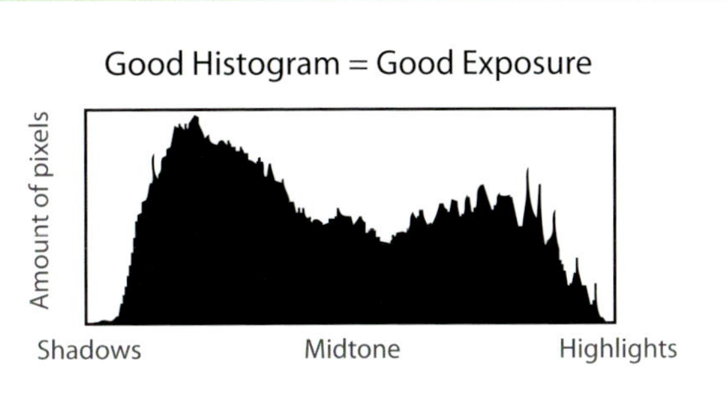

In a correctly exposed image, the histogram data drops off before reaching either edge. This medium-contrast scene has detail in both the highlights and shadows.

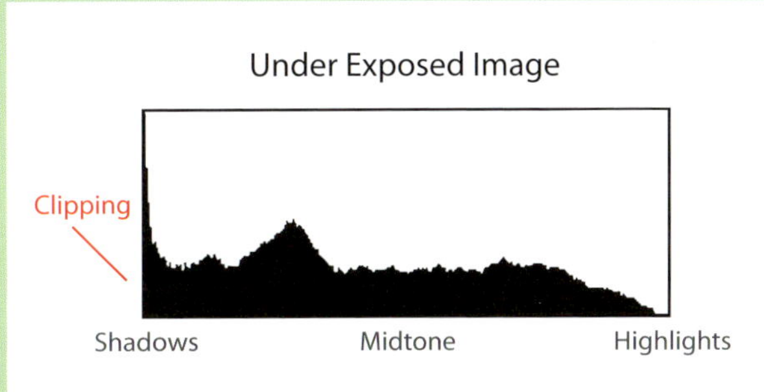

When the histogram data is too far to the left, the image is underexposed and the detail in the shadow areas is clipped. To correct this, you will need to increase the exposure.

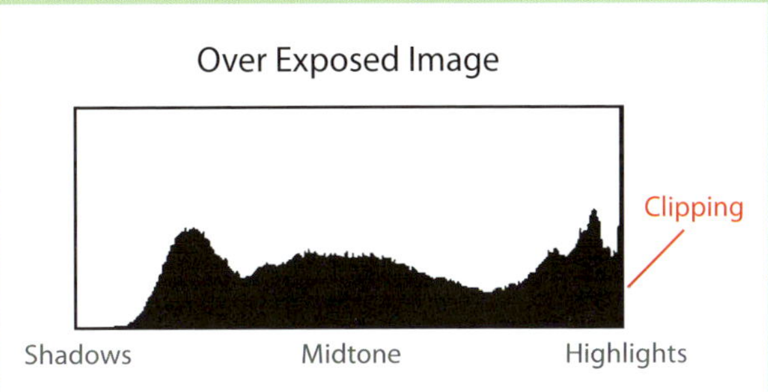

The histogram for this overexposed image shows clipping and loss of highlight detail. The bright areas are "blown out" and lack pixel data. To correct this, the exposure needs to be reduced so the histogram moves to the left and the data graph doesn't push against the edge.

3. EQUIPMENT

INSIDE MY CAMERA BAG

I don't believe that having the latest and greatest gear makes you a better photographer. I believe in having the right tools—quality tools—in my bag to capture the shot. Don't get me wrong; having good gear and quality glass is worth the investment, but it is not the end-all-and-be-all to making superior images. Equipment does not make the photographer—vision does. Using the "right" tools to capture your vision with success is all that you need. So even if you don't have top-of-the-line equipment, you can still make great images. With that said, I buy the best equipment I can afford to fit my style and vision. Buying used gear is a great way to get top equipment for less dough. Don't let the lack of equipment hold you back. Work with what you have—there will always be a new camera or gizmo to lust after next month.

My bag includes two Nikon pro camera bodies and Nikon 17–35mm f/2.8, Nikon 24–70 f/2.8, Nikon 70–200mm f/2.8, Nikon 28–300mm f/3.5–5.6, Nikon 105mm Macro, and Nikon 400mm f/2.8 lenses. I own a steady tripod, quality ballhead with a quick-release plate system, and a cable release. Also packed in my bag are several filters (more on them later), several Compact Flash cards, and an extra battery.

I prefer backpacks to shoulder bags. Backpacks allow me to keep my hands free when I hike and climb up and down hillsides with my gear evenly distributed and securely resting on my back. Finding one that fits comfortably can be challenging, but a good fit will make long hikes more pleasurable.

A strong, steady tripod is required for sharp images, slow-motion effects, and just about all landscape images. Tripods are necessary when bracketing images to ensure every frame is the same except for the exposure. Using a tripod forces me to focus on the composition and tweak it with precision. I made using my tripod a habit years ago, and I never leave home without it.

There are many types of tripods on the market, and it is really a matter of preference which style you prefer. Some have center columns and some do not. If you like to get right down onto the ground, the center column can get in the way and prevent you from getting where you want to be. Independent, adjustable legs are important when the ground is not level and you need to place it on the hillside, for example. Additionally, if you plan to do a lot of hiking, you may want to consider a lightweight carbon-fiber model.

Tripod heads are sold separately from the legs. Just like tripods, there are many styles to choose from. I prefer the large ballhead styles by Arca-Swiss and Really Right Stuff (RRS); Kirk makes a similar one. They are compatible with the RRS quick-release plate system that offers great quality, durability, and ease of use. These ballheads feature a large locking knob with a tension control that holds the camera in place. Additionally, many have a panning base for moving the camera from side to side, which is great for creating panoramics. Some even have leveling bubbles to ensure the horizon is straight.

Tripod heads are sold separately from the legs. Like tripods, there are many styles to choose from.

Quick-release plates make it simple to place your camera securely and quickly on the ballhead. I use the Arca-Swiss dovetail plate, which has a grooved channel that slides onto a large platform base and locks into place. Arca-Swiss, Kirk, and Really Right Stuff all make products that utilize this dovetail system. An L plate has a channel on the bottom and wraps around the side of the camera for either vertical or horizontal shooting. This allows me to frame a vertical composition with the ballhead upright for more stability because the weight is on top instead of tilted into the drop notch on the side. Really Right Stuff also makes a series of foot replacements (for lens collars) that have the channel integrated in the bottom for placing a large lens directly on the ballhead. Mounting a large lens directly on the ballhead balances the weight for less vibration and more stability.

Another useful accessory is a cable release. By using a cable release, camera shake is reduced because you don't have to touch the camera to release the shutter. This is very useful for long exposures when camera shake can be very evident. In lieu of a cable release, you can use the self-timer function on your camera to fire the shutter, but I find that to be a cumbersome alternative.

Filters. My filter collection consists mainly of polarizers and neutral-density filters. The effects of these filters can't be replicated digitally—at least not easily. Reducing the glare from water to reveal the rocks below the surface is one of the many reasons I use a polarizer; another is to darken blue skies. Solid neutral-density (ND) filters are great to slow down exposure times and create motion effects, while graduated ND filters balance the lighter areas with darker sections in the scene. Detailed examples of the effects of these filters can be found later in this book.

Miscellaneous Tools. It is a good idea to carry a few basic tools, or a multi-tool, in your bag should you need to make a repair. Rain gear is also helpful should the weather change. Your cell phone can also be a great resource. These days, I use my iPhone's stopwatch function to time exposures over 30 seconds. I also have apps for sunrise and sunset times, maps, and a compass.

So let's get out there and start shooting.

PART TWO: MAGIC LIGHT

4. CYCLE OF LIGHT

As the first light of the day begins to illuminate the upper atmosphere, the landscape is not completely lit or completely dark. Many photographers look at the sunrise time and plan to arrive then or a few minutes earlier. Let's face it, getting out of bed at 5:00AM or earlier is no fun, but photographs captured at this time can be worth the effort. Photographers arriving during nautical twilight, when the sun is between 6 and 12 degrees below the horizon, can capture unique

▼ The first light of the day was captured at Wild Goose Island on St. Mary's Lake in Glacier National Park at 6:17AM with a 44-second exposure.

TIME OF DAY: 6:17:46AM | FOCAL LENGTH: 35mm | ISO: 160 | APERTURE: f/20 | SHUTTER SPEED: 44 seconds

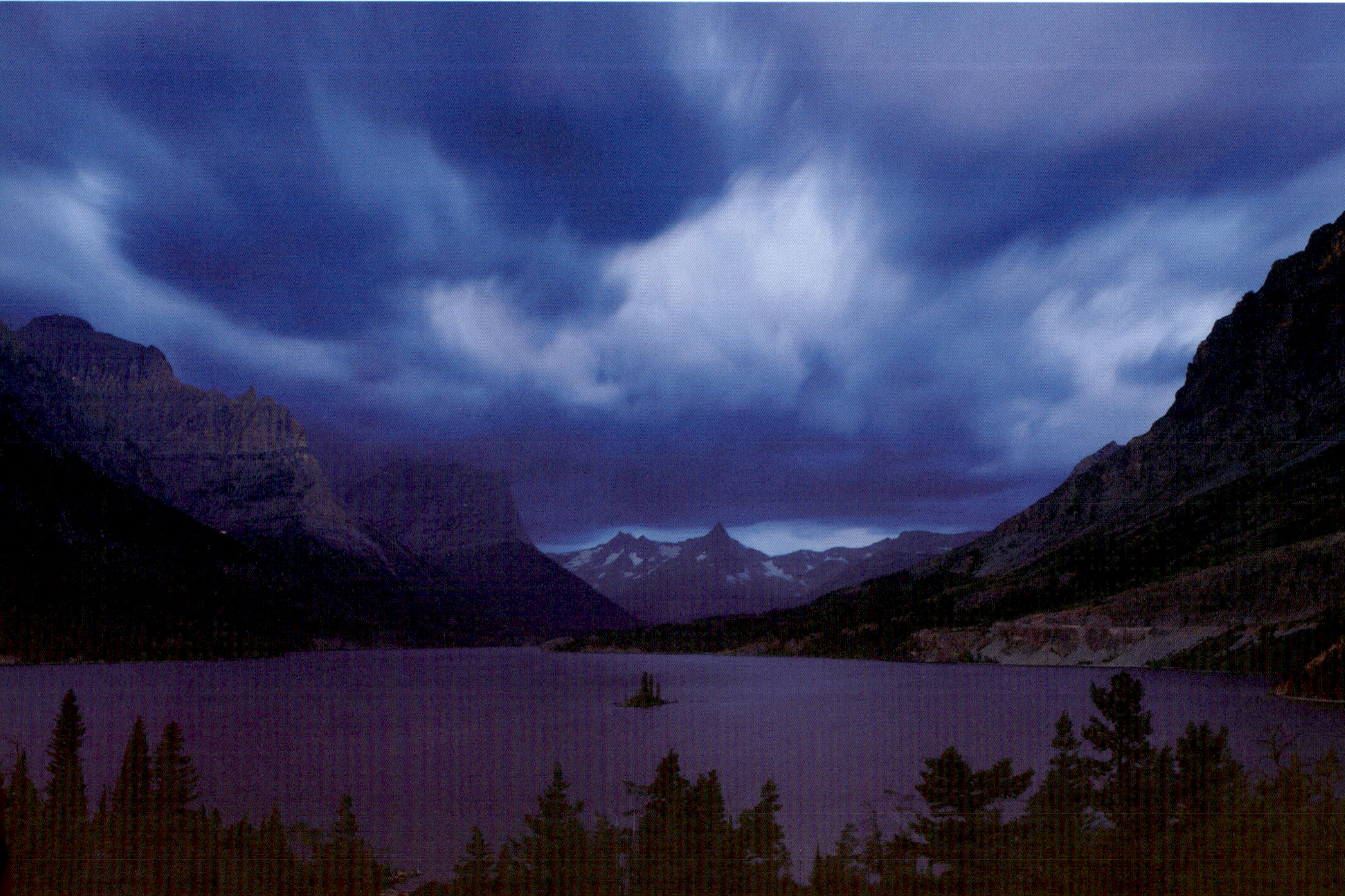

▲ Deep, dark-blue exposures are common during the blue hour. The light at this time of day changes quickly, so it is a good idea to arrive at your location with plenty of time to set up and shoot. If possible, scout out your sunrise location the night before to save time looking for a shot in the morning.

TIME OF DAY: 6:10:19am | FOCAL LENGTH: 35mm | ISO: 160 | APERTURE: f/16 | SHUTTER SPEED: 58 seconds

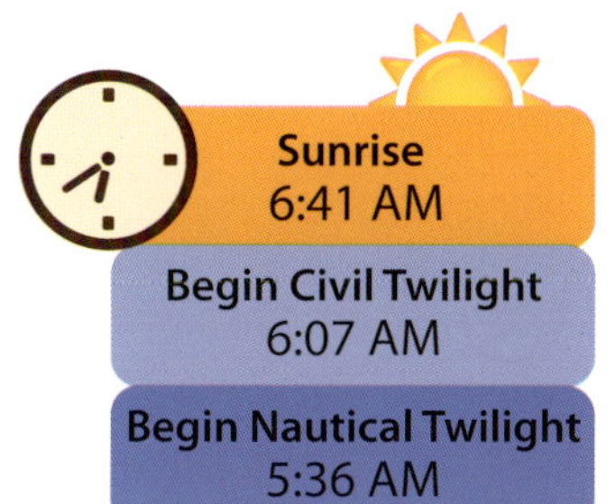

images before the sun rises over the horizon. This period of time at the edge of the day is also known as the *blue hour* because of the deep-blue tones present.

These images of Wild Goose Island were taken as nautical twilight transitioned into civil twilight. As you can see, the light changes dramatically at this hour of the morning. Notice how the image taken seven minutes earlier during nautical twilight is very blue and the mountains and trees show less detail. As the light transitioned toward dawn, there was more light on the mountainside with increased contrast. A long exposure of 44 seconds softened the water movement and produced a nice "brush stroke" effect in the moving clouds.

A tripod and a cable release are essential tools when the light is very low and long exposures are required. The maximum shutter speed that most cameras allow is 30 seconds, but these images required a longer exposure. To extend the exposure beyond 30 seconds, I set the camera to Bulb. I then used my iPhone and its stopwatch app to time the exposure. A quick check of the histogram allowed me to view the results.

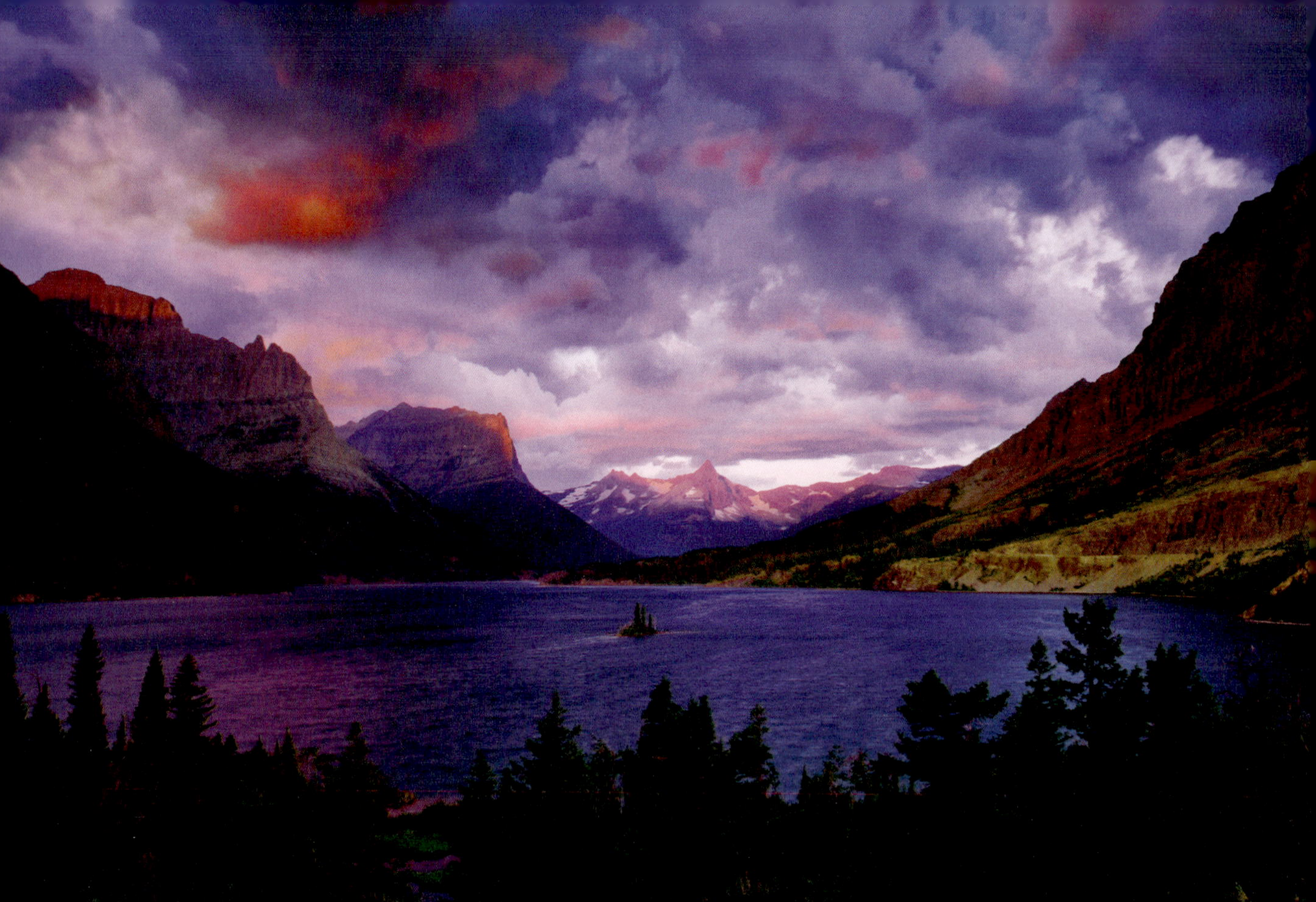

DAWN

Many of Glacier National Park's great locations require hiking. However, this location provides one of the easiest photo ops in the park—it is right along Going to the Sun Road, complete with a little photo sign marking the spot. Usually, I try to get more creative and unique shots than a marked, roadside photo location offers, but this spot makes a great twilight/sunrise location with easy access for early mornings. Also, because it is close to the road, it is relatively safe from bears. Sure, I could have bush-whacked down the shore, but this area is known to have a heavy bear population, so I decided to remain safe and still get a great shot.

Typically, color in the sky starts during civil twilight, approximately 30 minutes before sunrise when the sun is 6 degrees below the horizon. During this time, terrestrial objects such as trees, rocks, and water are clearly distinguishable. Vivid colors may occur in the sky opposite the actual sunrise. The

▲ High clouds are illuminated with vivid colors in the opposite direction of the sun at dawn (also called *civil twilight*) in Glacier National Park. Always look behind you to see what the sky is doing in the opposite direction.

TIME OF DAY: 6:39:08AM | FOCAL LENGTH: 35mm | ISO: 160 | APERTURE: f/16 | SHUTTER SPEED: 4 seconds

▶ The reddish light of alpenglow appears on the mountain peaks as the color in the sky fades before sunrise at Wild Goose Island.

TIME OF DAY: 6:43:53AM | FOCAL LENGTH: 35mm | ISO: 160 | APERTURE: f/16 | SHUTTER SPEED: 1.3 seconds

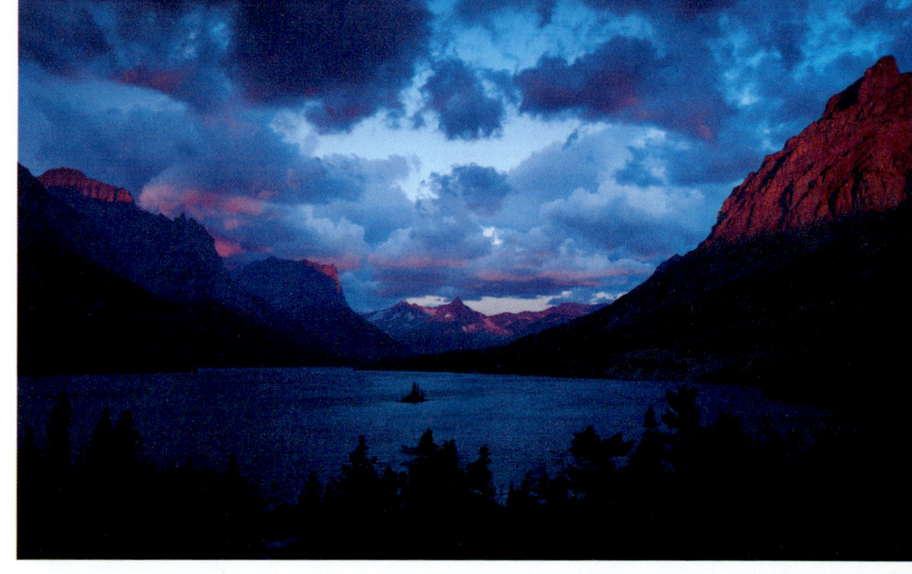

▶ I arrived early and was rewarded with blue and violet colors, as civil twilight began at 6:28AM and lasted until sunrise at 6:58AM on this October day at Lake Durant in the Adirondack Mountains.

TIME OF DAY: 6:33:02AM | FOCAL LENGTH: 29mm | ISO: 100 | APERTURE: f/18 | SHUTTER SPEED: 30 seconds

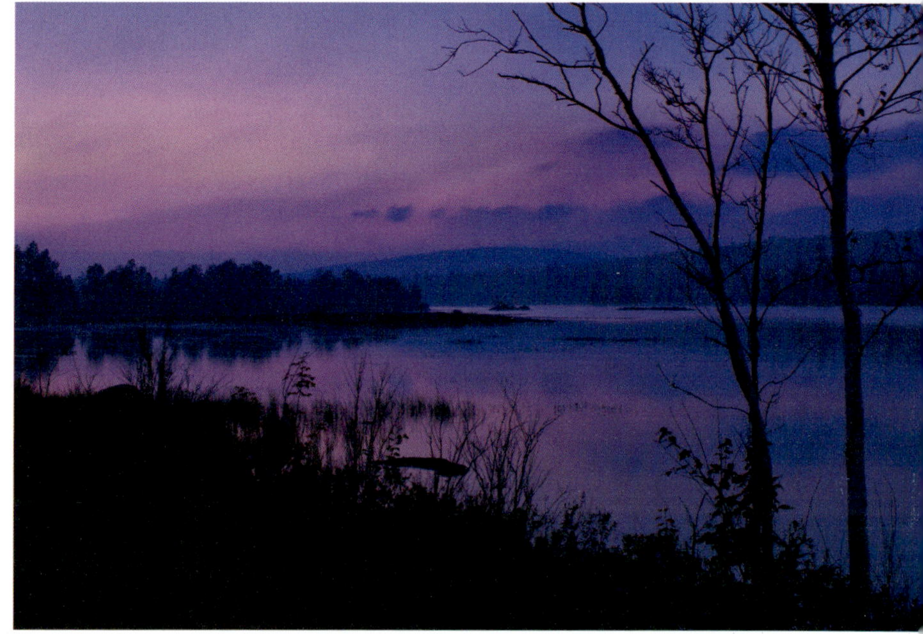

appearance of *alpenglow*—the reddish glow on the mountain peaks—occurs when the sun is just below the horizon during civil twilight in the opposite direction of the sunrise.

For this shoot, the sun was rising behind my left shoulder producing striking colors in the cloudy sky and alpenglow on the mountain peaks. Alpenglow is another reason to arrive early and be prepared because its effect changes rapidly.

On this day, the peak color in the sky faded before the predicted sunrise time. It is often a good idea to arrive a half hour or more before the official sunrise time so you are prepared for the show. This is especially true in the mountains where there are opportunities for alpenglow in addition to colorful skies.

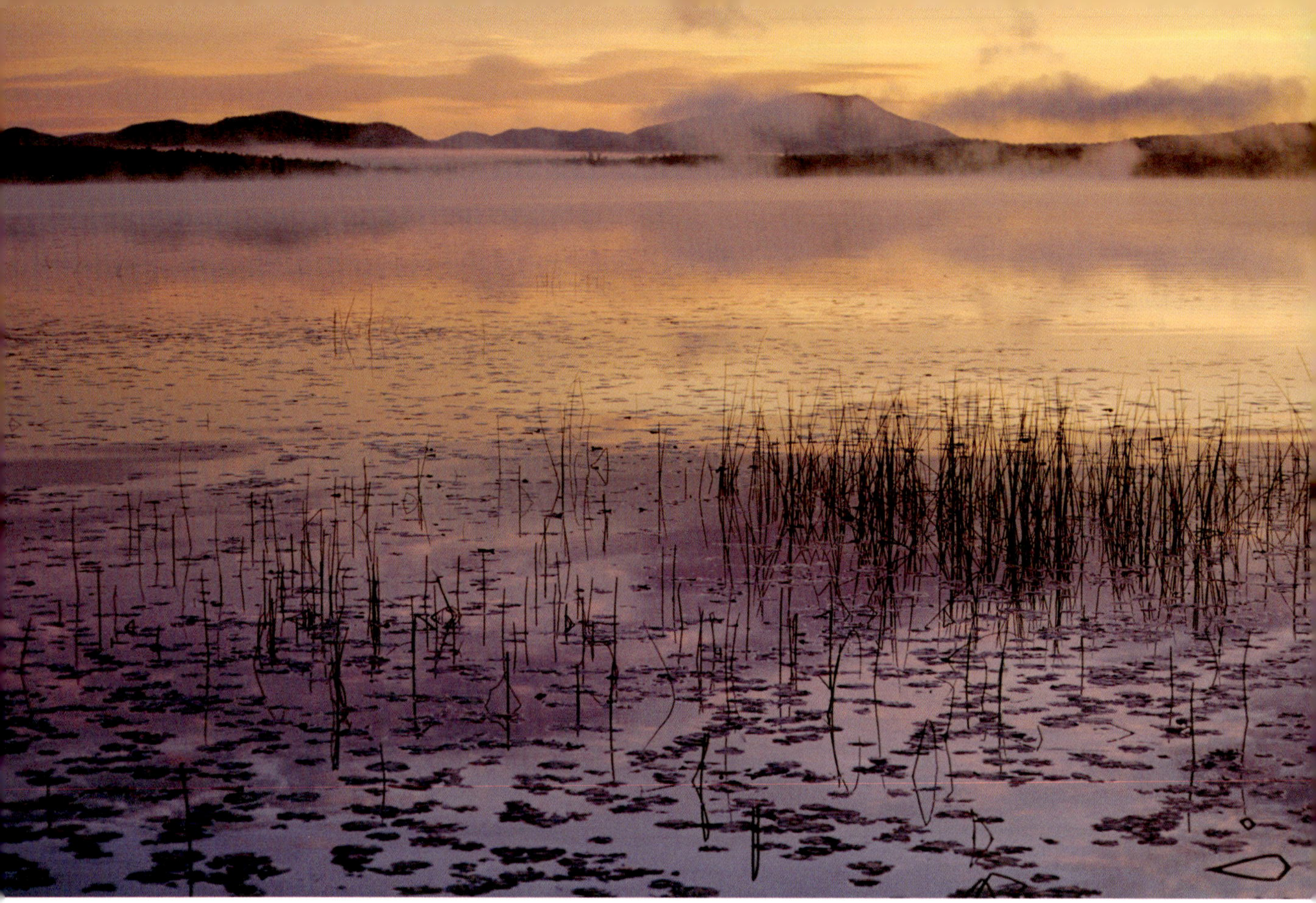

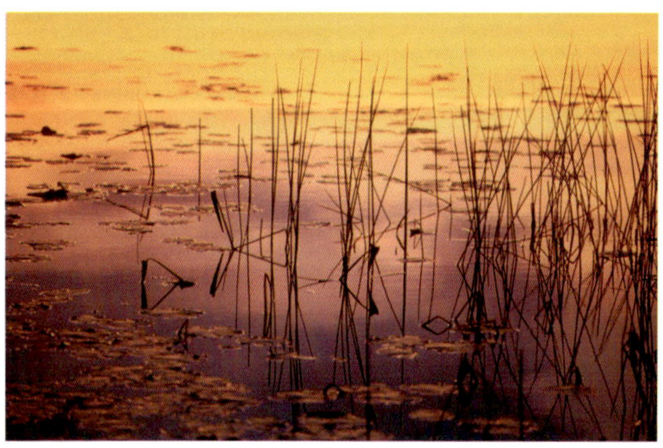

▲ Spectacular sunrises and sunsets are more abundant at certain times of the year. Autumn's cool nights and warm water created mist over the Raquette Lake in the Adirondacks, adding another element to this eye-catching sunrise.

ISO: 50 | Fujichrome Velvia | APERTURE: Not available | SHUTTER SPEED: Not available

◄ Zooming into a section of the reeds emphasized the beautiful colors of sunrise.

SUNRISE

At sunrise and sunset, the sun's rays have a longer path through the atmosphere—passing through more particles and molecules that change the direction of the rays and cause them to scatter. This scattering effect pushes away the blue and violet colors, leaving behind the oranges and reds. Later in the day when the sun is high in the sky, its rays travel a shorter distance and through less atmosphere, resulting in the short blue wavelength of daylight.

In the fall of 2000, I made my first trip to the Adirondack Mountains. During this time,

I was lucky enough to photograph sunrise along Raquette Lake. Four rolls of film were quickly shot on this beautiful morning. Unfortunately, I don't remember all the technical details of what I did on that morning, but I am certain I used a tripod. In addition to providing stability for sharp images, using a tripod helps me to slow down and work the composition with greater precision. I would have metered on the middle-toned area in the foreground to achieve a precise reading, which is critical when using slide film because there is little margin for error. Velvia was my choice for slide film because of its ability to reproduce saturated colors.

As the sun began to rise, the colors in the sky started to transition from violet to yellow. The clouds and mist scattered the light, creating a beautiful mix of colors. The reeds and lily pads in the foreground added texture and dimension to the scene and draw the viewer into the image. The rising mist between the mountains added another level of interest.

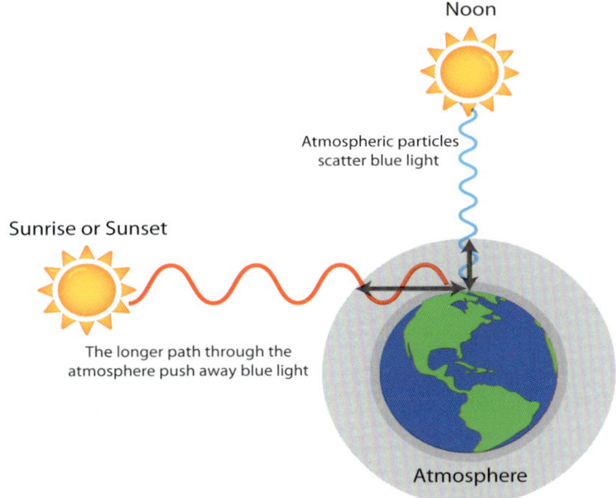

◄ The sun's rays travel a longer distance and through more atmospheric particles at sunrise and sunset, which scatters the long red and orange wavelengths of light. The sky is blue because tiny particles preferentially scatter blue light in all directions.

▼ Colors shift to rich golden tones as the sun rises over Raquette Lake. Photo courtesy of Mary Lou Smith.

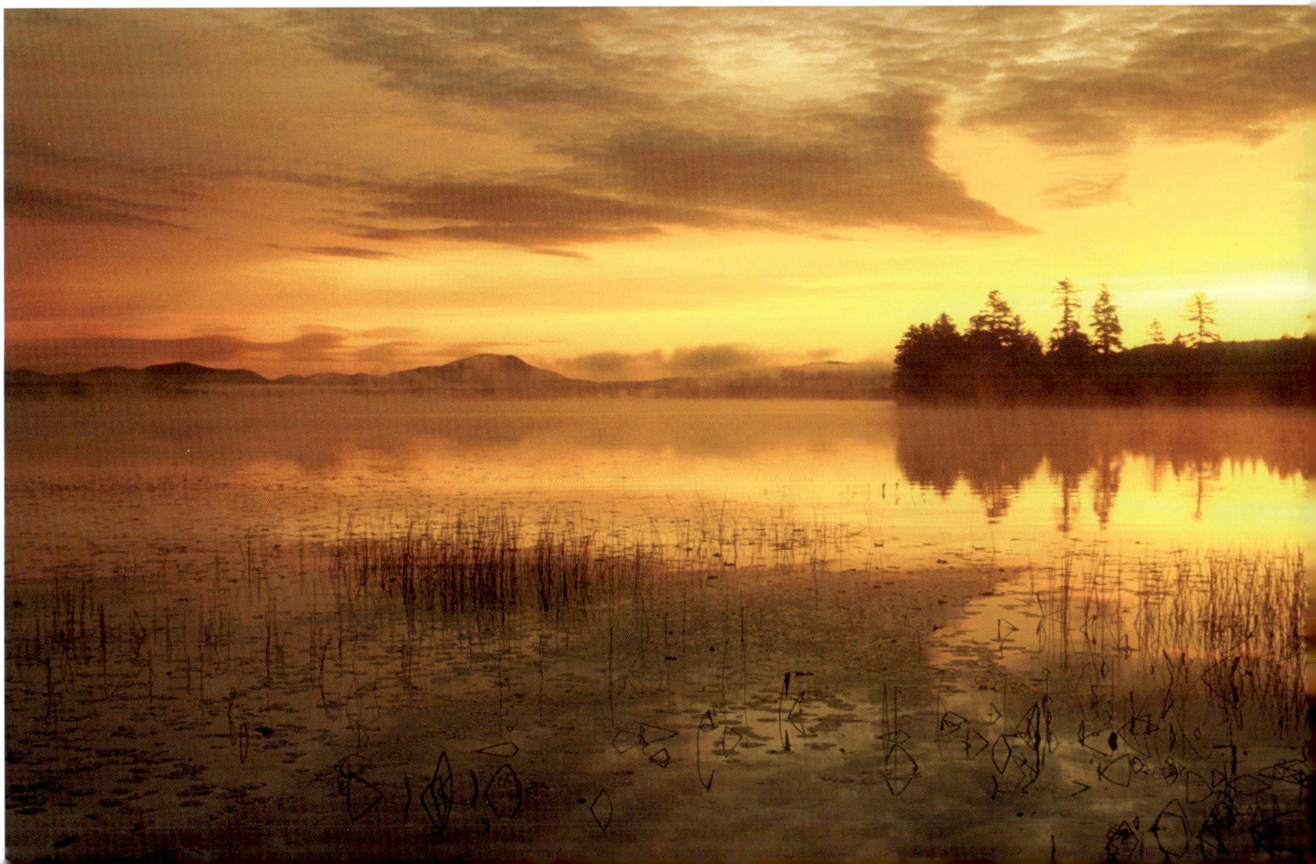

MAGIC HOUR

The light at the edges of the day, approximately the first hour after sunrise and the last hour before sunset, is known as the *golden hours.* Although the length of the "hour" depends on the global location and the time of year, the quality of light is magical—hence its other name, *magic hour.* During this time, the light is soft, diffused, and warm, without harsh shadows or bright highlights. The golden color of the low sun enhances the warmth of the landscape, especially when contrasted with a cool blue sky. As the low angle of sunlight falls onto land, it creates a warm golden glow that is very attractive for many landscape images—particularly in autumn, when the golden light enhances the warm colors of the changing leaves.

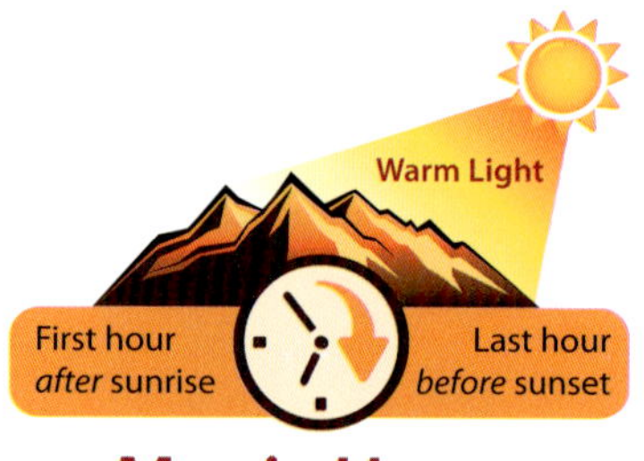

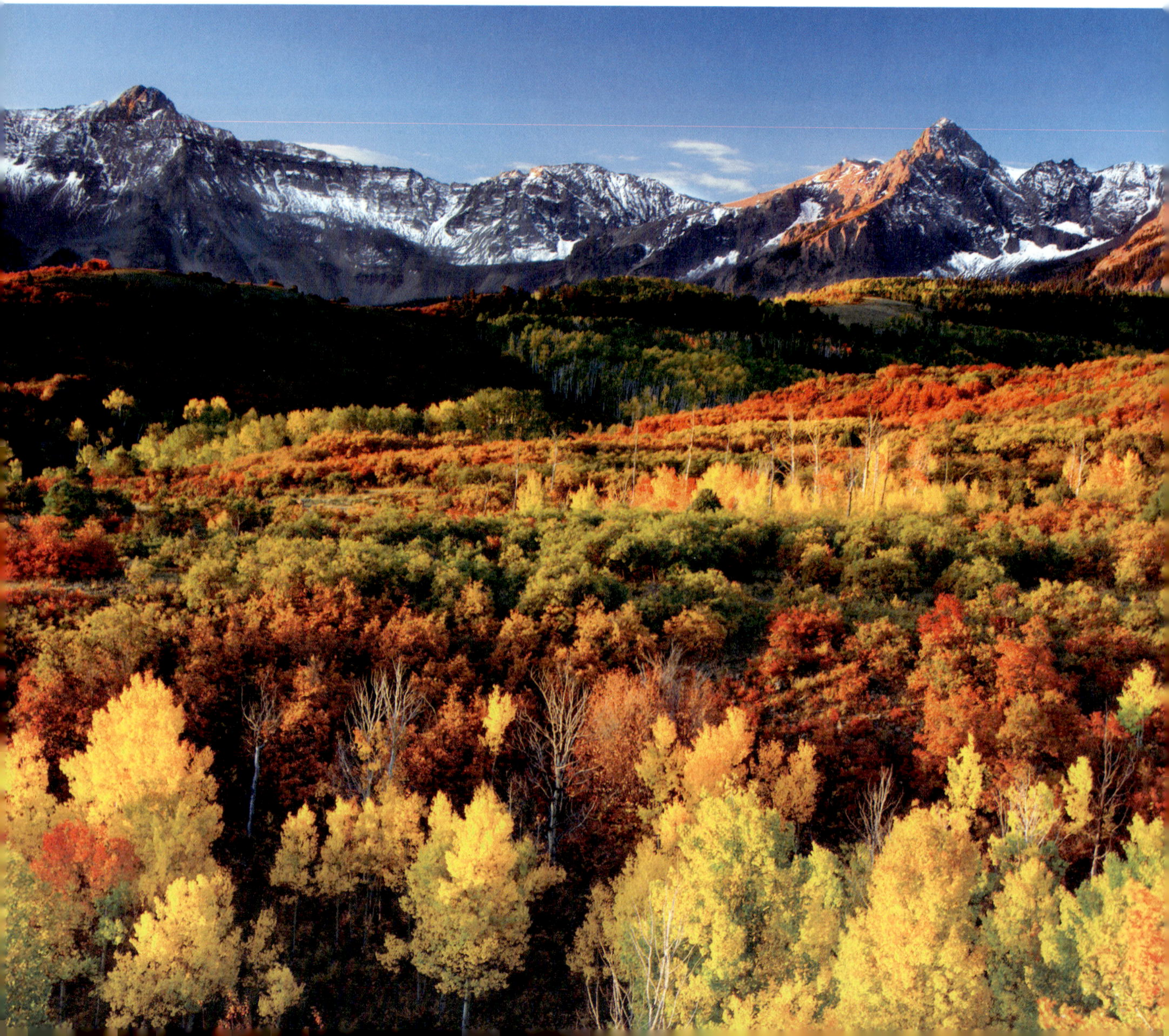

As I photographed Dallas Divide in autumn during the golden hour, the fall colors of the trees took on a golden glow. The magic hour was the optimal time to bring out the warmth of yellow and orange aspen leaves and showcase the changing seasons. As side lighting from the sun started to light Mears Peak in the distance, it created warm light on the mountain with open shade on the opposite ridges.

Open shade refers to an area not in direct sunlight that is illuminated by the blue sky, with a resultant blue cast in the shadows. Since part of the mountain is in open shade, there was a blue tint to the snow. This blue cast was easily removed in postproduction with Photoshop.

EARLY-MORNING LIGHT

Silverton, Colorado, is a National Historic Landmark that features summer train rides on the Durango and Silverton Narrow Gauge Railroad. This small town, nestled in the San Juan Mountains, attracts tourists and photographers alike. My companions and I piled into a 4-wheel-drive Jeep and headed up Gray Copper Gulch from the center of town. Not

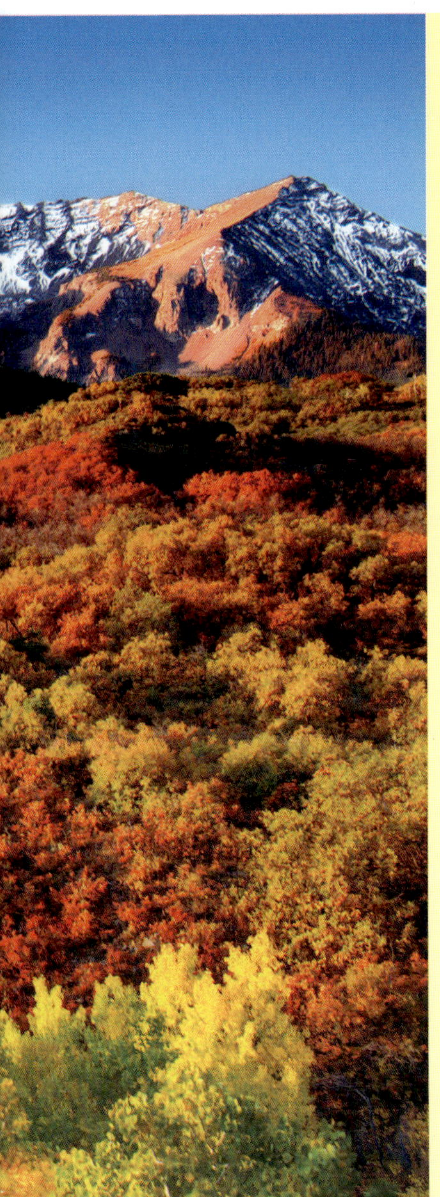

◄ Dallas Divide is a great location to see the changing seasons in front of Mears Peak near Telluride, Colorado.

TIME OF DAY: 7:23:06AM | FOCAL LENGTH: 58mm | ISO: 200 | APERTURE: f/22
SHUTTER SPEED: 1.3 seconds

▼ Magic hour imparted a beautiful golden light to Buttermilk Falls in the Adirondack Mountains. It helps to know your location. I knew that the light on this waterfall is best during the hour after sunrise when the trees reflect in the water and provide warmth to the scene.

TIME OF DAY: 8:57:14AM | FOCAL LENGTH: 25mm | ISO: 100 | APERTURE: f/22
SHUTTER SPEED: 1/1.2 second

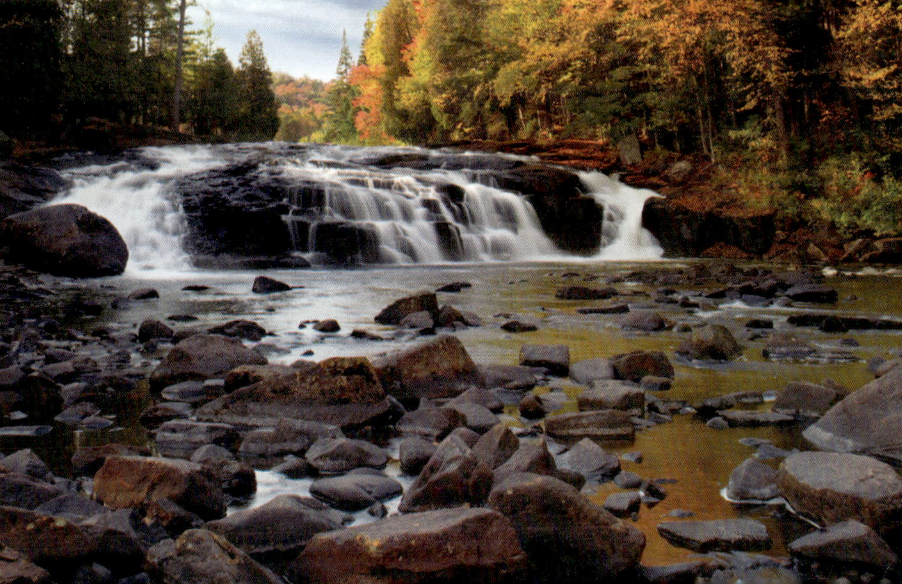

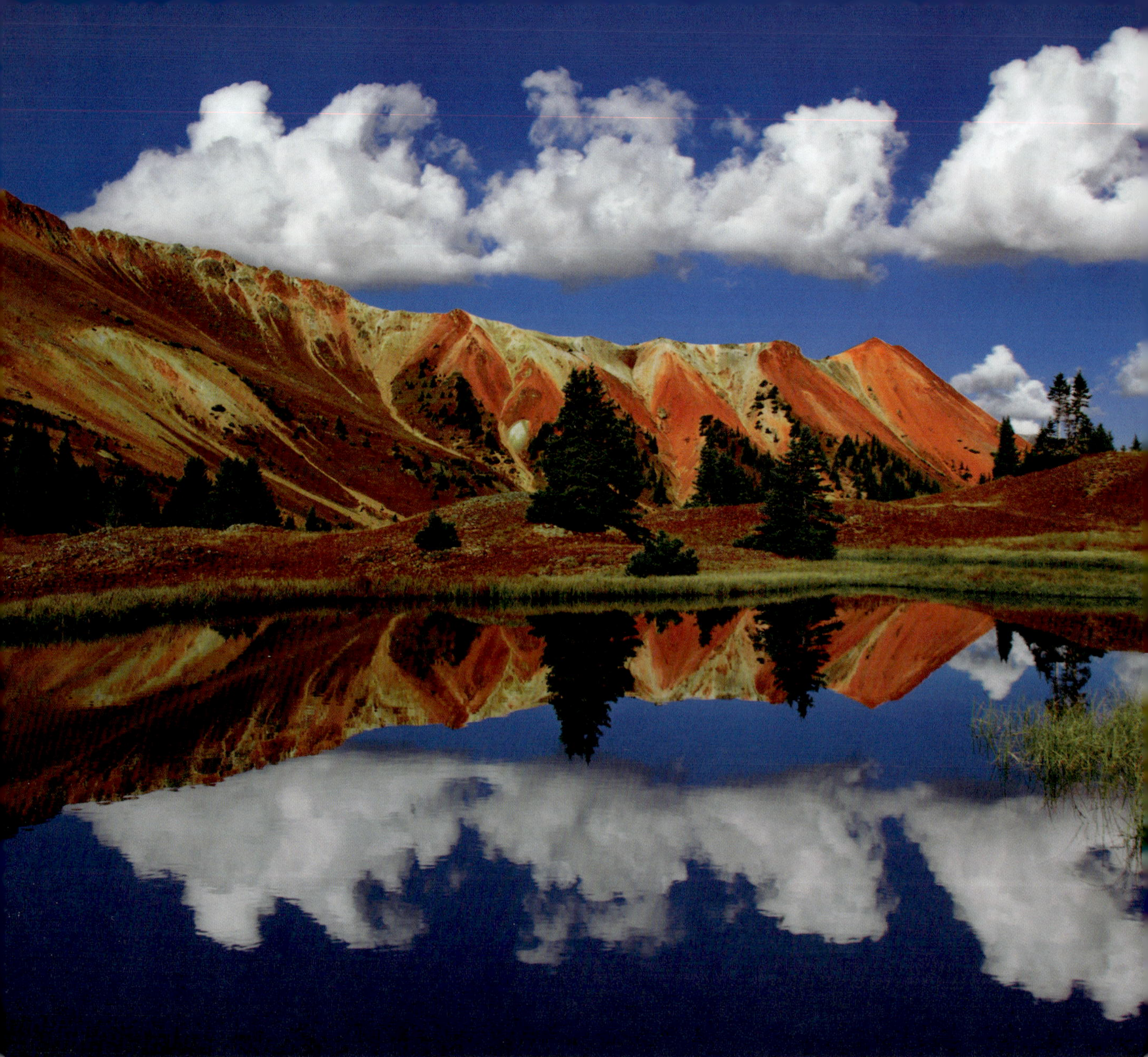

wanting to start the off-road journey in the dark, we arrived at these small mountain tarns in the early morning.

The sun was low and behind my back, creating a front-lit situation that cast very long shadows. The trick at this time of day is to be aware of your own shadow and make sure it is not in the frame. Working with a wide-angle focal length of 35mm or less is especially challenging because so much of the scene is visible in the frame. A careful composition with a cable release allowed me to stand away from the camera and tripod so my

▲ Red Mountain was reflected in a mountain tarn (a small body of water at a high elevation) during the early morning. The puffy clouds added texture and dimension to the scene.

TIME OF DAY: 9:51:59AM | FOCAL LENGTH: 32mm | ISO: 200 | APERTURE: f/18 | SHUTTER SPEED: 1/60 second

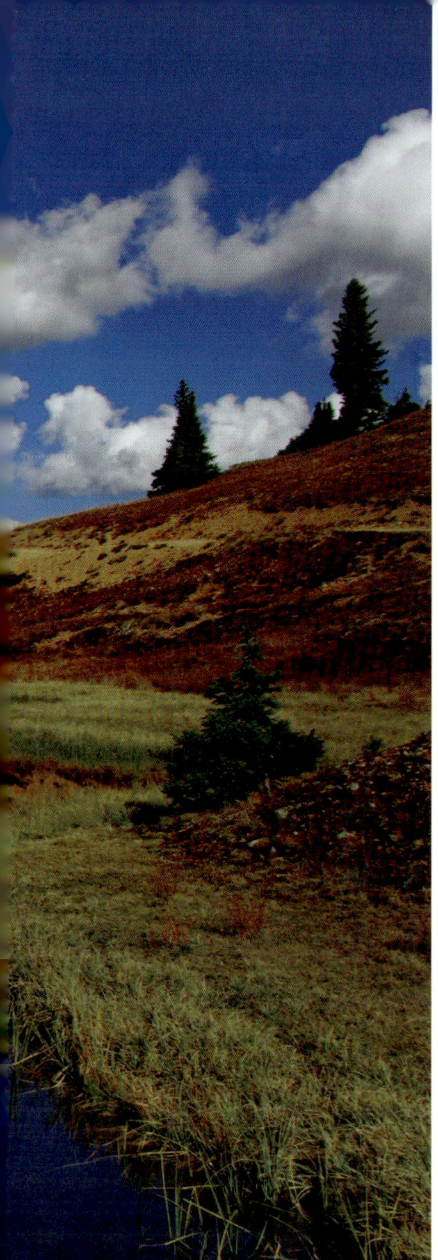

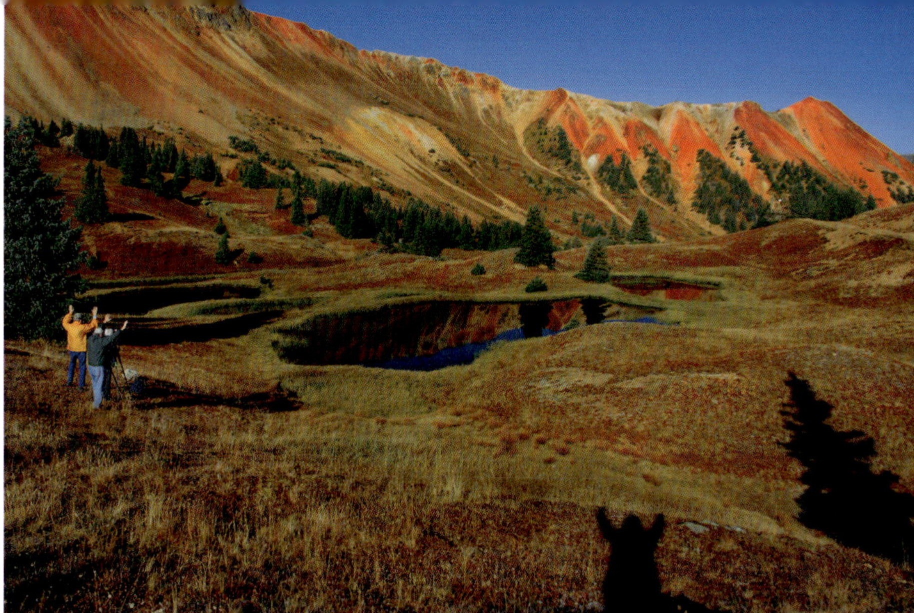

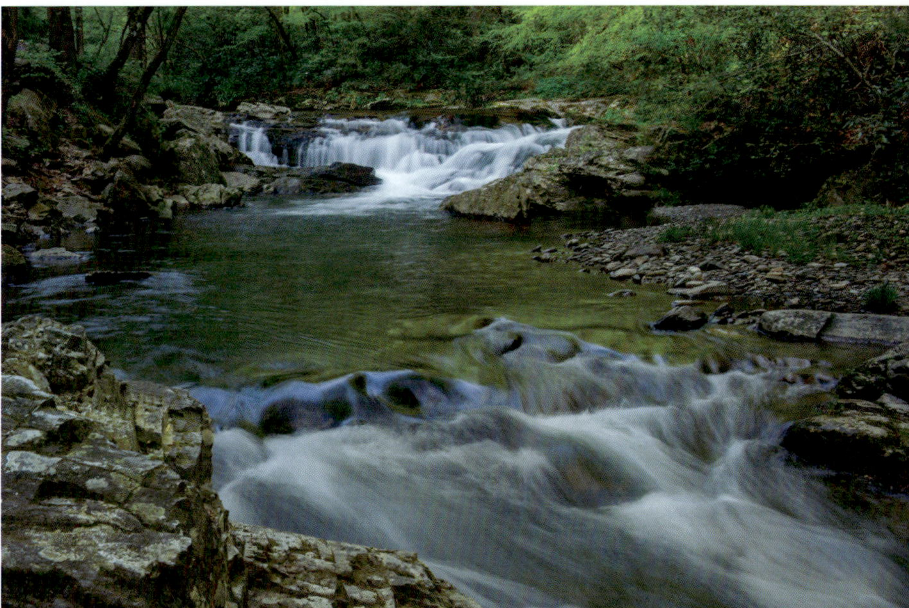

shadow was not visible. Look at the long shadows in the whimsical inset photo, and you can see how easy it is to include them in the frame (yes, we did this on purpose!).

At high elevations the air is cleaner, with less pollution and particles; this changes the red and blue levels present, raising the blue levels. A circular polarizer can remove some of the blue haze and darken the sky. However,

▲ (top) At this time of day, when the shadows are very long, it can be a challenge to keep your own shadow out of the frame. In this image, my fellow photographers and I decided to have fun with our shadows.

▲ (bottom) Early morning is also a good time to find reflections, as the sun is relatively low in the sky. In this image, trees lit by the low angle of the morning sun reflected into the cascades along Laurel Creek in the Smoky Mountains.

TIME OF DAY: 10:30:28AM | FOCAL LENGTH: 36mm | ISO: 100
APERTURE: f/20 | SHUTTER SPEED: 1/2.5 seconds

at this altitude, it is easy to over-polarize and have one side of the sky much darker than the other. This can be very noticeable when using a wide-angle lens. Additionally, at high altitudes it is possible to polarize the sky to the point that it is almost black. Remember that polarizers are adjustable, so a small amount of polarization may be adequate to darken the sky without creating an unwanted gradient.

MIDDAY SUN

Sometimes when hiking or traveling long distances or with non-photographers (who just don't "see" when the light is best), photographing in the harsh midday sun is unavoidable. There are some subjects, such as slot canyons, that require overhead sunlight to reach down into them, but this is the exception and not the rule for landscape photography.

The "Big Sky" of the southwest was new to me, growing up in the northeastern United States. I really wanted to capture the feeling of a large, wide-open landscape with a sky that seemed endless. Driving to Arizona, my friend and I arrived at Monument Valley close to noon. Fortunately, for this midday image, there were plenty of big, puffy clouds. The clouds not only added to the big-sky feel (notice how they get smaller as

I really wanted to capture the feeling of a large, wide-open landscape with a sky that seemed endless.

▼ Successful midday images are possible with plenty of puffy clouds to filter the light and create intriguing shadows across Monument Valley in Arizona.

ISO: 50 Fujichrome Velvia | APERTURE: Not available | SHUTTER SPEED: Not available

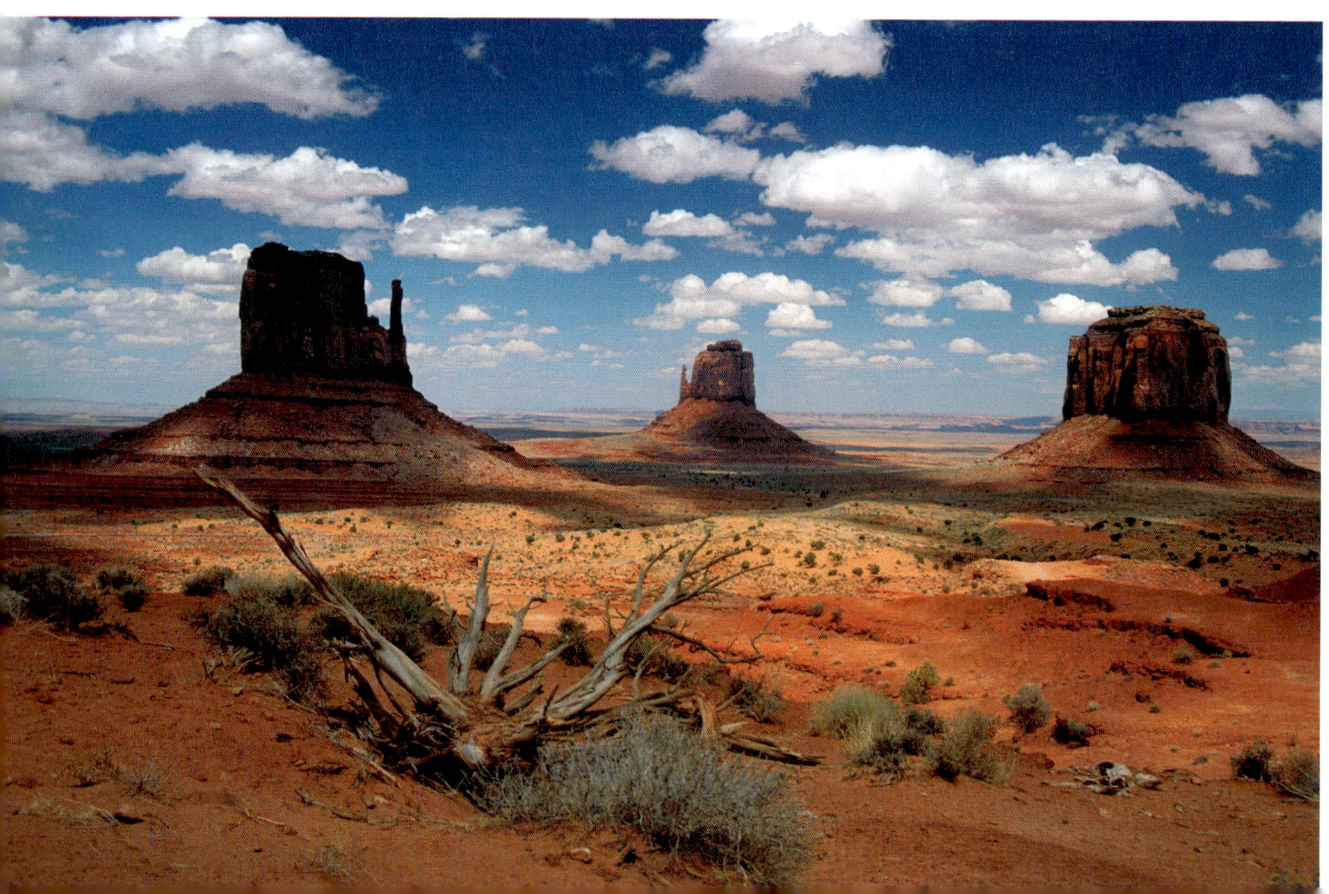

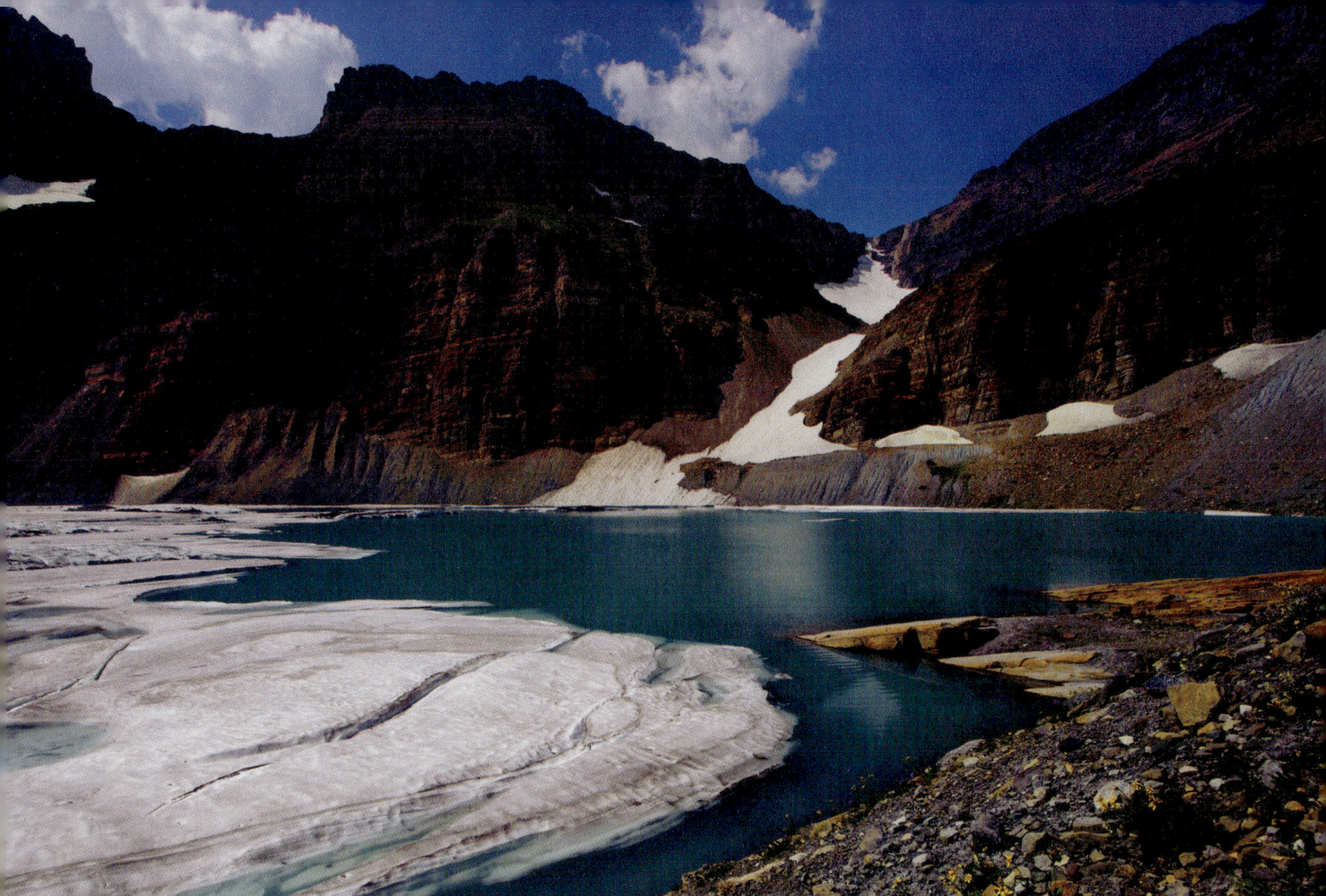

▲ Fed by the melting waters of Grinnell Glacier, Upper Grinnell Lake, located at the base of the Continental Divide, was photographed at midday after a long hike to reach this incredible destination.

TIME OF DAY: 1:48:42PM | FOCAL LENGTH: 19mm | ISO: 100 | APERTURE: f/14 | SHUTTER SPEED: 1/80 second

> "The key to successful photography is taking time to really see. It may sound simple, but this is the hardest thing we do—training the eye to see the nuances in colors, compositions, and imperfections."[6]
>
> **Jack Dykinga**
> *Pulitzer Prize-winning photographer*

they get farther away), they also filtered the light. When faced with high overhead sunlight, look for puffy clouds in your scene to reduce the contrast, create interesting shadows, and add dimension to the landscape.

The Mittens, free-standing sandstone buttes, produced intriguing shadows and texture across this region of the Colorado Plateau on this day. The use of the deadwood and

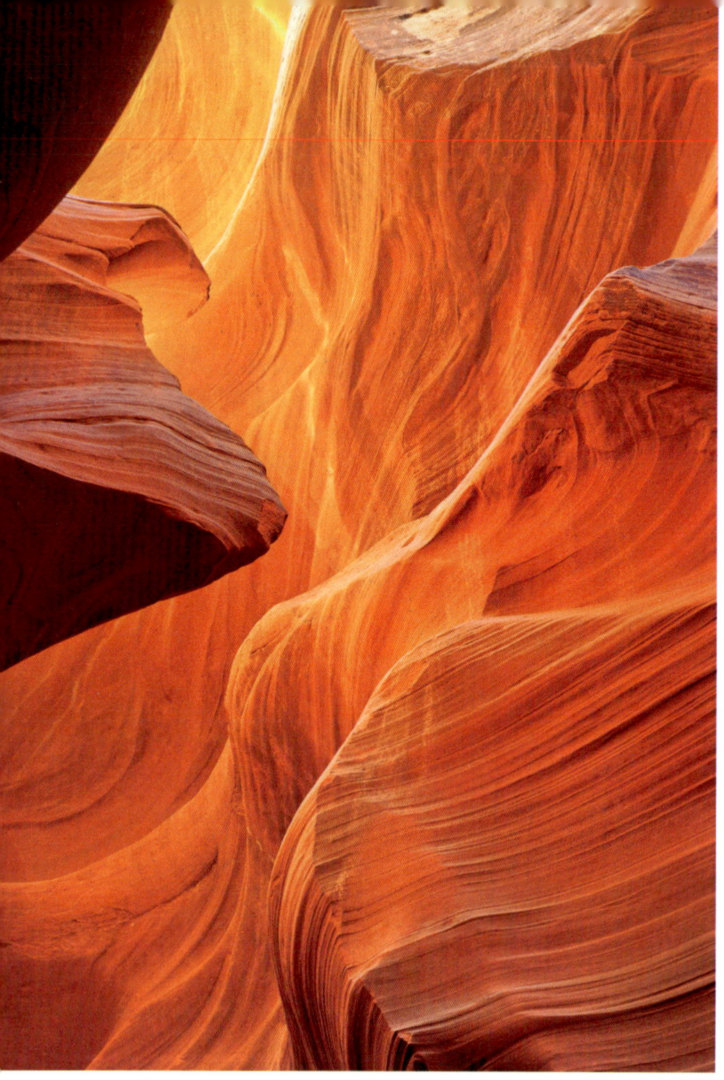

◄ Antelope Canyon in Arizona is one subject that requires midday overhead light to reach down into the canyon walls. Photo courtesy of Michael Lustbader.

► Reflections and warm light from the late-day sun give the Middle Prong of the Little Pigeon River in the Great Smoky Mountains a golden hue.

TIME OF DAY: 5:54:41PM | FOCAL LENGTH: 24MM | ISO: 100
APERTURE: f/20 | SHUTTER SPEED: 1 second

sagebrush as foreground elementsadds interest and depth to the stark desert landscape of Monument Valley. I strategically positioned my camera so the branches of the wood pointed to the Mittens, drawing the viewer's gaze into and through the scene.

Remote locations that require hiking to reach are another instance when overhead midday sun may not be avoidable. This was the case for my "moderate" hike up 1600 feet over 4+ miles (one way) to Upper Grinnell Lake and Grinnell Glacier in Glacier National Park. The prize at the end of this incredible journey was a beautiful glacially fed turquoise lake.

Unfortunately, the light was not great upon arrival and there was haze in the area from recent forest fires. To make the best of the situation, I used a polarizer to remove some of the haze and glare on the water. With a little help from Photoshop to bring out the detail in the distant mountain, I was able to capture a successful image of this very special place.

LATE-AFTERNOON LIGHT

Late afternoon is another great time to get your camera out and photograph the low angle of the sun's rays. At this time of day the shadows are very long, creating dimensionality and drama across the landscape. Reflections and silhouettes can also occur at this time. The light becomes warmer as the golden hour and sunset approaches.

When photographing in the Greenbrier area of the Great Smoky Mountains during the spring, you will find that the rivers flow strong and trees glisten a bright green. This color can be "added" to the rivers when the late-day sun reflects color from nearby surroundings into the water. These reflections transform grayish water into a colorful visual treat.

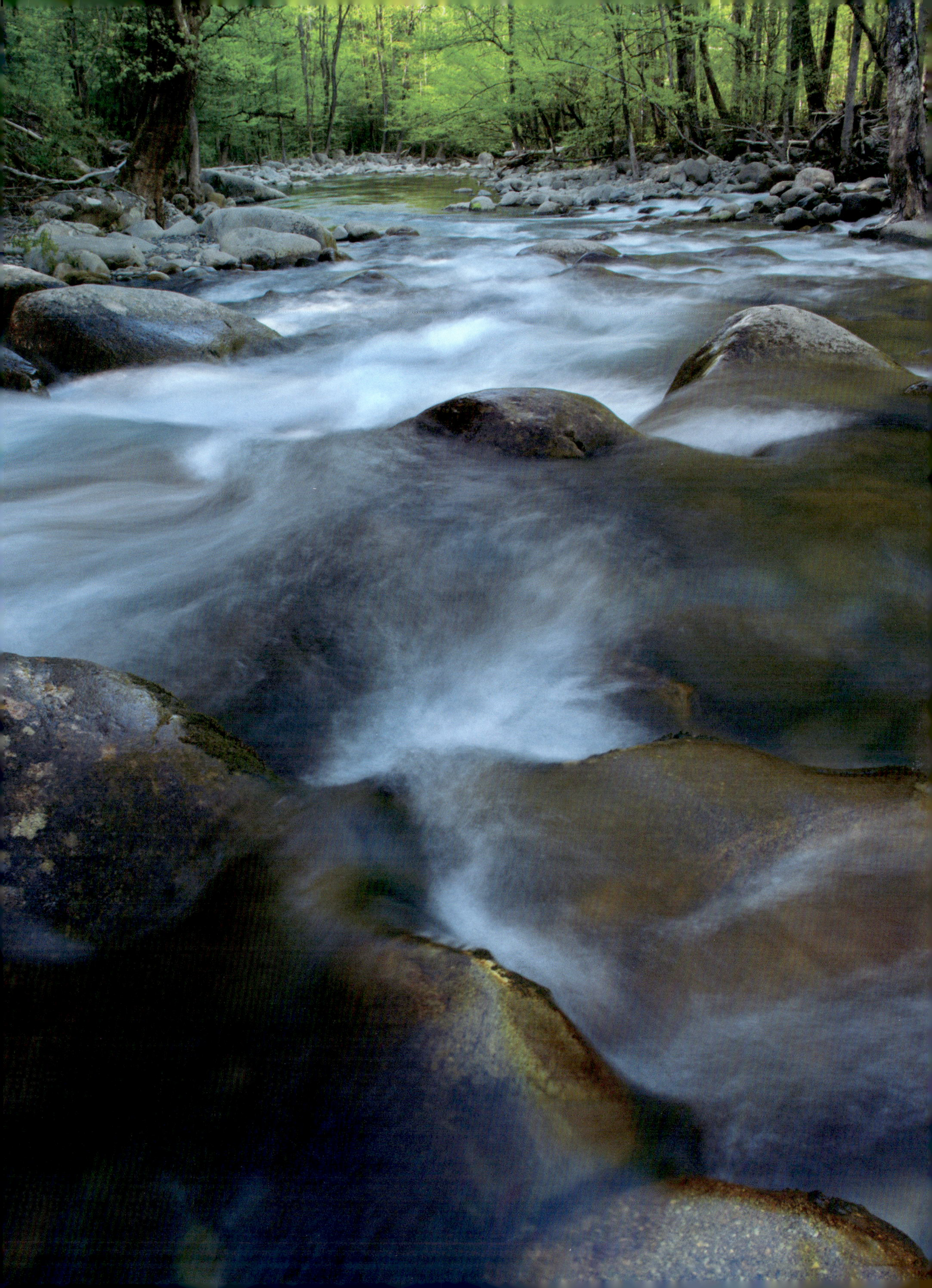

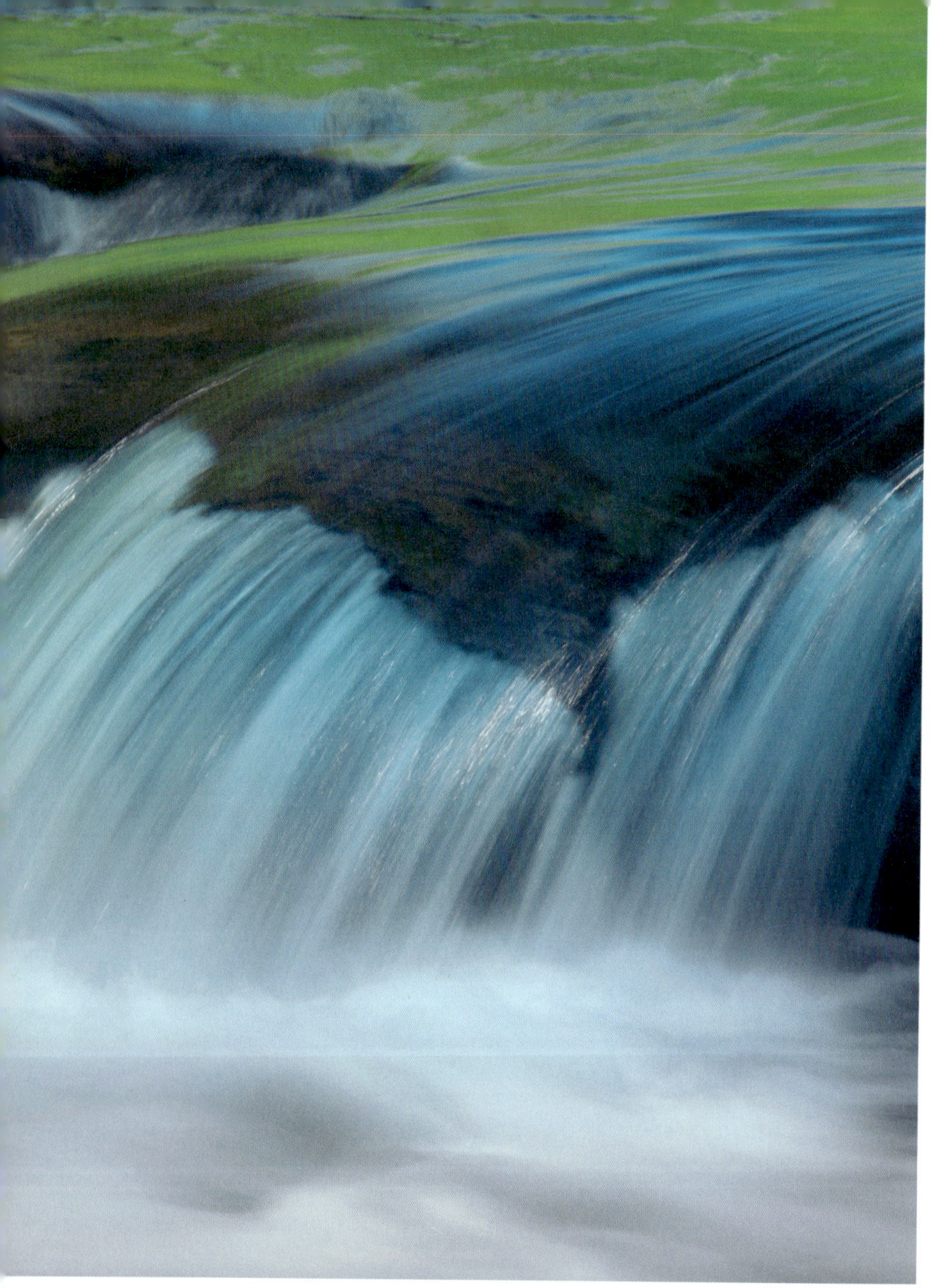

◄ Spring green adds reflected color to this cascade of water in the Greenbrier area of the Great Smoky Mountains.

TIME OF DAY: 4:38:54PM | FOCAL LENGTH: 210MM | ISO: 100 | APERTURE: f/14 | SHUTTER SPEED: 1/5 second

▼ (bottom left) The late-afternoon reflected light of Lake Durant provided a nice contrast to the colors of the autumn season change. The warm tones of the late-day sun are accented in the fall when the leaves change from green to the warm colors of yellow, orange, and red.

TIME OF DAY: 5:34:22PM | FOCAL LENGTH: 44MM | ISO: 100 | APERTURE: f/25 | SHUTTER SPEED: 1/5 second

▼ (bottom right) A two-stop hard-edge graduated filter placed over the sky helped to balance the exposure between the foreground and the sky.

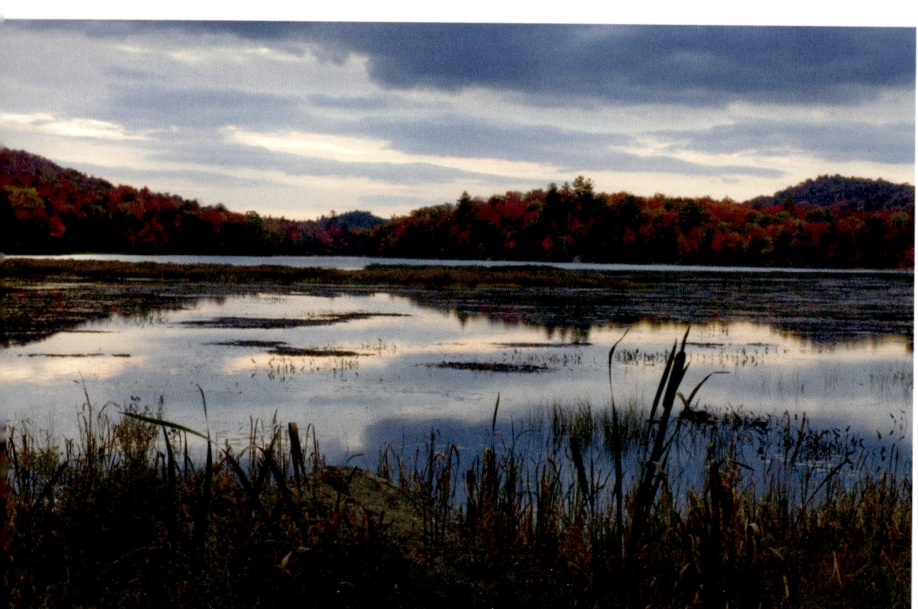

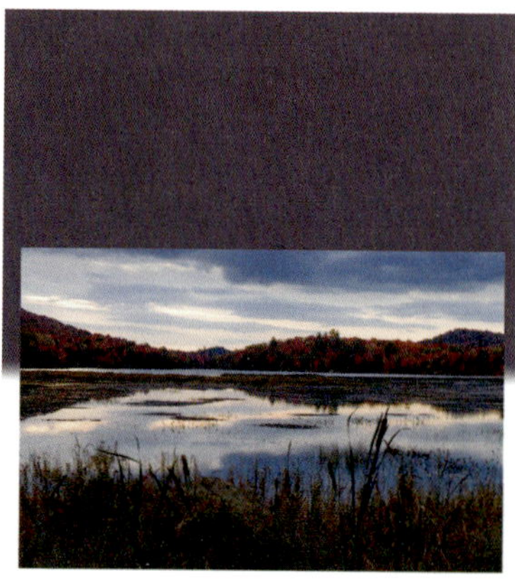

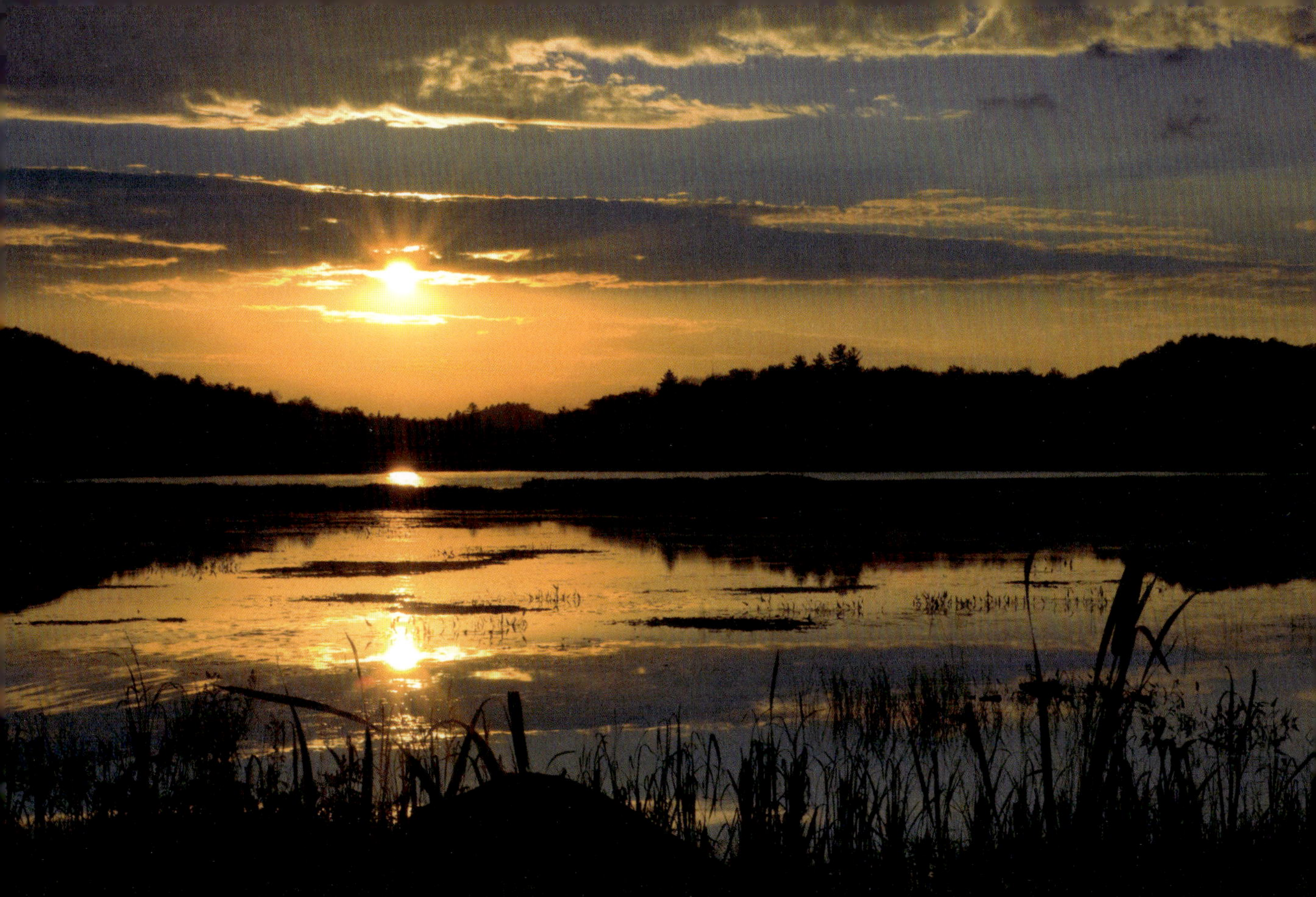

▲ Cattails add to the story with a silhouette as the sun drops over Lake Durant.

TIME OF DAY: 6:18:39PM | FOCAL LENGTH: 44MM | ISO: 100 | APERTURE: f/29 | SHUTTER SPEED: 1/30 second

I found Lake Durant in the Adirondack Mountains to be another good location for late-day photo opportunities. I climbed down the steep bank where several cattails and tall grasses lined the water's edge. They made a nice foreground element and provided texture and dimension to the scene. The sky was brighter than the foreground, so I placed a two-stop hard-edge graduated filter in front of the lens, aligning the dark edge of the filter with the distant shoreline.

Anytime the sun is partially hidden behind an object, you might see a starburst effect.

Late-day sunlight also creates good silhouettes. I continued to keep the cattails in my foreground because they added interest as a silhouette. The sun peeking out from behind the clouds created the starburst effect. Anytime the sun is partially hidden behind an object, you might see a starburst effect. To make the rays appear to radiate outward, use a small aperture such as f/22.

EVENING GOLDEN HOUR

Fall in the Adirondack Mountains is a magical time. The mountains dance with color as the seasons change. Iconic Adirondack chairs sit along the water's edge ready for visitors to watch the show. The main roads weave along the lakes with open access to many lakeside views. Hiking boots and canoeing will get you deep in the heart of the mountains, but there are plenty of other photo opportunities that don't require an outdoor adventure.

As I gain more photography experience, I realize it requires a lot of effort to get to several locations. It's sometimes necessary to climb mountains and hike off the beaten path to get "the shot." The irony is one of my award-winning photos was taken along the roadside.

Blue Mountain Lake is located at the intersection of Route 28 and Route 30 in the Adirondack Mountains of New York. As I drove by this location, magic light "happened," and I stopped at the side of the road to capture it. The low angle of the sun lit up the autumn foliage on the mountainside and this beautiful orange glow reflected into Blue Mountain Lake. Its magic was brief—only a few minutes—just long enough for me to capture an award-winning image.

My Nikon N90 (loaded with Fujichrome Velvia slide film), a 70–200mm lens with a polarizer, and a tripod was all I needed to capture this moment. This image proves that all is not lost if you cannot climb mountains or paddle a canoe. Roadside shots can be magical too.

▼ This image of the Dock at Blue Mountain Lake during the evening golden hour won second place in *Adirondack Life*'s 2001 annual photography contest. The low angle of the sun lit up the mountainside and filled the lake with golden reflections.

FOCAL LENGTH: 70–200mm | ISO: 50 Fujichrome Velvia
APERTURE: Not available | SHUTTER SPEED: Not available

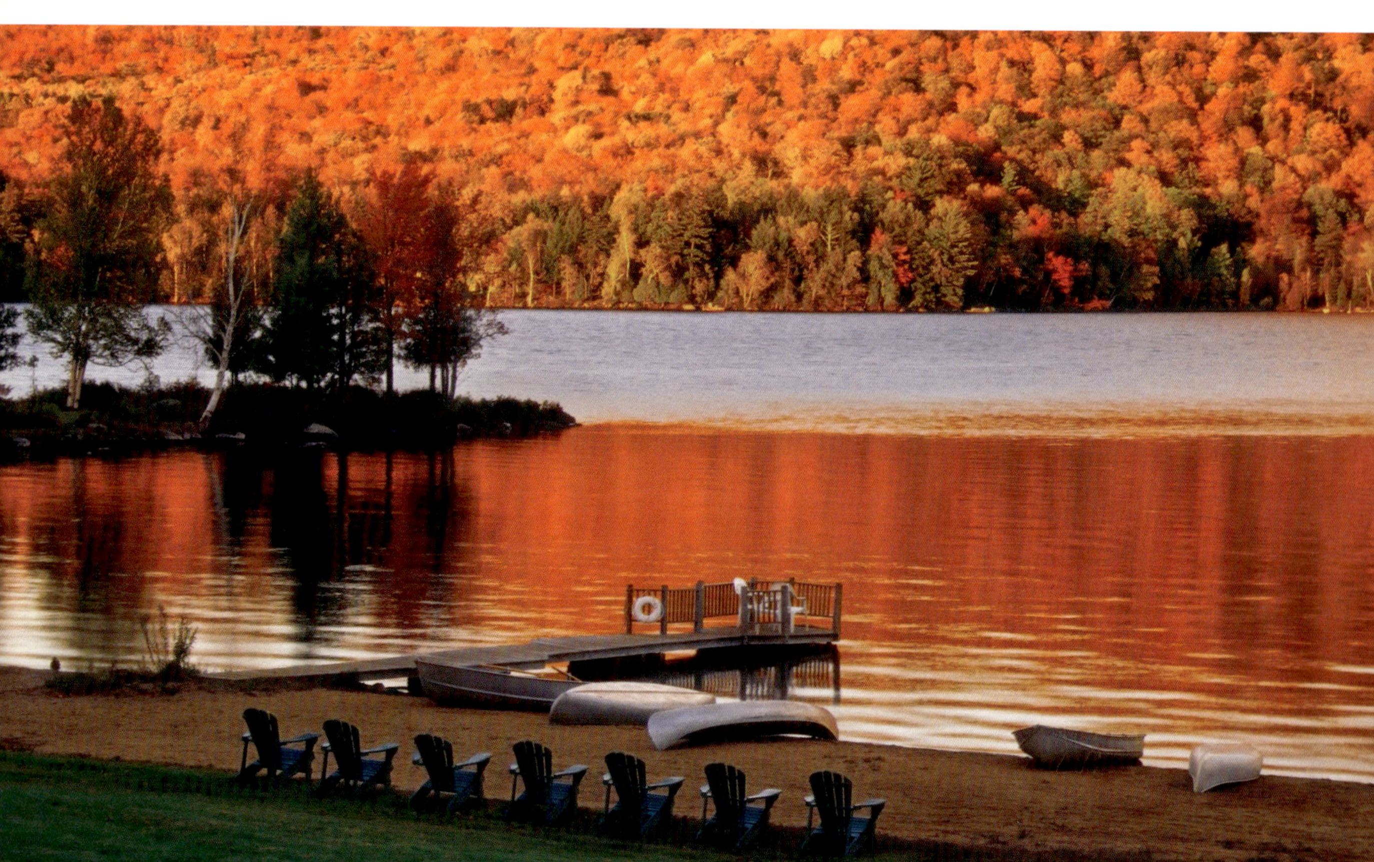

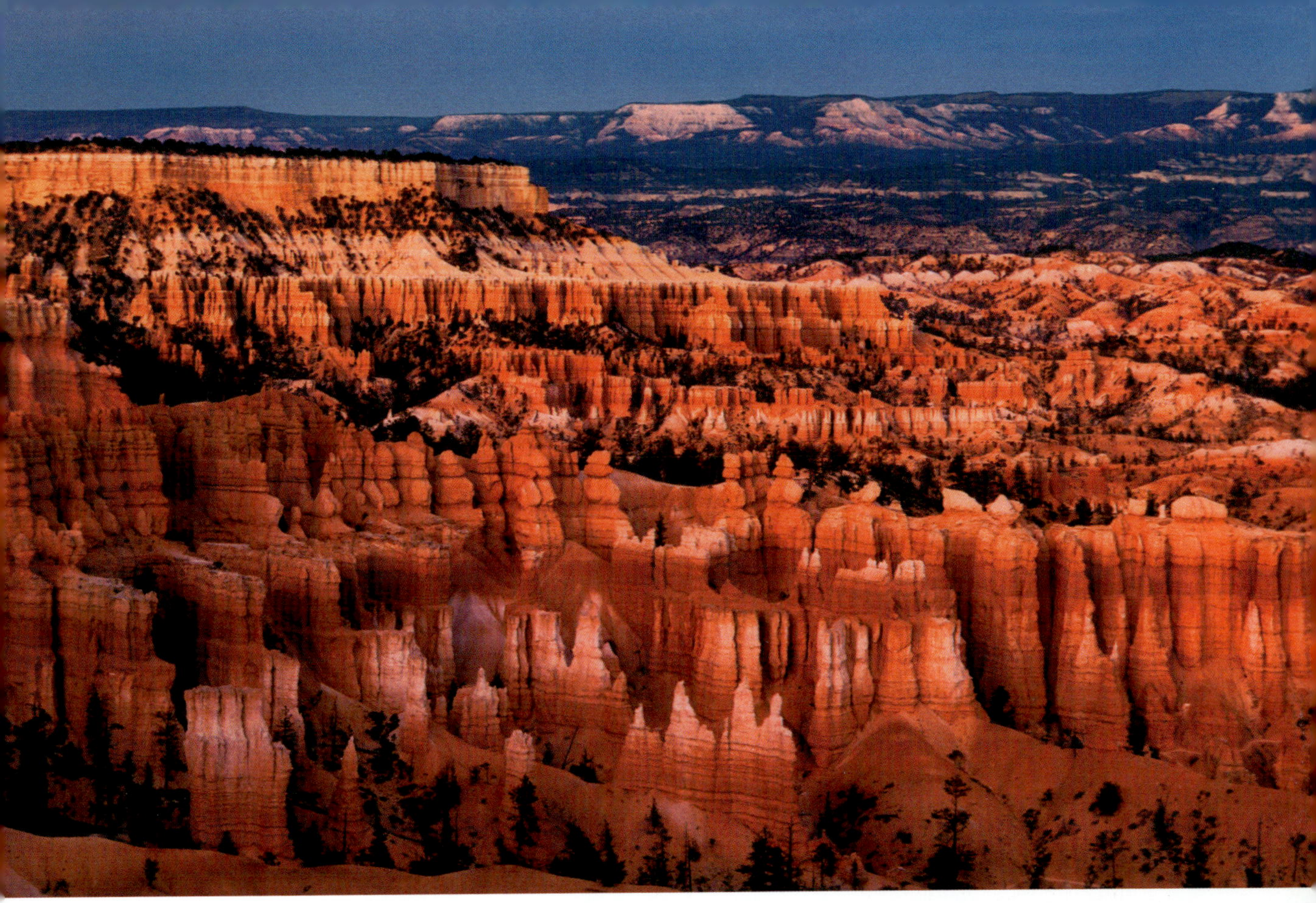

▲ The Hoodoos, rock pillars created by years of erosion, in Bryce Canyon, Utah glow in the warm light of golden hour. The Hoodoos spired texture is accented by the low-angle side light from the late-day sun.

ISO: 50 Fujichrome Velvia
APERTURE: Not available
SHUTTER SPEED: Not available

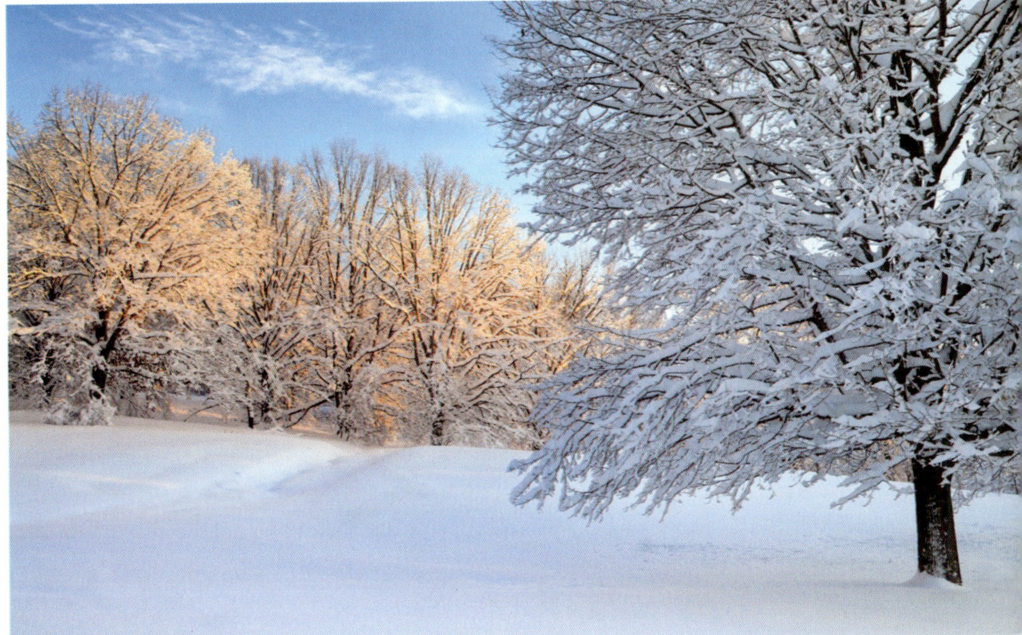

► Golden light can occur during any season, as seen in this photograph, captured after a winter snowstorm in South Park, Pennsylvania.

FOCAL LENGTH: 25mm
ISO: 200 | APERTURE: f/7.1
SHUTTER SPEED: 1/125 second

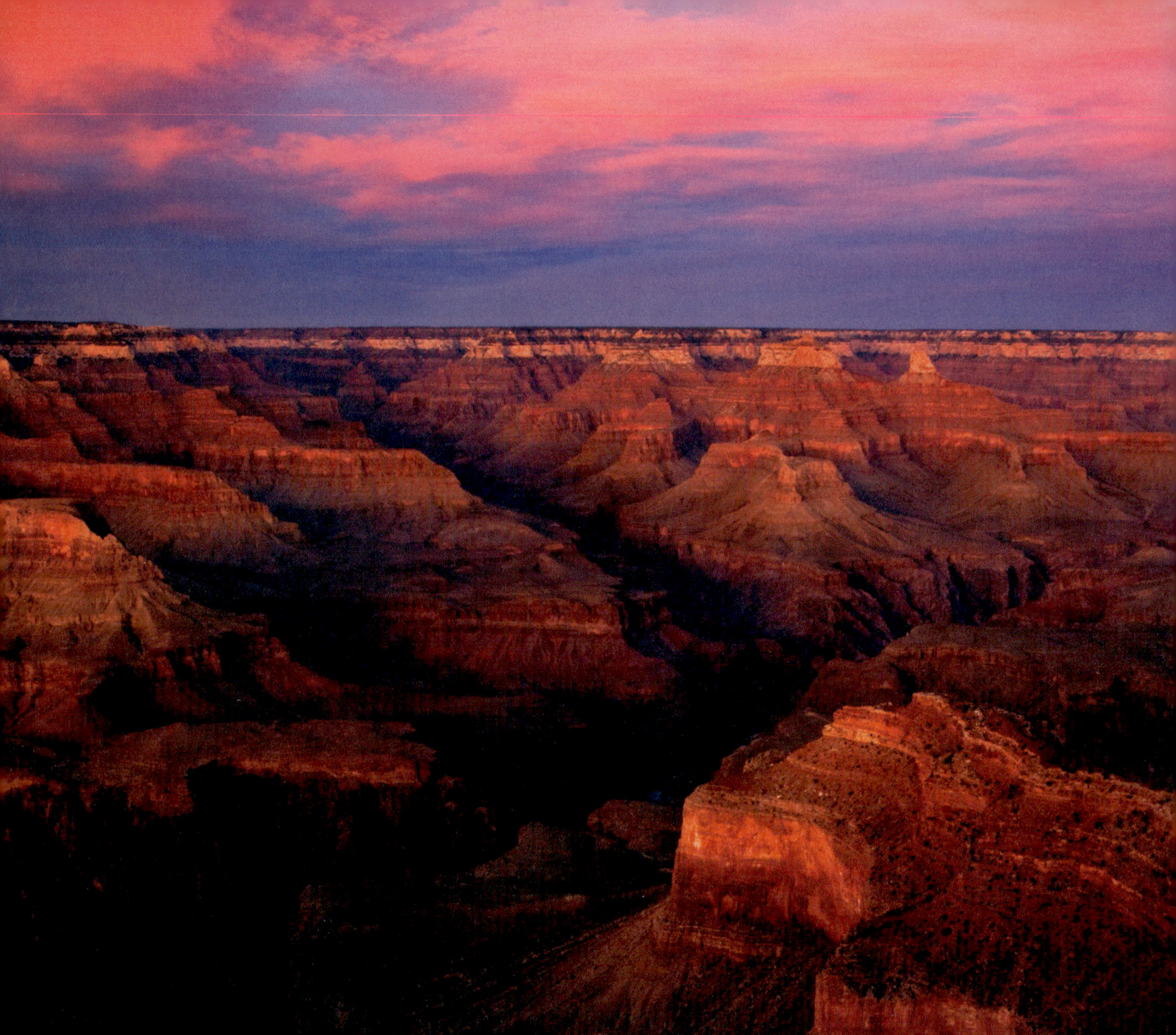

SUNSET

The Grand Canyon is easily one of the most iconic destinations in America. As far as the eye can see, its expansive views are not matched anywhere. The South Rim is the most popular location, with about 4 million visitors a year. It is open year round, and while the nights can get cold in the winter, it is far less crowded than in the summer. I visited the park in November when the crowds were low and there was open access to shooting locations.

▲ The two-billion-year-old sandstone of Grand Canyon radiates with color and texture at sunset. Hopi Point offers views to the south and west as the remaining light of the day produces a grand finale of color.

TIME OF DAY: 5:35:59PM | FOCAL LENGTH: 20mm | ISO: 200 | APERTURE: f/20 | SHUTTER SPEED: 2.5 seconds

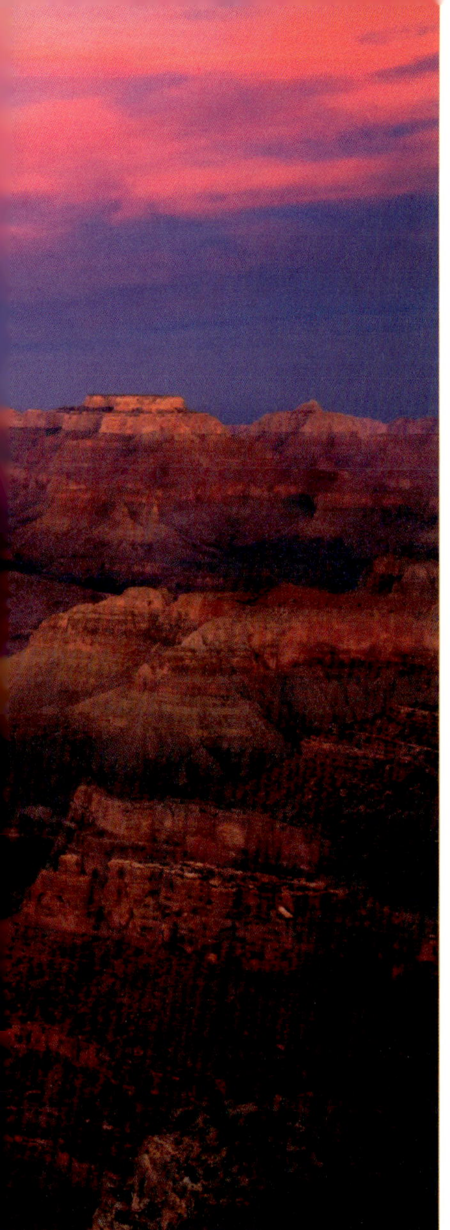

Sunrise and sunset are the best times to photograph the canyon; the low angle of the sun accents the canyon's colors, and shadows define the shapes and textures of gorge. I set up near Hopi Point and was prepared to shoot just before sunset. Hopi Point, named after Native Americans who lived along the Colorado River, is one of the most popular sunset vantage points. Its wide vista offers views to the south and west. The sky was illuminated with color as the finale of the setting sun created an interplay of light, shadow, and colors between the deep canyon walls and the clouds above.

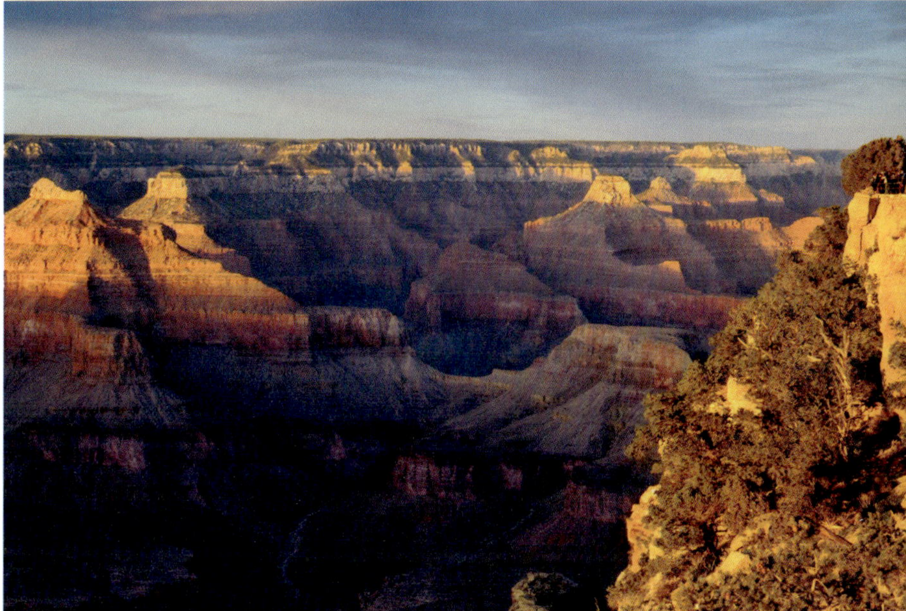

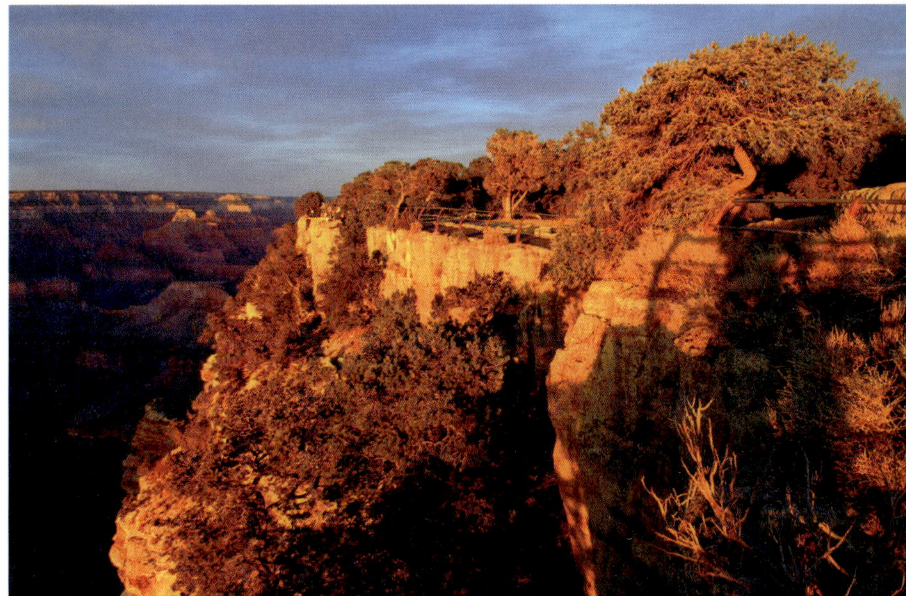

► (top) At 5:16PM, the low angle of the sun fell into the uppermost ridges of the Grand Canyon.

TIME OF DAY: 5:16:54PM | FOCAL LENGTH: 45mm | ISO: 200 | APERTURE: f/20 | SHUTTER SPEED: 1/3 second

► (bottom) At 5:20PM, a golden glow fell briefly on the upper edge of the canyon wall.

TIME OF DAY: 5:21:29pm | FOCAL LENGTH: 18mm | ISO: 200 | APERTURE: f/20 | SHUTTER SPEED: 1/5 second

Remember when photographing sunrises and sunsets to look behind you. The sky can be more interesting and colorful opposite the sun. Hopi Point's horseshoe-shaped overlook offered multiple views in different directions, so when I looked behind me I saw the golden glow on the upper rim. This light changed quickly, so working fast was essential. Notice how quickly the color changed on the upper wall within a five-minute span. The sun set at 5:27PM that November day. The main image was captured at 5:35PM as the light echoed off the canyon walls below.

DUSK

Many photographers stop shooting after sunset, pack their bag, head to dinner, and miss the blue hour. The colors in the sky turn a beautiful cobalt blue—distinctive from the rest of the day—during this time. Although the duration of the blue hour varies according to the time of year and the distance from the equator, the quality of light is exceptional.

Traveling with follow photographer and friend Perri K. Schelat, I set up to capture the civil twilight (the time after the sunset when the sun is 6 degrees below the horizon) and the blue hour at Lake McDonald in Glacier National Park. A few minutes before the sun officially set at 8:38PM, the colors started to transition into cool blue tones. The sky was still lighter than the foreground rocks, so I used a 3-stop graduated filter at a slight angle to balance the sky with the foreground. I spot metered on the sky just above the small cloud for proper exposure. Even at this time of night, a polarizer is effective at reducing the glare on the water and revealing the rocks below the surface.

Additionally, the blue hour allowed us the chance to experiment and explore creative possibilities in the low available light. For example, Perri used a flashlight on the rocks in the foreground. She moved the light beam all over the rocks to "paint" them with light. Each time it was different—making it a fun experiment. Even during nautical twilight (when the sun is between 6 and 12 degrees below the horizon) the sky and its reflection were brighter than the foreground rocks, so illuminating the rocks with flash or strobe brought out some of the details in the rocks. At this time of day, a tripod and cable release are an absolute must because exposure times are very long—sometimes several minutes.

► Detail in the foreground sedimentary rocks was illuminated by the overhead sky just after sunset at Lake McDonald in Glacier National Park.

TIME OF DAY: 8:39:32PM | FOCAL LENGTH: 28mm | ISO: 125 | APERTURE: f/14 | SHUTTER SPEED: 2.5 seconds

> "Light . . . and an intense perception and awareness, an intuition for tuning in to the cycles of nature's forces—these are the illusive tools I work with to create photographs."[7]
>
> **David Muench**
> *Heralded American-landscape photographer*

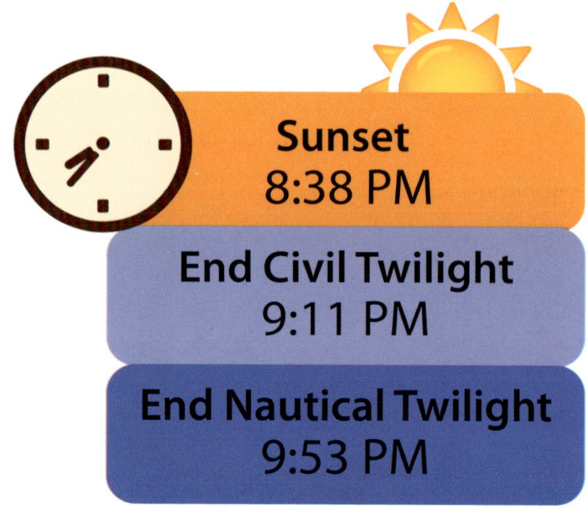

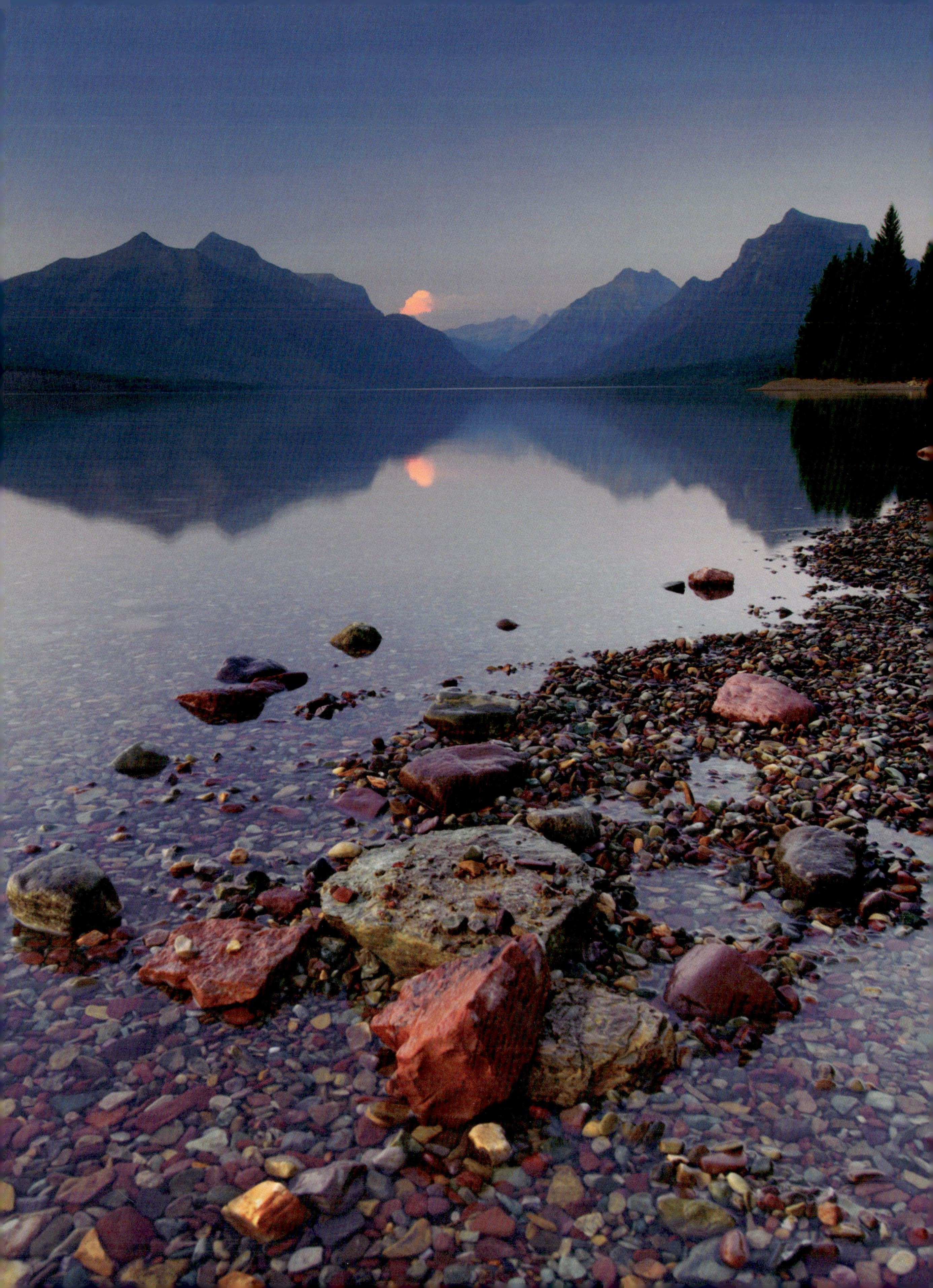

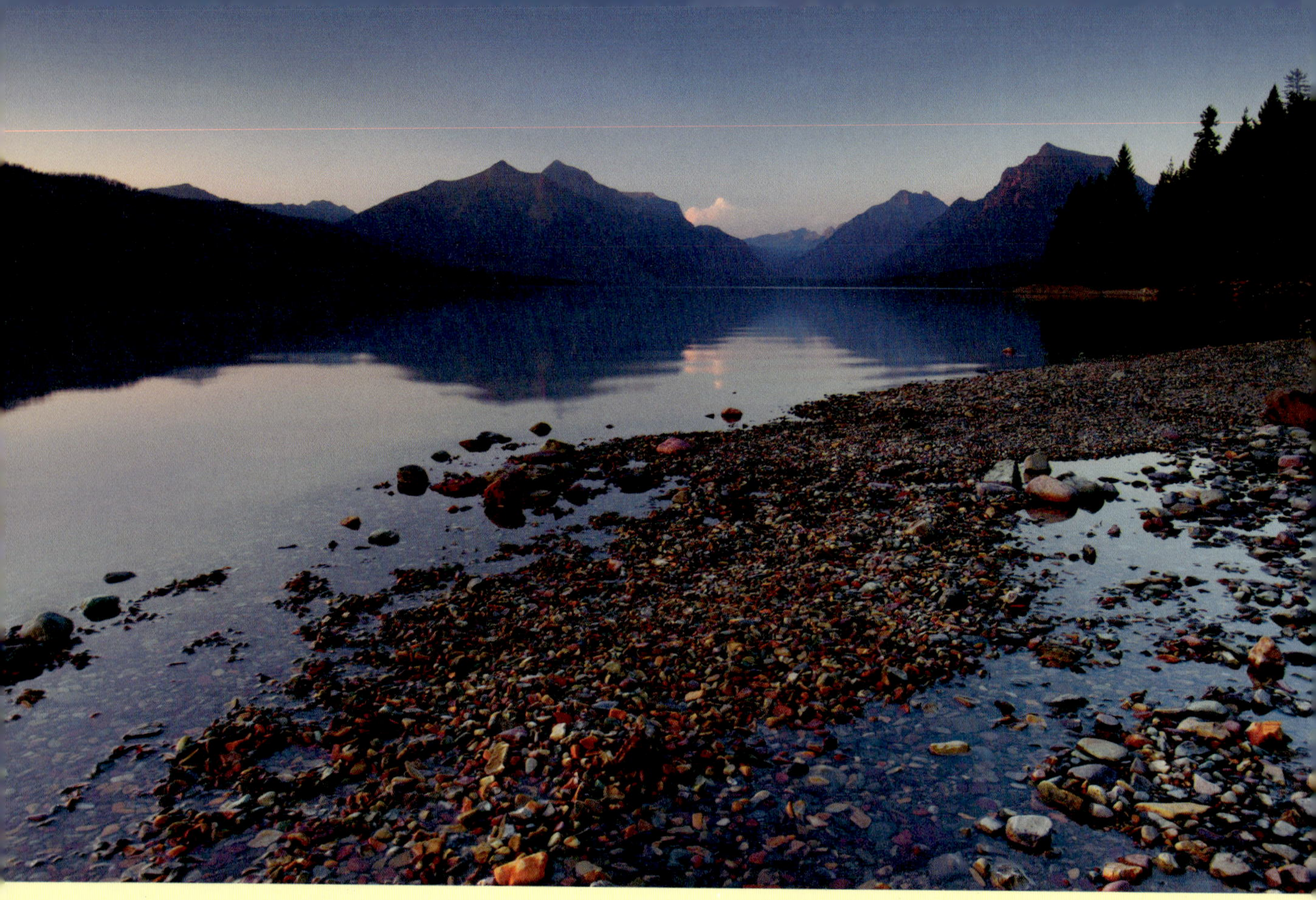

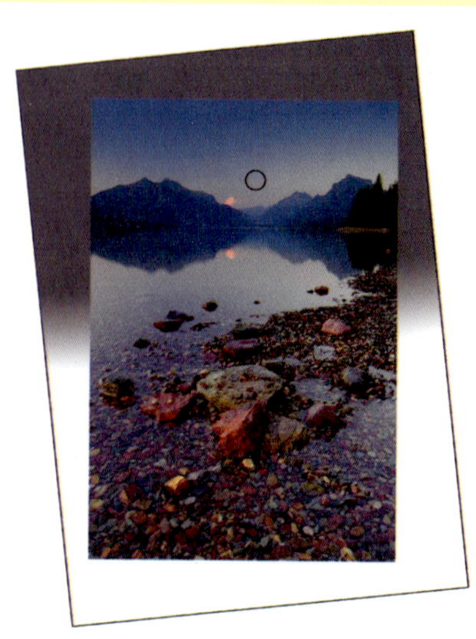

▲ Many scenes work well in both horizontal and vertical formats, so if time permits, try it both ways.

TIME OF DAY: 8:32:08PM | FOCAL LENGTH: 25mm | ISO: 125 | APERTURE: f/14
SHUTTER SPEED: 1/1.7 second

◄ A three-stop graduated filter used at a slight angle over the sky and water area helped to balance the exposure and avoid the foreground being underexposed. A polarizer reduced the glare on the water and revealed the color of the rocks below.

► During the blue hour, rocks and trees have less distinction as their texture and details fade. In this image, a flashlight was used to paint the rocks with light. This brought out some of the detail in the foreground.

TIME OF DAY: 9:25:21PM | FOCAL LENGTH: 35mm | ISO: 125 | APERTURE: f/16
SHUTTER SPEED: 89 seconds

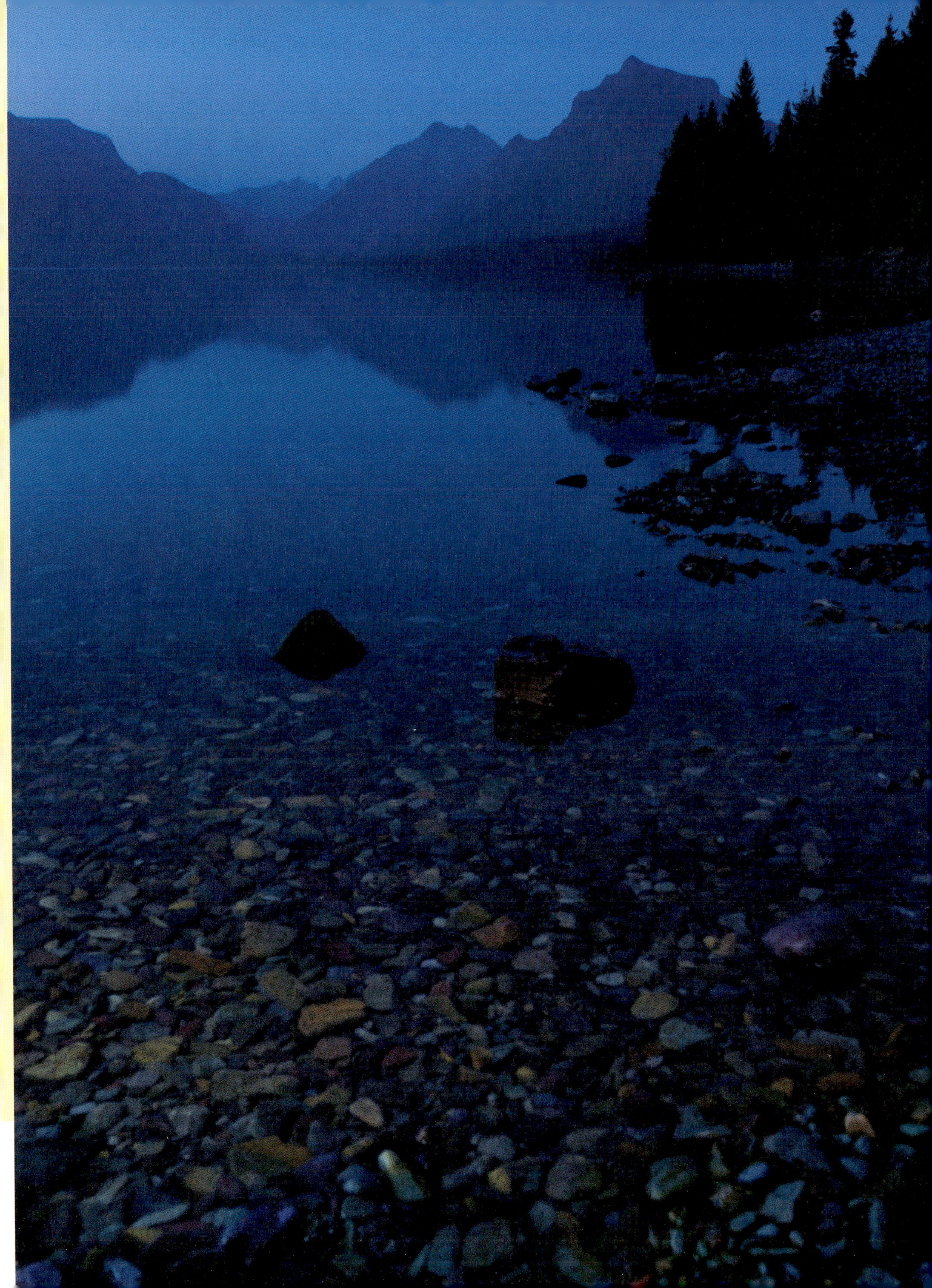

5. DIRECTION OF LIGHT

FRONT LIGHT

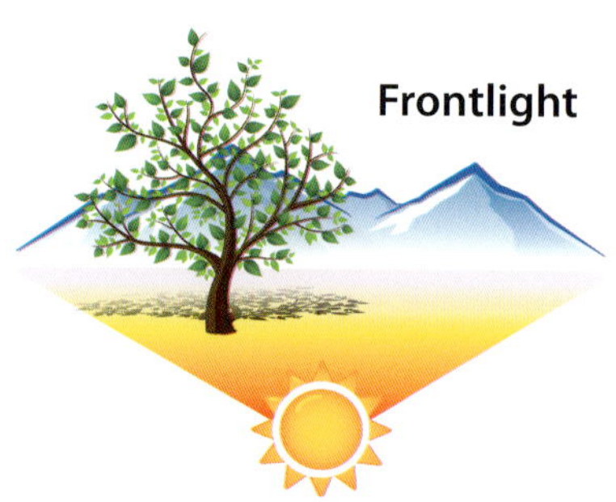

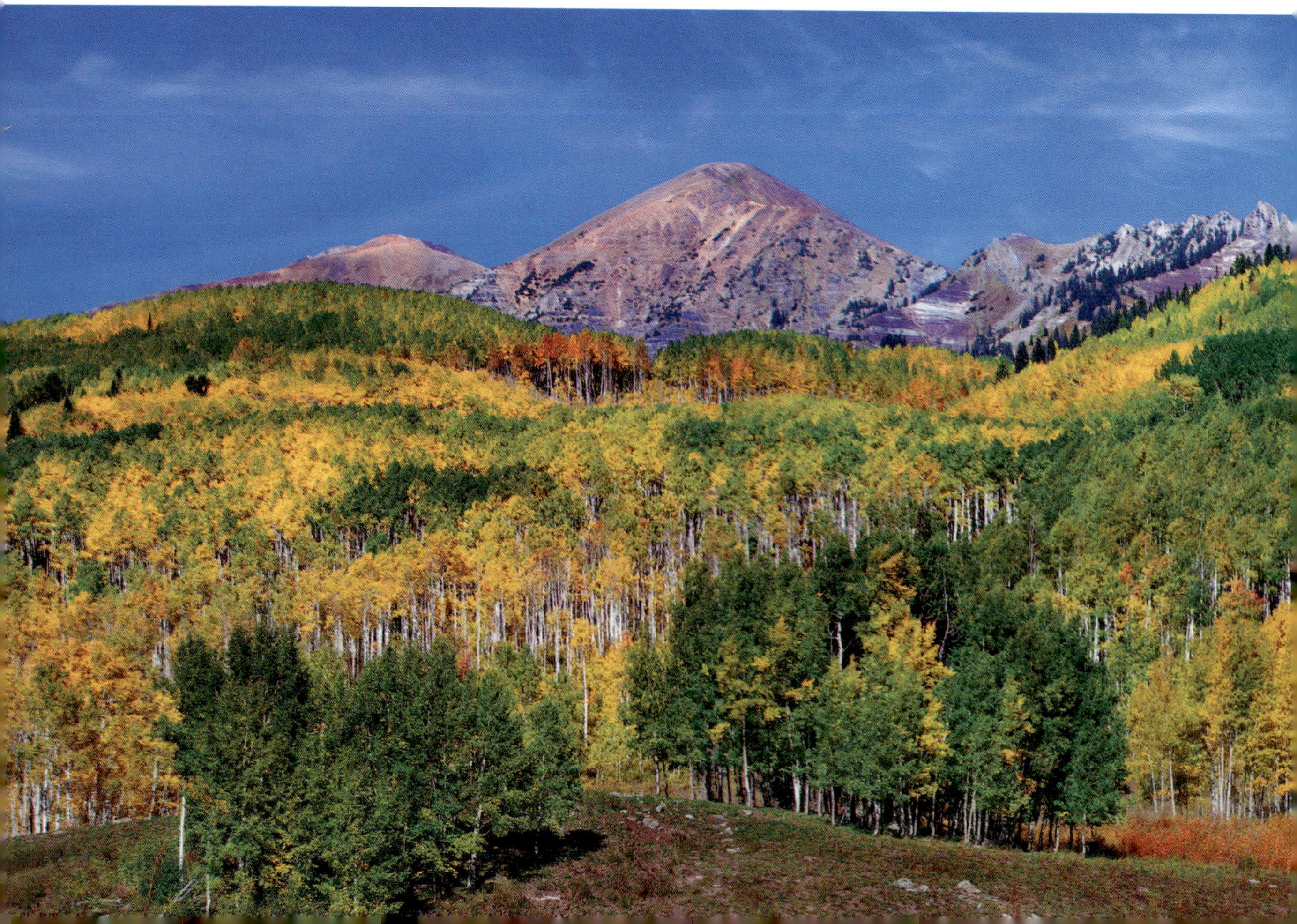

In my early days of photography, I was taught to shoot with the sun at my back. I bet you were taught the same. *Front light*—when the sun is behind you—is generally the easiest light to photograph. It provides even light across the scene, making it simple to obtain the correct exposure. This light is sometimes referred to as *flat* because it lacks contrast and depth. While front light may be considered flat, it does reproduce vibrant colors. When the sun is low in the sky, front light can be very dramatic.

Front lighting emphasized the colors of the aspen trees along Kebler Pass in Colorado. The colors weaving across the mountainside in front of Ruby's Peak were a good subject for a panoramic image. The stitching together of images was easy because there were no dramatic changes in the light across the entire scene.

The stitching together of images was easy because there were no dramatic changes in the light . . .

I turned my camera vertically so I could shoot more frames from left to right at a larger file size—nine images were used to create this panoramic! Using a small hot-shoe bubble level, I maneuvered my tripod and camera to a level position. Starting on the left side, I carefully panned across the scene, making sure to have an overlap in each frame by keeping an eye on a tree, rock, or some "marker" for the capture. If you don't have an overlap, Photoshop won't be able to stitch the images together. Using Photoshop's Photomerge function is easy and fun to watch as it stitches the images into one panoramic image. For more on this topic, see chapter 12.

▼ With the sun at my back, front lighting on the Dyke area of Kebler Pass in Colorado enhanced the seasonal color change. The even lighting across the scene was great for creating a nine-frame panoramic image.

FOCAL LENGTH: 110mm | ISO: 200 APERTURE: f/20 | SHUTTER SPEED: 1/25 second

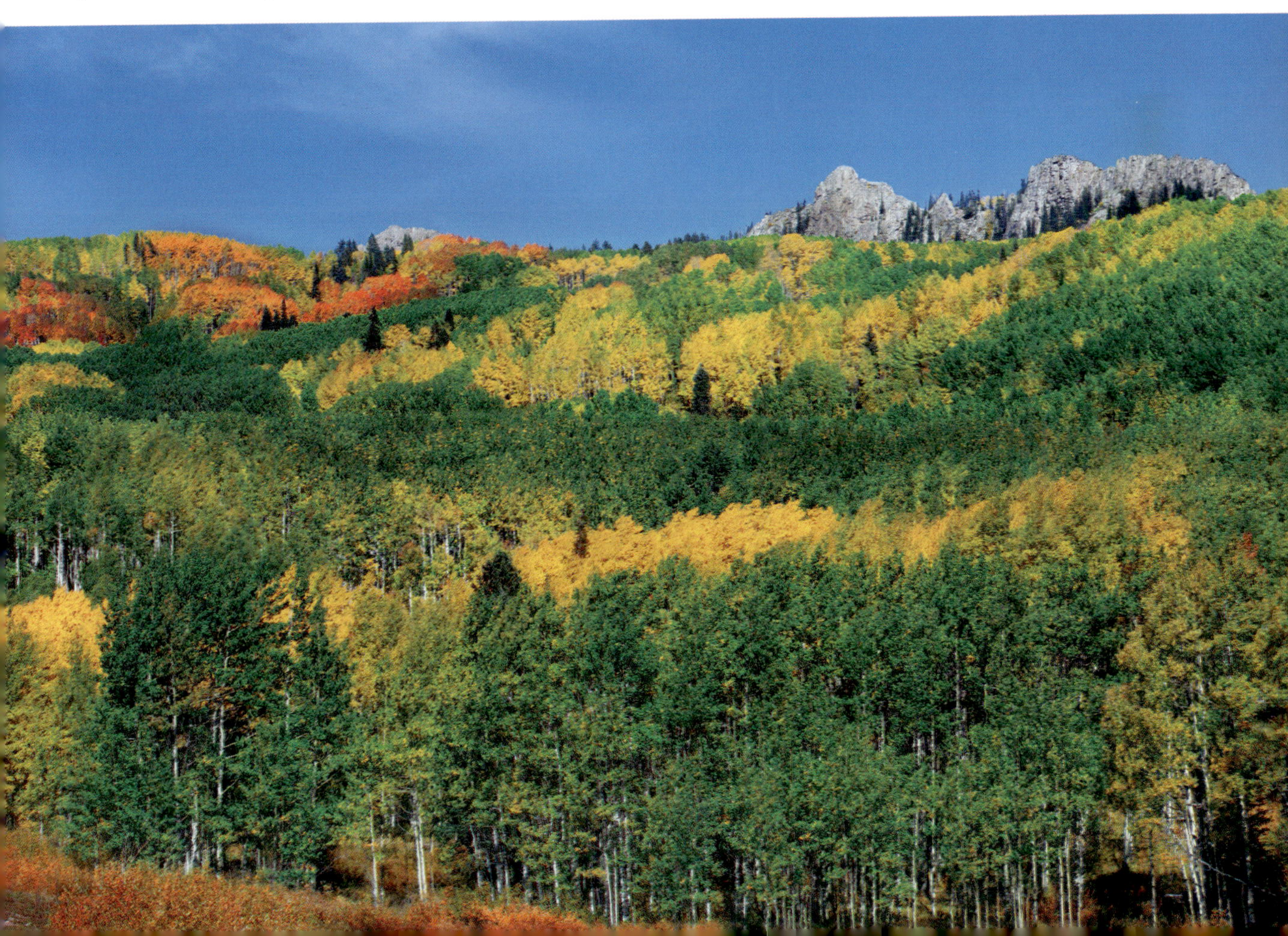

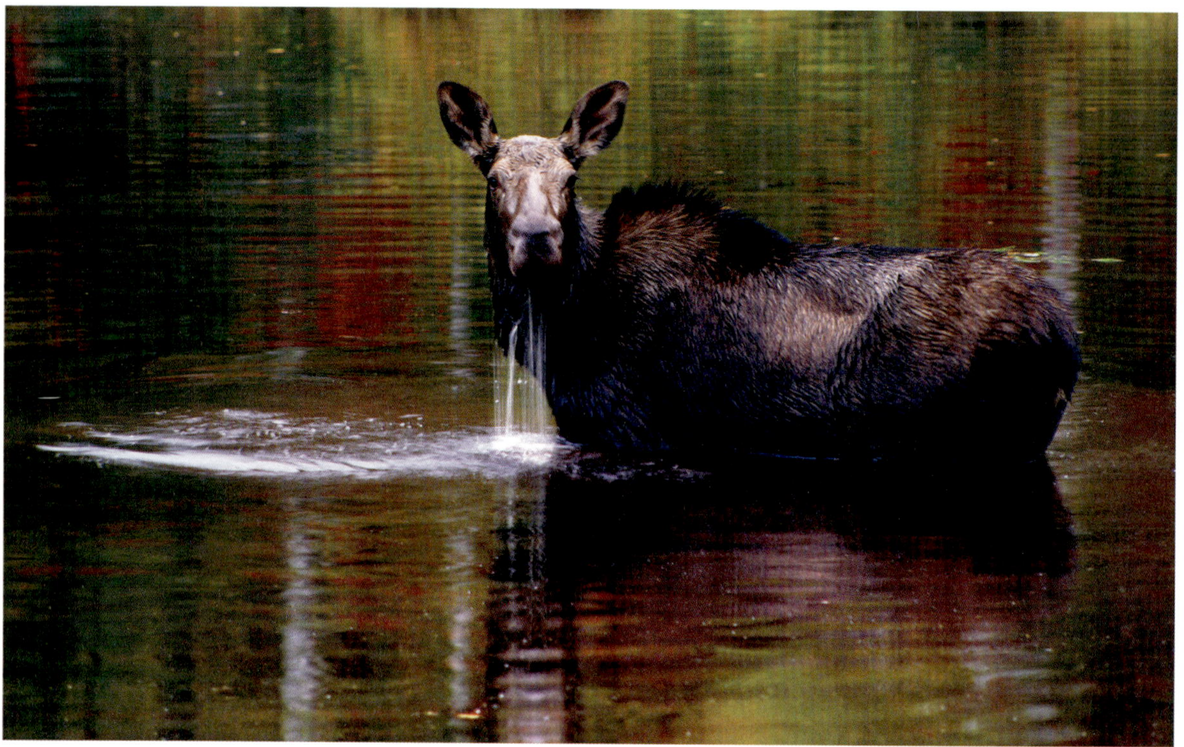

▲ Front light provided even light on this moose and created the reflection in the water.

ISO: 50 Fujichrome Velvia | APERTURE: Not available | SHUTTER SPEED: Not available

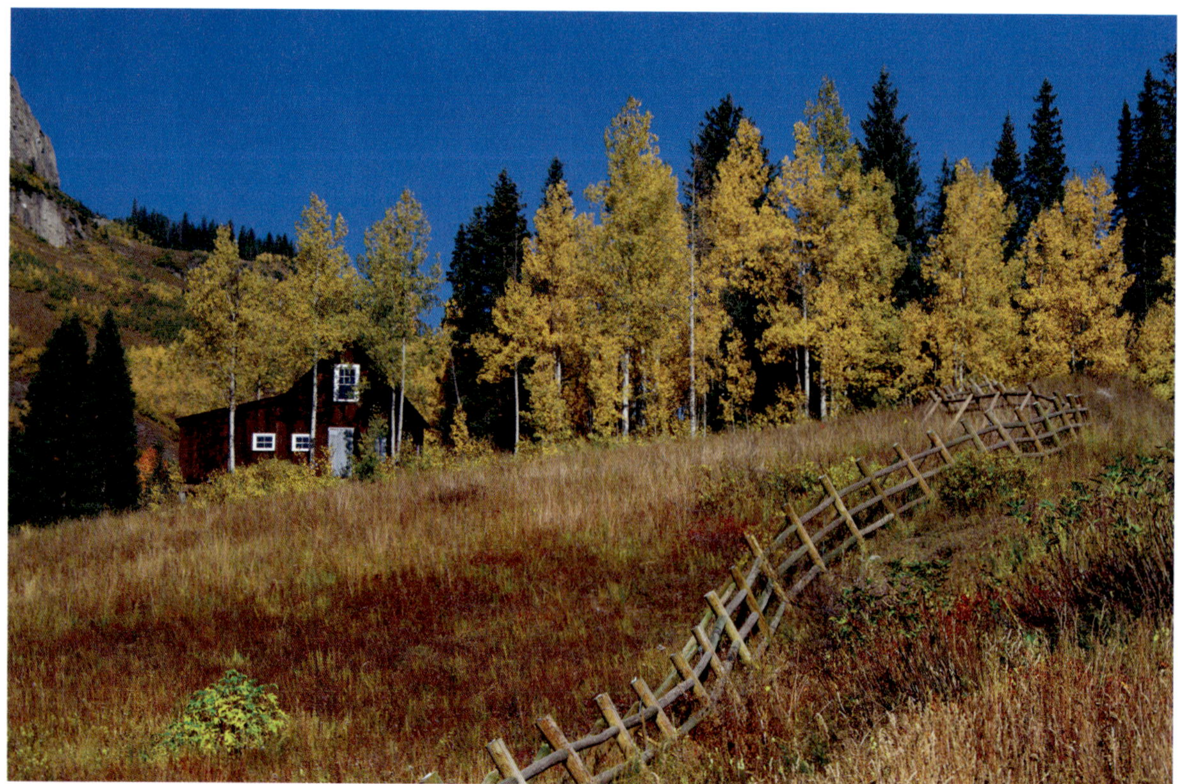

▲ The dark-blue sky against golden aspens was accented by front light. Although the image may lack dimension, the bold colors produced by the use of front light can make an image interesting and impactful.

FOCAL LENGTH: 90mm | ISO: 200 APERTURE: f/20 | SHUTTER SPEED: 1/40 second

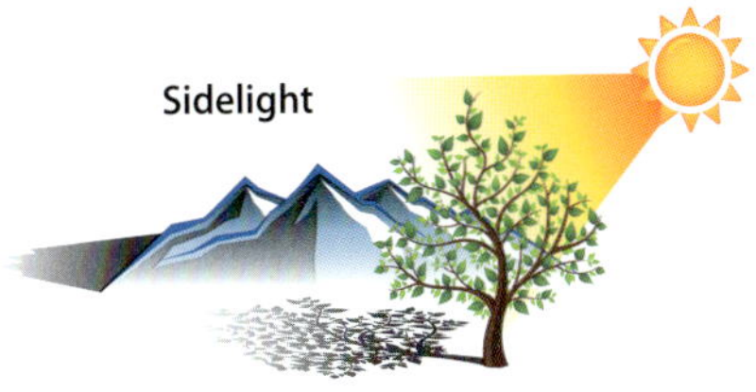

► The low angle of the setting sun produced side light that emphasized the form and texture at Great Sand Dunes National Park in Colorado.

FOCAL LENGTH: 30mm | ISO: 125
APERTURE: f/20 | SHUTTER SPEED: 1/15 second

Side light happens when the angle of the light falls sideways across the scene.

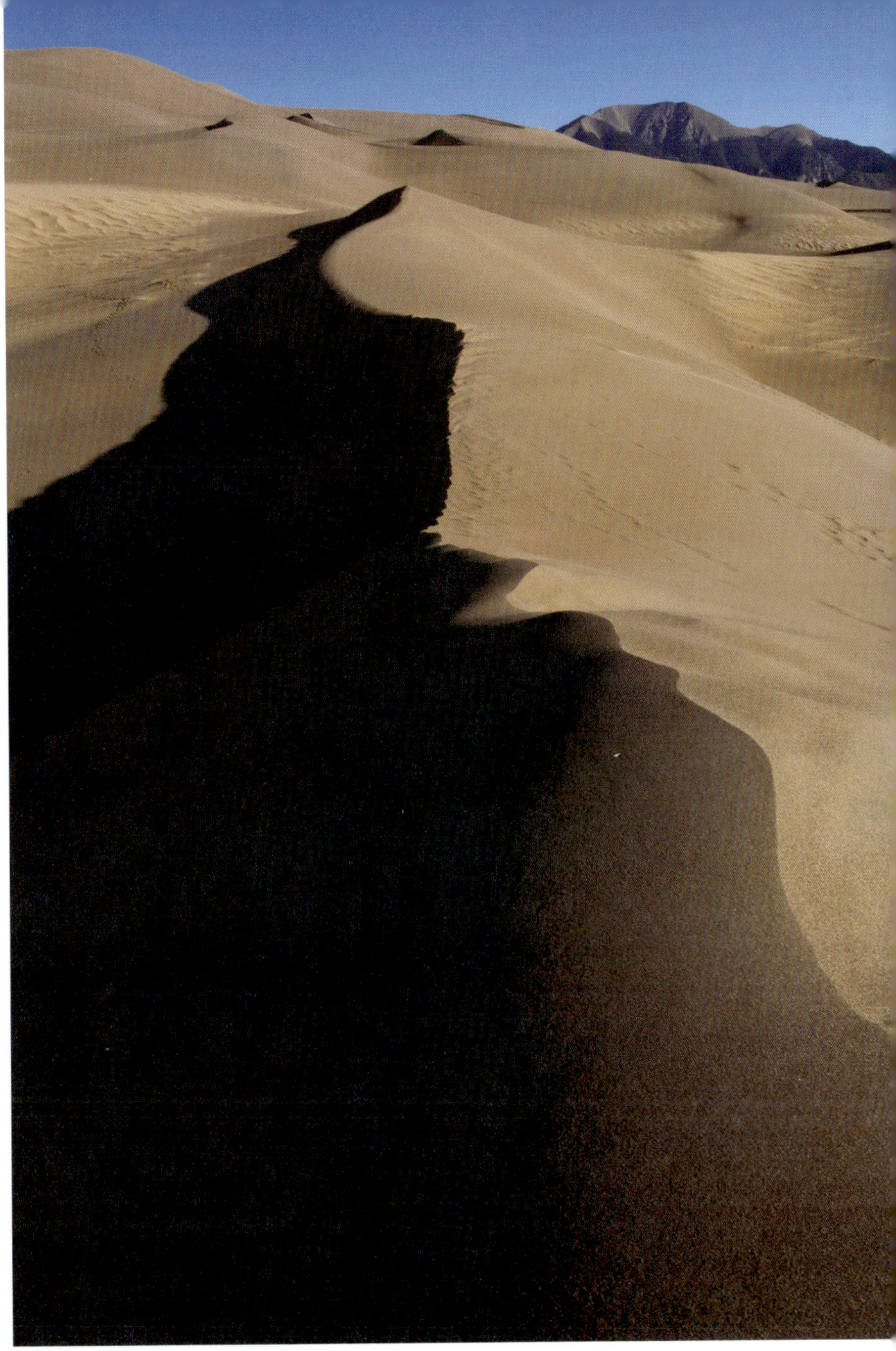

SIDE LIGHT

Side light happens when the angle of the light falls sideways across the scene. The interplay of light and shadow emphasizes contours in the landscape and creates drama with texture, depth, and form. Strong directional light when the sun's rays are low will produce very long shadows that further accent the texture.

Great Sand Dunes National Park appears three-dimensional when lit from the side in the late afternoon. Sand dunes are interesting and challenging to photograph. I love the fact that they constantly change in the blowing wind, although the sand particles can be brutal on camera equipment. When photographing sand dunes, I recommend never changing lenses in the field. Pick a zoom range that you are comfortable with and stick to it or carry another camera body with a different focal length lens. I chose a 28–300mm on the first evening because it offered a wide zoom range for a variety of composition possibilities. It was my first visit to the park and I wanted a focal length range that covered a lot of scenarios.

The interplay of light and shadow emphasizes contours in the landscape and creates drama.

The next morning, I chose my 17–35mm lens for a different look and because I wanted to focus on the texture in the foreground. Using a very wide-angle focal length allowed me to focus very close to a line in the sand and accent its texture as the dune flowed into the frame. In case you didn't know, wide-angle lenses have the ability to focus very close to a subject. I can get 10.8 inches away with my 17–35mm. Wow!

Red Rock Canyon National Conservation Area in Nevada is another location where the texture and rock formations benefit from side light. The warm side light hits the rocks from the left, creating long shadows on the right. The combination of light and shade brings out the fine details and texture of the rocks. Additionally, the warm tones of the rocks are emphasized during the golden hour before sunset.

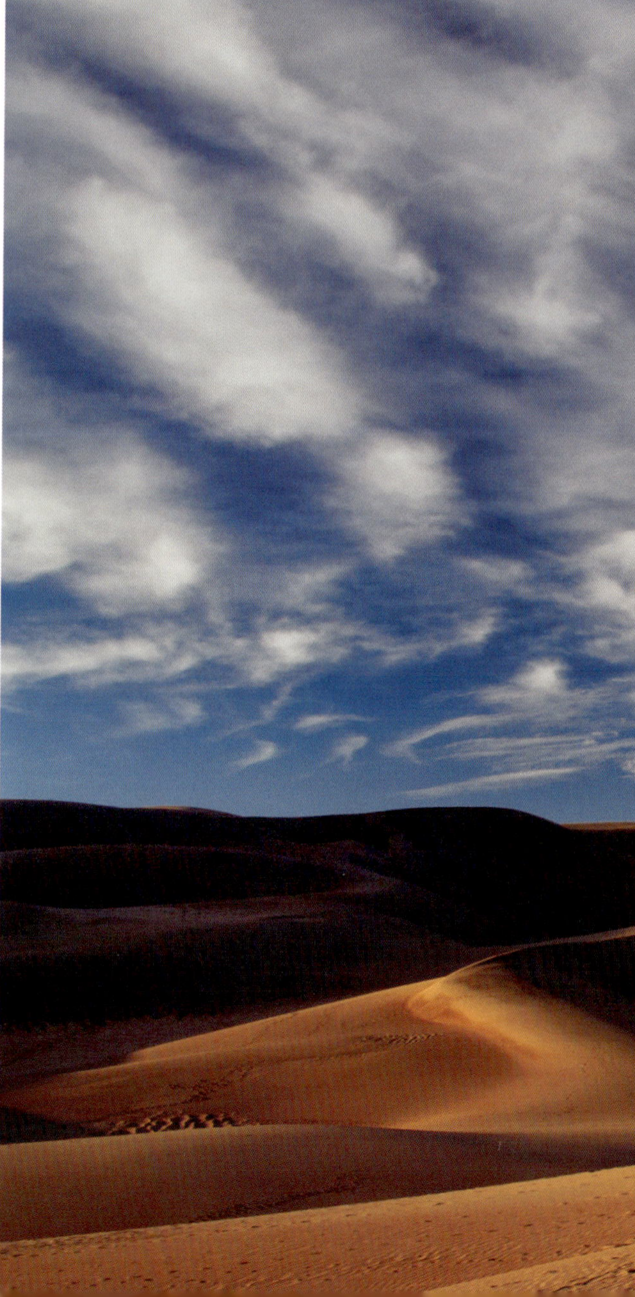

► Sand dunes offer the photographer plenty of form, texture, and contours that are accented in late-afternoon side light. The late-day sun added warmth to the color of the dunes.

FOCAL LENGTH: 28mm | ISO: 160 | APERTURE: f/20 | SHUTTER SPEED: 1/10 second

► The texture and shapes of Red Rock Canyon are emphasized when light comes from the side.

FOCAL LENGTH: 22mm | ISO: 200 | APERTURE: f/22
SHUTTER SPEED: 1/8 second

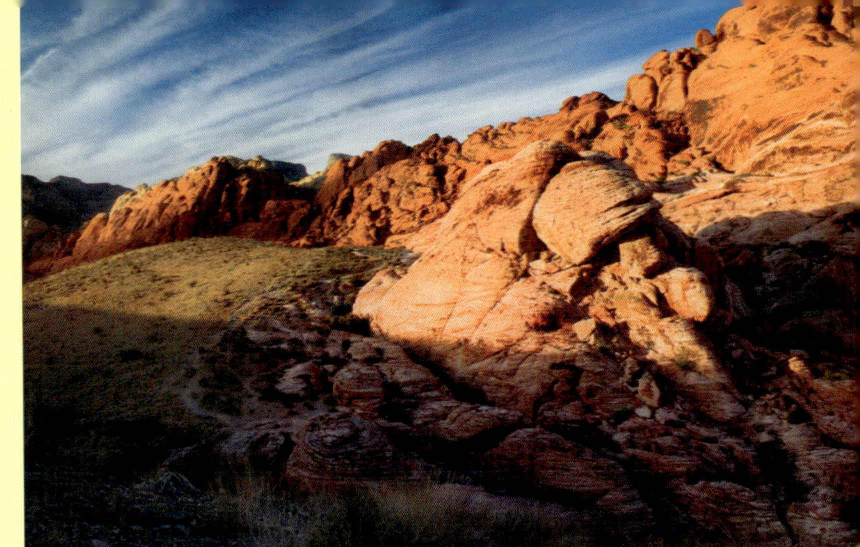

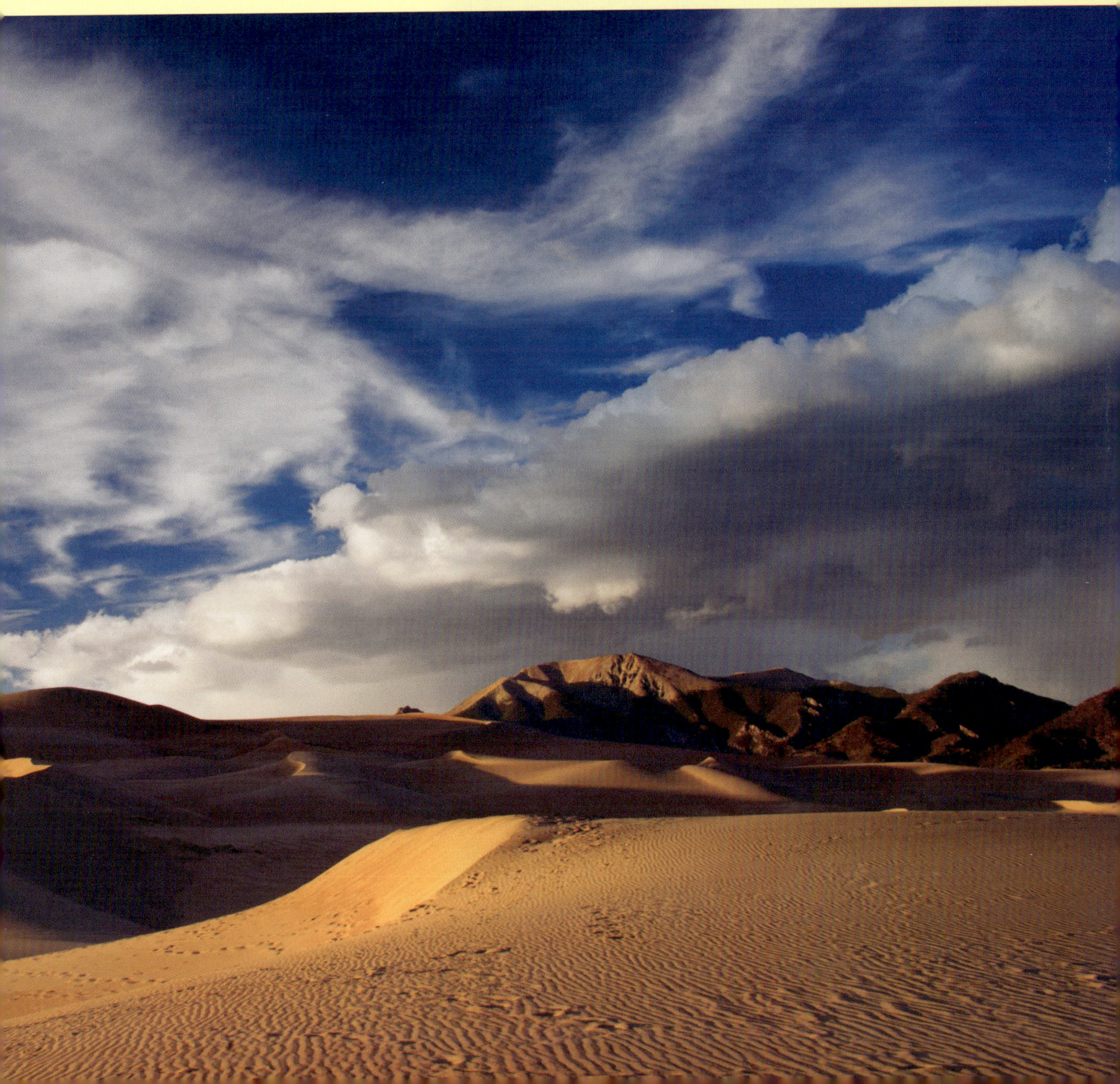

BACK LIGHT

Back light occurs when the subject is illuminated from behind and you are facing the light source. You may have learned that it is wrong to point your camera into the sun; however, this is not true. Successful and dramatic images can be made with the proper use of back lighting. Back lighting allows you to capture silhouettes because the contrast between light and dark is high (this is wonderful for creating a mood). When the sun's rays catch the edge of a subject it produces a rim light that accents the shape or texture of things like cactus spines, flowers, and trees. Translucent subjects like fall leaves shimmer when backlit.

When I saw this tree in the local park, backlit by the late-day sun, I immediately had a vision of the image I wanted to create. The background needed to be dark so the tree would really pop, further accenting the translucent effect of the back lighting. I positioned my tripod so the sun was behind the tree and not showing in my frame. The hillside was in the shade but not too far way, so I chose an aperture of f/5.6 for a shallow depth of field. Additionally, I wanted a soft, glowing effect on the leaves. Since the background was relatively close to the tree, this was not possible in a single image—although it was possible with a multiple exposure. I set my Nikon D3's multiple-exposure function to two frames and shot one exposure in focus and one out of focus. I was able to achieve my goal using this technique, along with a little Photoshop tweaking.

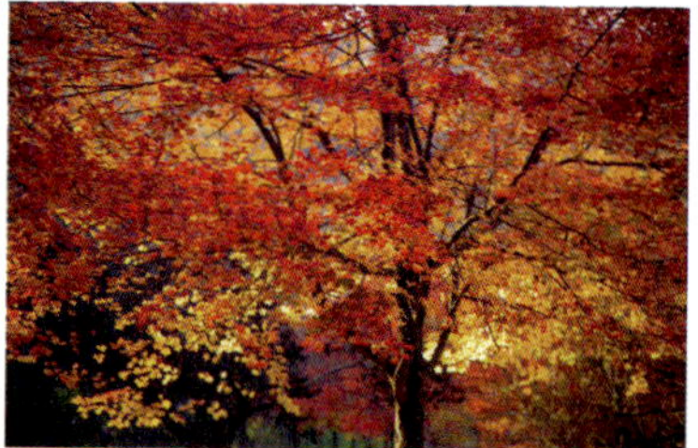

▲ This single exposure of a backlit maple tree lacks the "pop" seen in the featured image that utilized my camera's multiple-exposure function.

▼ Translucent subjects, such as fall foliage, appear to shimmer when backlit. In-camera multiple exposures added to the glowing effect.

FOCAL LENGTH: 250mm | ISO: 100
APERTURE: f/5.6 | SHUTTER SPEED: 1/15 second

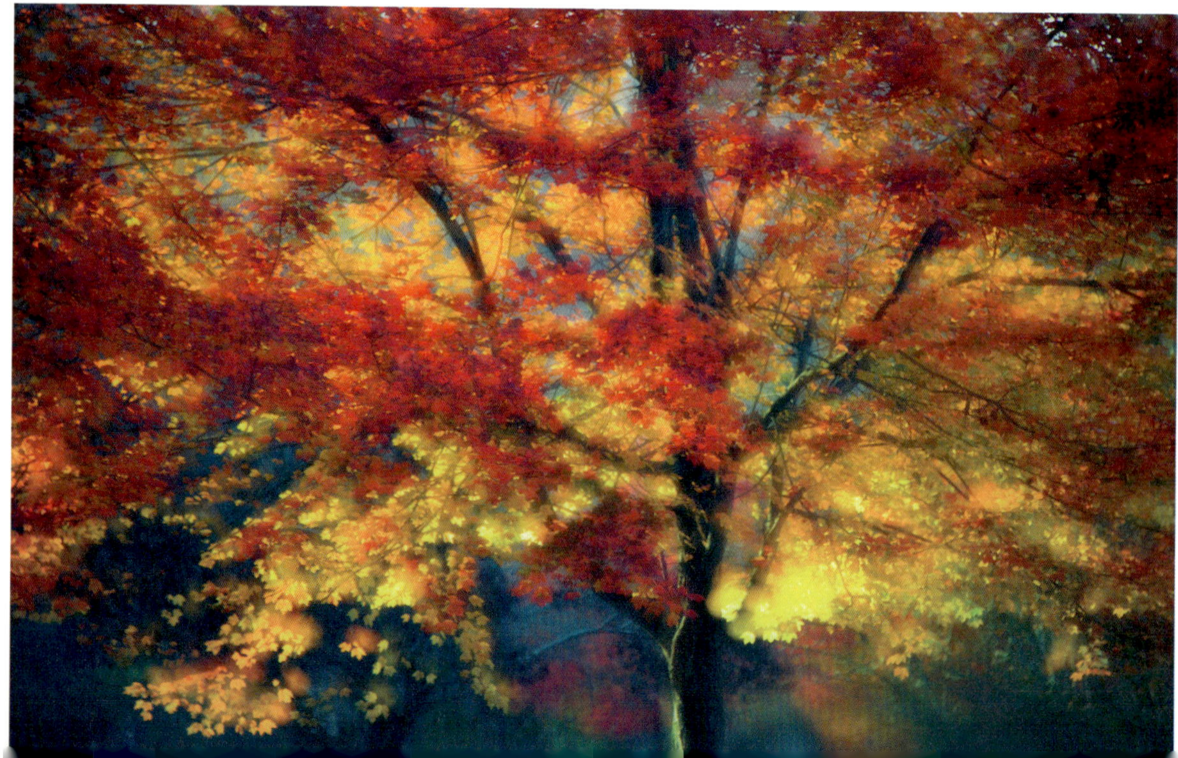

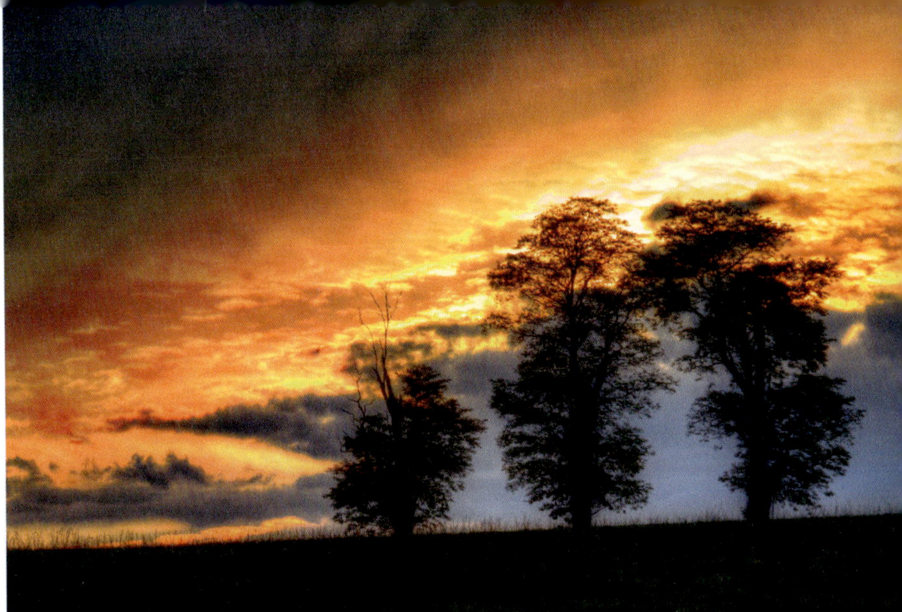

► The contrast of the setting sun created a silhouette of three trees on the horizon. Always consider the shape of the subject when creating silhouettes and look for distinctive forms that separate from the background.

FOCAL LENGTH: 135mm | ISO: 100
APERTURE: f/22 | SHUTTER SPEED: 1/30 second

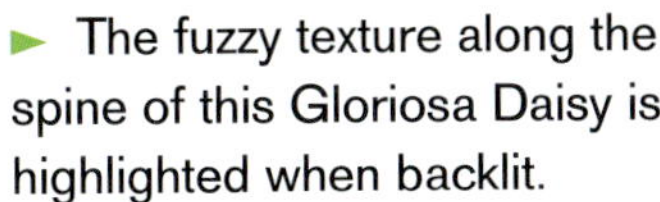

► The fuzzy texture along the spine of this Gloriosa Daisy is highlighted when backlit.

FOCAL LENGTH: 200mm Macro | ISO: 400
APERTURE: f/11 | SHUTTER SPEED: 1/30 second

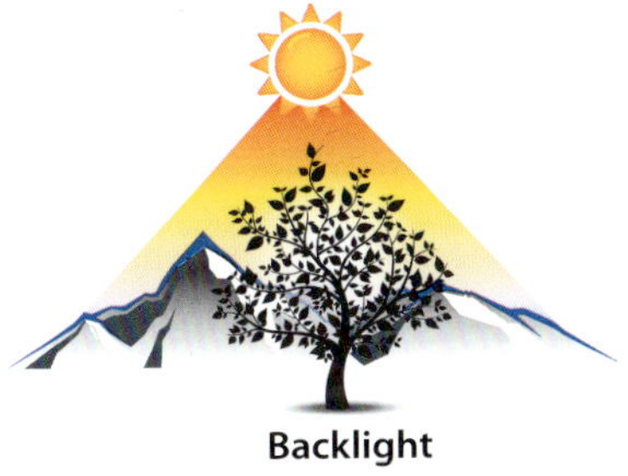

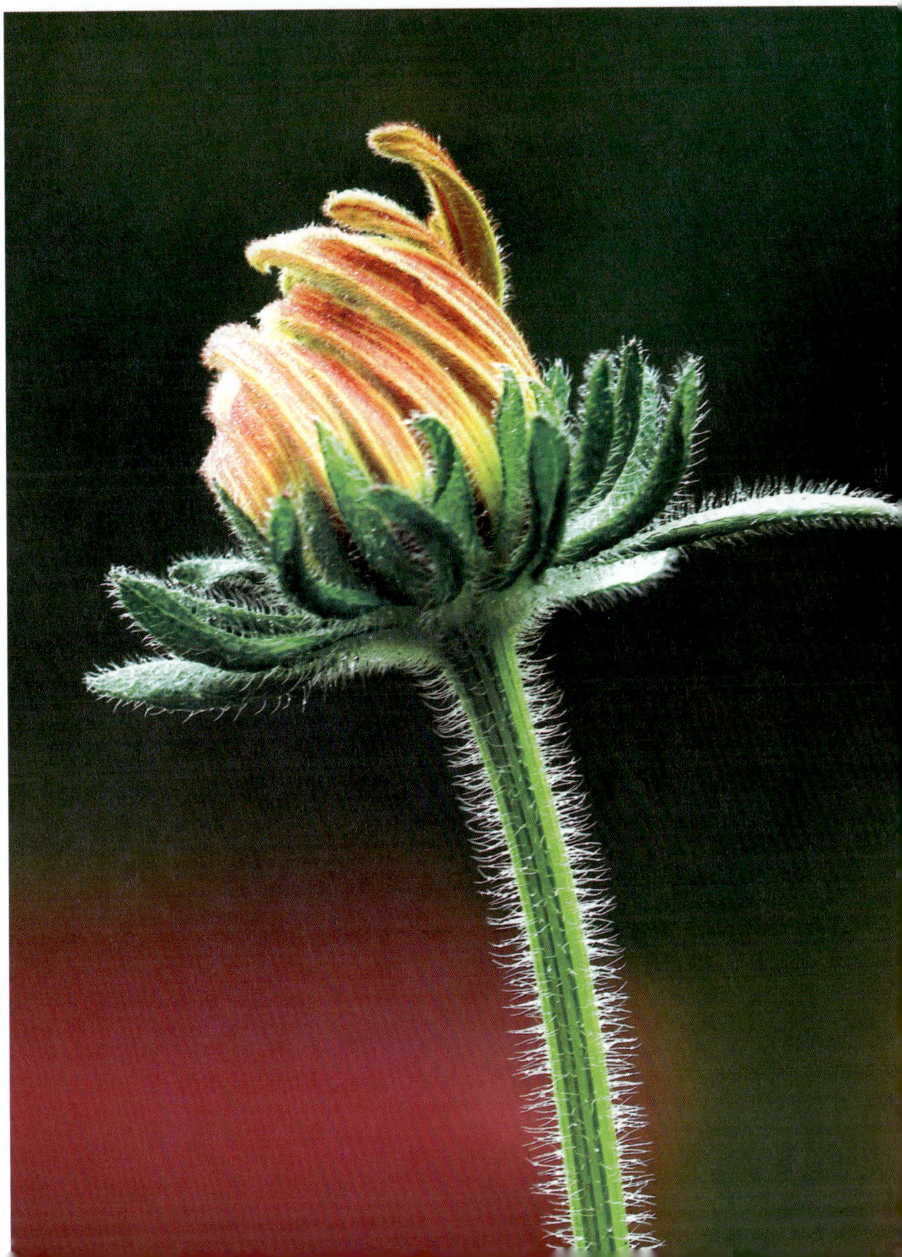

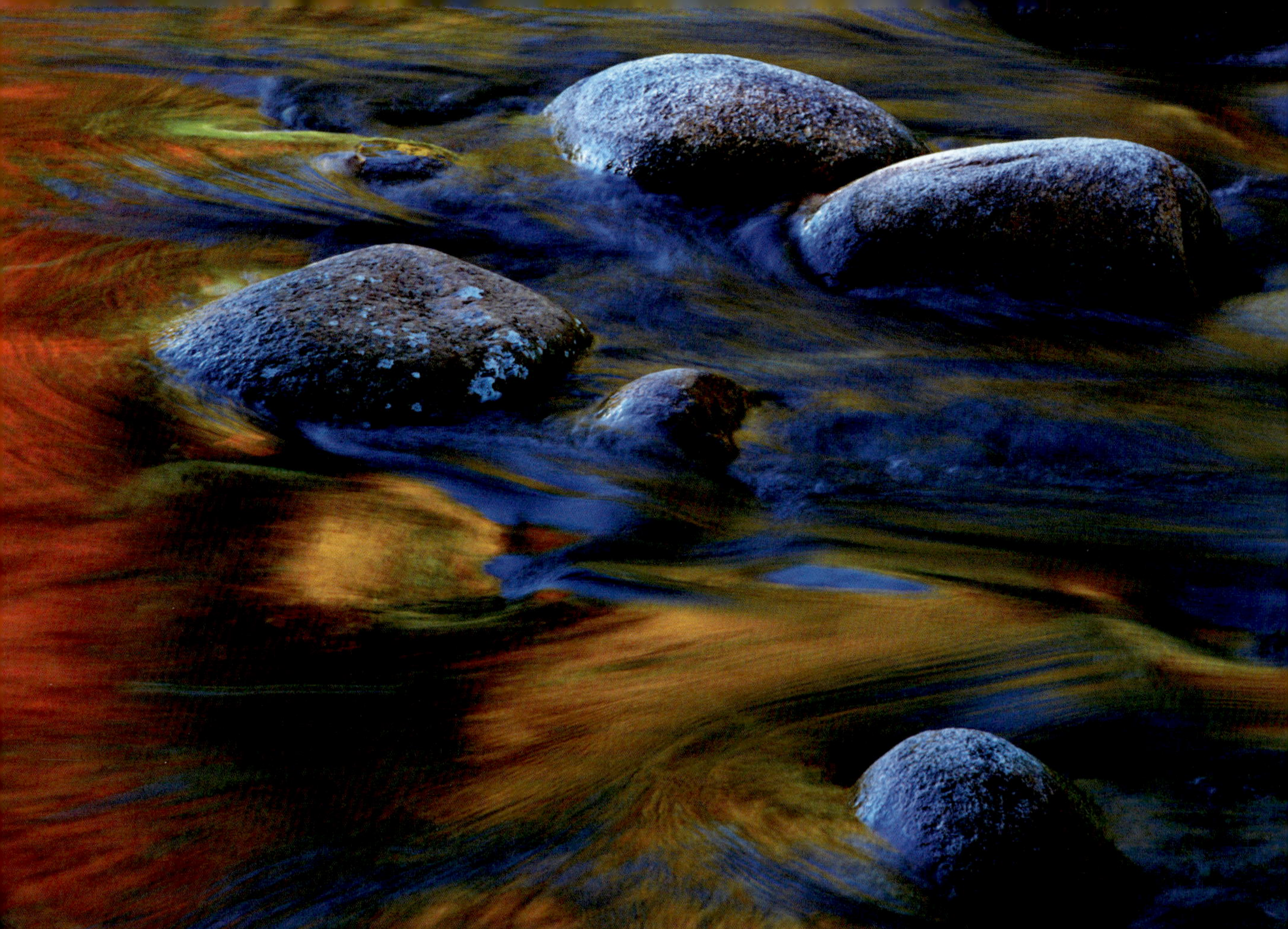

▲ Using a slow shutter speed blurred the water movement and blended the reflected autumn colors seen in the Wild River of Maine.

ISO: 50 Fujichrome Velvia | APERTURE: Not available | SHUTTER SPEED: Not available

REFLECTED LIGHT

Reflections are everywhere—glass buildings, car windows, eyeglasses, and my favorite, water, are just a few. Learning to see reflected light in water is not always easy. Some colors, like blue, are harder to see than the brighter colors of yellow or orange. The intensity of the reflection can change with the quality of light, making it easier or harder to see, as well.

Start by photographing any reflection and notice how the camera records it.

Colors "pop" in reflected light, and once you learn to see them, you will have a powerful creative tool at your disposal.

Start by photographing any reflection and notice how the camera records it. Reflections are usually darker with increased color saturation than the subject being reflected. Another added benefit is reflections have less contrast than the subject in direct sunlight. The more you practice seeing reflections and studying your results, the easier it will become to include reflections in your images. In the words of Freeman Patterson, “Clear, still water surfaces produce perfect reflections, which you may want to record. However, you’ll find even greater challenges and exciting opportunities for natural abstracts, if you photograph reflections in gently swelling or rippled water. Observe the water surface carefully until you begin to see the possibilities.”[8]

The movement of the water combined with a slow shutter speed “mixed” the reflected colors.

Wild River in Maine was a fun place to photograph reflections and be creative at the same time. This river had strong currents flowing around several large rocks. The sky was blue and the autumn foliage was at its peak, with lush reds and yellows lining the shore. The movement of the water combined with a slow shutter speed “mixed” the reflected colors. The result is a colorful image that is artistic and unique.

I used the typical setup—my camera on a tripod, cable release, and a polarizer. However, this image was captured with Fujichrome Velvia slide film, so I don’t have the camera data available to know the actual shutter speed.

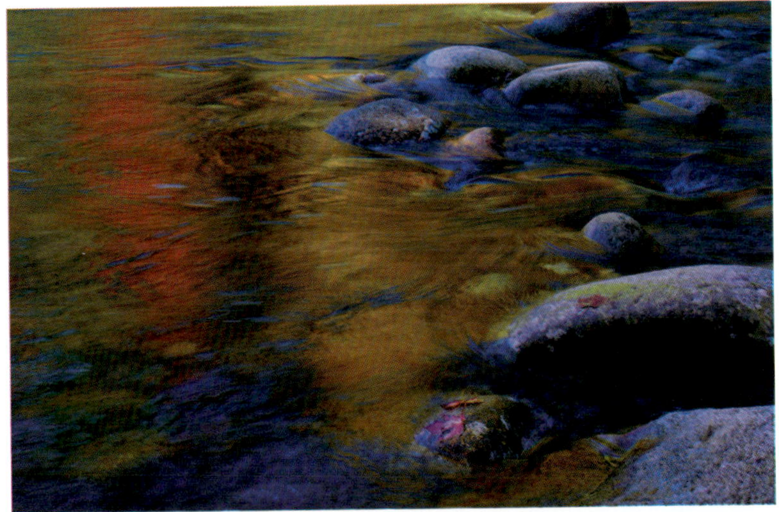

► A wider view shows the green, reds, and yellows of the fall season. Blue can be one of the most difficult colors to see in reflections, but the camera has no problem capturing it. Moving your camera position will change the angle of the reflection and the color within the edges of the viewfinder.

FOCAL LENGTH: Not available | ISO: 50 Fujichrome Velvia | APERTURE: Not available SHUTTER SPEED: Not available

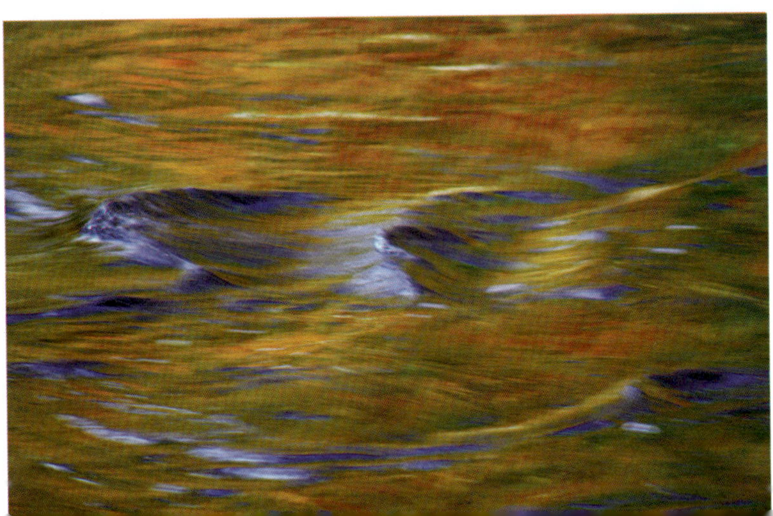

► Reflected colors pop when the foliage on the shore is in sunlight and the water is in the shade.

FOCAL LENGTH: Not available | ISO: 50 Fujichrome Velvia | APERTURE: Not available SHUTTER SPEED: Not available

6. QUALITY OF LIGHT

SOFT LIGHT

Soft light is diffused, even sunlight from a large light source. When the sun is hidden behind clouds or better yet it is a cloudy/overcast day, the light is considered soft. Clouds diffuse the sunlight, spreading it out to illuminate the landscape with an even, soft, low-contrast light. This light lacks noticeable shadows and bright highlights, allowing the camera to record a wide dynamic range (the contrast range from the brightest to darkest area).

Soft light preserves details and makes subtle color changes appear more saturated. While the scene may not look as pretty to the human eye, a digital camera sensor will record soft light with amazing results. Photographer Galen Rowell said, "When the sun goes behind a cloud, many landscape photographers put away their cameras. Contrasts necessary to give distant features a sense of power and form tend to disappear in soft light. ... Yet at the same time, color film [and a digital sensor] reaches its zenith; more aspects of the landscape can be photographed successfully in soft light than any other time."[9] Intimate details, small landscapes, flowers, waterfalls, and portraits all benefit tremendously from soft light. When the sky is gray and doesn't have any texture, it is wise not to include it in the image. When the light is soft and the sky has texture and interest, go ahead and leave it in!

For the shot of Tupper Lake in the Adirondack Mountains, the sky was not completely overcast, but the sun went behind a large cloud bank. With the sun behind the clouds, the full

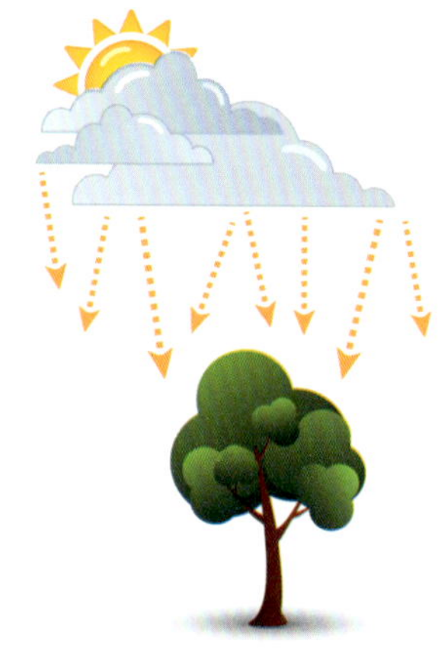

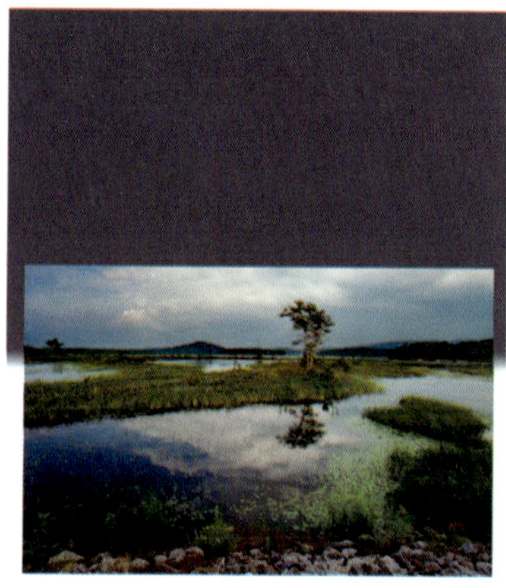

▲ Using a two-stop graduated neutral-density filter revealed the texture in the clouds by holding back the exposure two f-stops. This essentially darkened the sky for a nicely balanced exposure.

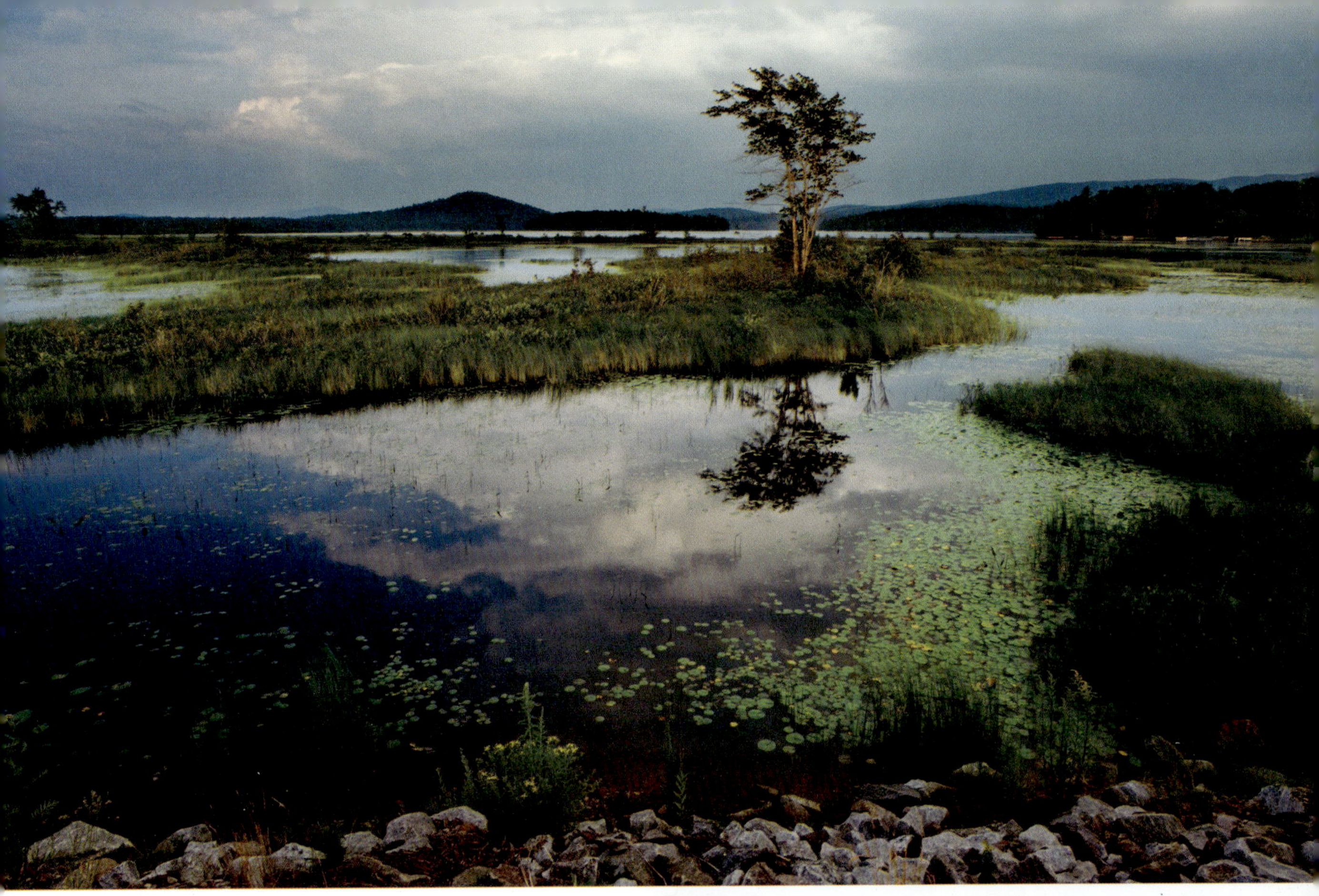

▲ Soft diffused light over Tupper Lake created a tranquil mood. Cloudy skies diffused the hard light of the sun by retransmitting and thereby softening the light.

TIME: 7:47:12PM | FOCAL LENGTH: 20mm | ISO: 400
APERTURE: f/18 | SHUTTER SPEED: 1/60 second

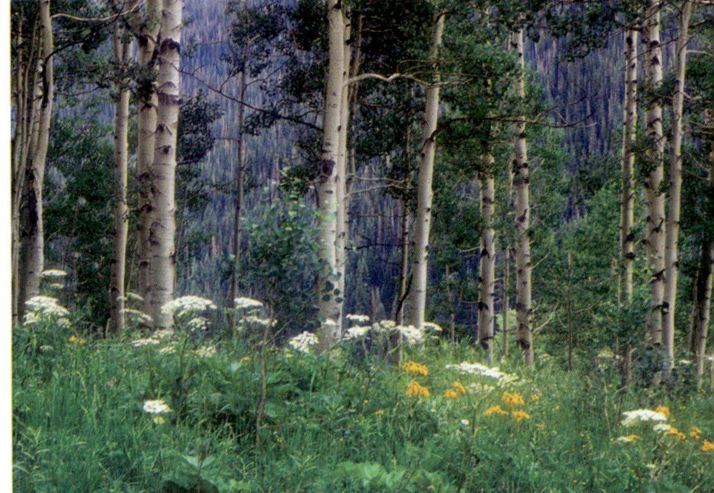

► Soft light revealed the details and depth of the trees in this aspen grove.

ISO: 50 Fujichrome Velvia | APERTURE: Not available | SHUTTER SPEED: Not available

dynamic range of shades and colors in the foreground grasses, water, and rock was easily captured in a single image. Compared to a gray overcast day, this bright cloudy sky still had some blue tones that were reflected in the water. Additionally, the texture in the sky was retained by using a two-stop graduated neutral-density filter to hold back the exposure of the sky and balance it with the foreground.

HARD LIGHT

Hard light occurs when the light source is small, direct, and far from the subject (e.g., the sun on a clear day). When there are no clouds or other modifiers to diffuse the light, the transition from shadow to highlight is sudden and dense. Shadows are deep and dark with well-defined edges that produce high contrast levels that can stretch the dynamic range beyond the camera's capture capabilities. More often than not, High Dynamic Range (HDR) images are created from hard-light scenes.

The peak contrast and hardness happens around noon, when the sun is directly overhead.

The size of the light source compared to the subject also determines whether the light is hard or soft. An on-camera flash produces hard light because it is small and close to the subject. The sun, however, is so far away from earth that on a clear day it acts as a small light source. The peak contrast and hardness occurs around noon, when the sun is directly overhead. As the day progresses, the hard light becomes less intense because a lower angle of light produces less contrast with longer shadows.

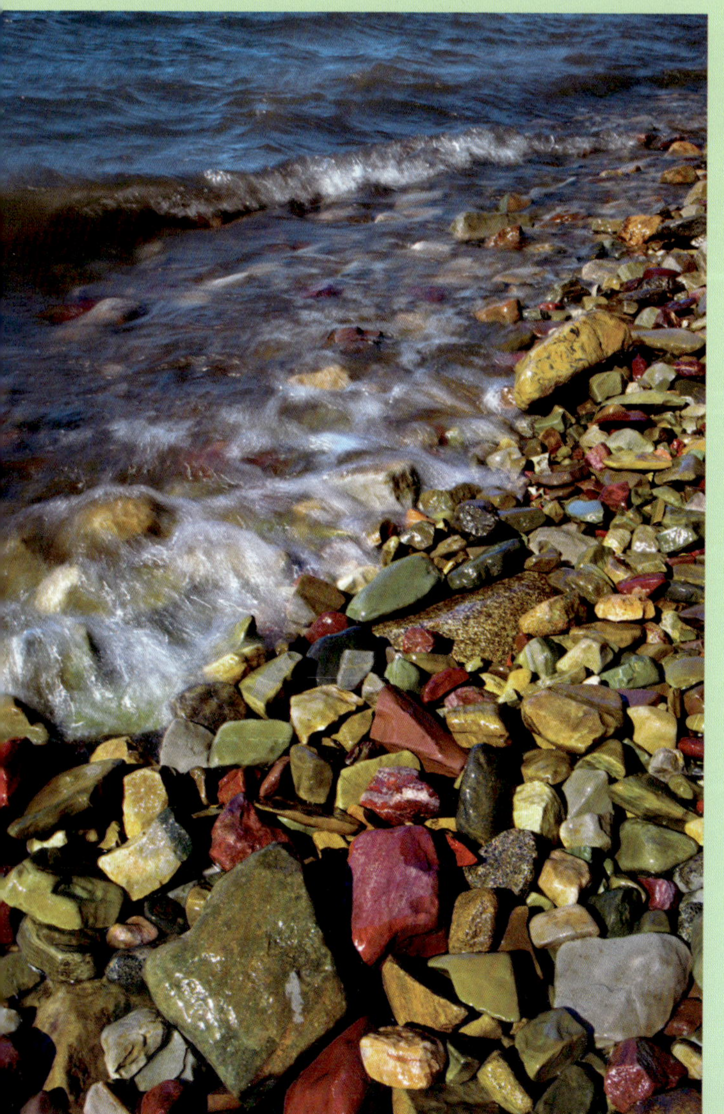

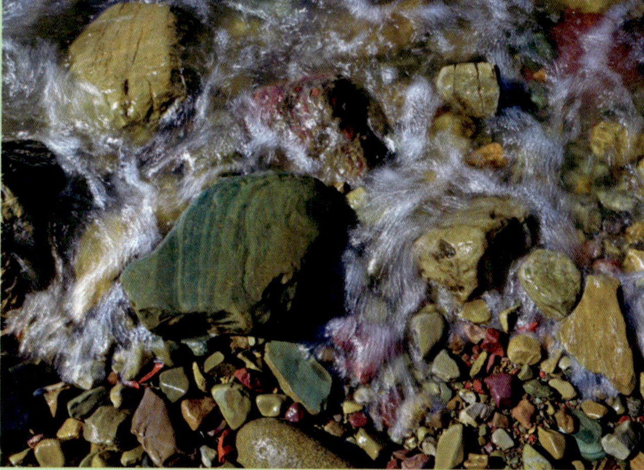

▲ Water washing onto the shoreline reduced some of the harsh shadows on the sedimentary rocks. A shutter speed of 1/15 second revealed the details in the water movement.

TIME OF DAY: 10:57:24AM | FOCAL LENGTH: 32mm | ISO: 100 | APERTURE: f/20 | SHUTTER SPEED: 1/15 second

◄ The sharp, well-defined edges of the sedimentary rocks in Lake Sherburne, Glacier National Park have short and harsh shadows when photographed in the hard light of midday.

TIME OF DAY: 10:52:32AM | FOCAL LENGTH: 32mm | ISO: 100 | APERTURE: f/22 | SHUTTER SPEED: 1/10 second

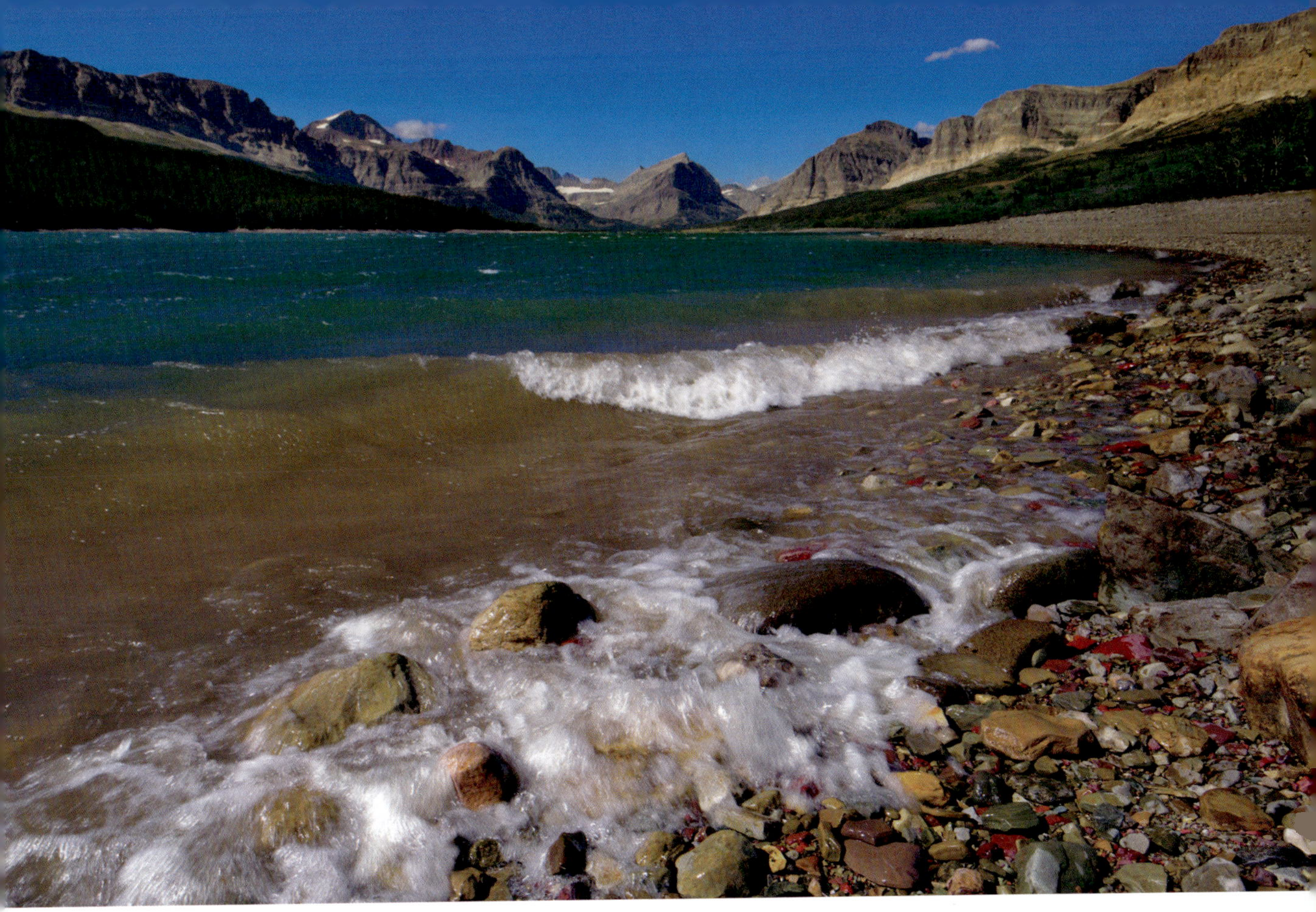

▲ The waves crashing into the shoreline saturated the colorful sedimentary rocks along Lake Sherburne in Glacier National Park. Silt from the melting snow and glacial water gives the lake its aqua color.

TIME OF DAY: 11:13:59AM | FOCAL LENGTH: 20mm | ISO: 100 | APERTURE: f/11 | SHUTTER SPEED: 1/60 second

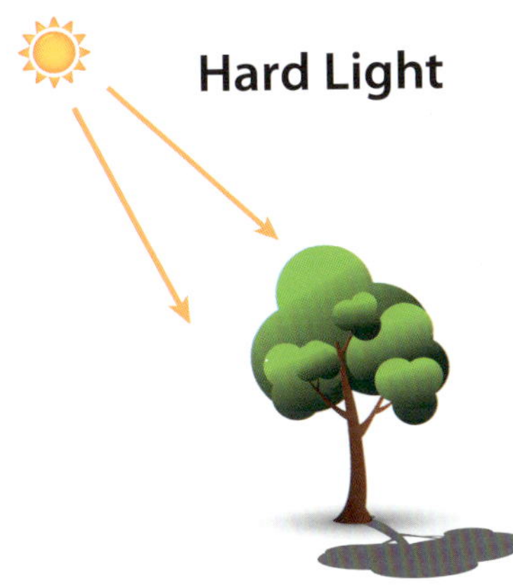

When photographing in hard light, choose your subject carefully. Sherburne Lake in Glacier National Park is filled with sedimentary rocks of all sizes and colors. These hard objects are suitable subjects for hard light. Photographed near midday without a cloud in the sky, the shadows are short, dense, and crisp. Midday sun is considered "white" or colorless, so the daylight white balance setting applies no color correction and renders colors accurately.

I shot several frames to capture the waves rolling in at just the right moment. In this case, the shoreline was too long and large to wet down all the rocks, but whenever possible, wet down the rocks in water scenes—it will dramatically increase the color saturation.

6. COLOR OF LIGHT

COOL LIGHT

Blue, green, and violet are considered cool colors, the same colors that can be found in water, meadows, and the sky. These colors are tranquil, relaxing, and calm. Calm lakes and blue sky have a soothing effect. The color blue can also be associated with cold, winter, and icy-blue waters. Cool colors appear to recede or move away from the viewer. A small room will feel larger if painted with a cool blue color, for example.

At twilight, scenes are generally full of deep-blue tones. During this time, the sun is below the horizon and the landscape is in shade, illuminated only by the sky reflecting a cool blue light down onto the land.

Cool light can also be found in open shade—an area that is out of direct sunlight, such as the shade from a building or mountain. Open shade occurs on sunny days when there is a large area of shade.

Overcast and stormy skies can also have subtle blue undertones from cool light. The common factor in all these scenarios is that the landscape is not directly illuminated; it is in shade or in diffused light. Shade is cool—not

▼ The cool light of early morning is a good time to capture images of the mist rising before disappearing from the heat of the day. In this image, morning mist rises along the mountain ridges in the Cades Cove area of the Great Smoky Mountains.

TIME OF DAY: 8:14:54AM | FOCAL LENGTH: 230mm | ISO: 100
APERTURE: f/22 | SHUTTER SPEED: 1/15 second

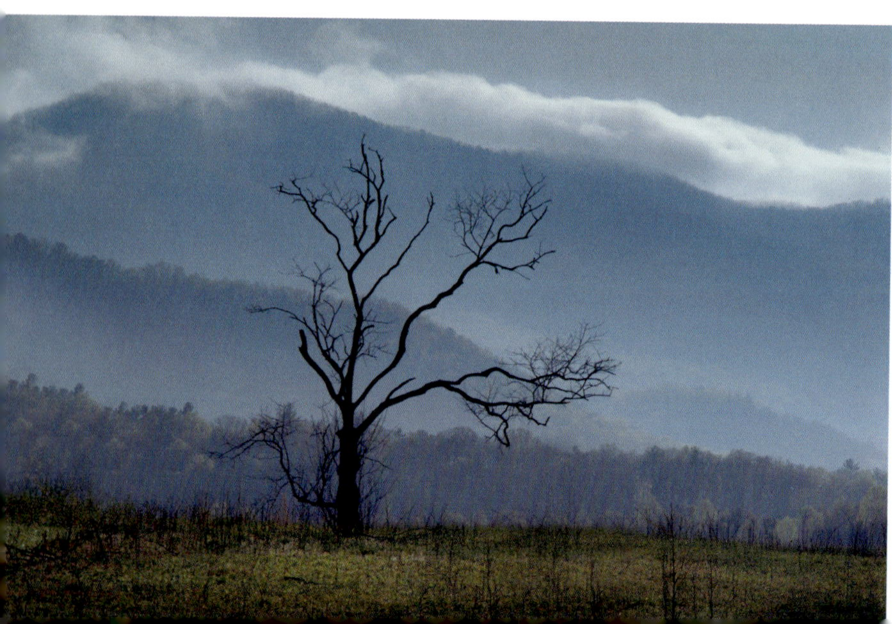

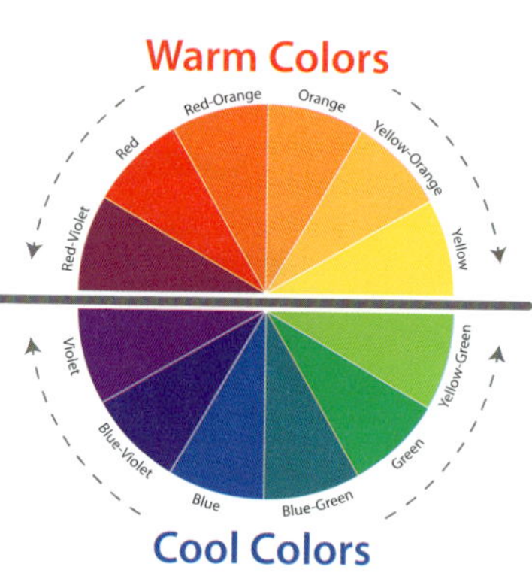

(top) Blues and violet colors are considered cool colors that create a feeling of tranquility.

ISO: 50 Fujichrome Velvia | APERTURE: Not available | SHUTTER SPEED: Not available

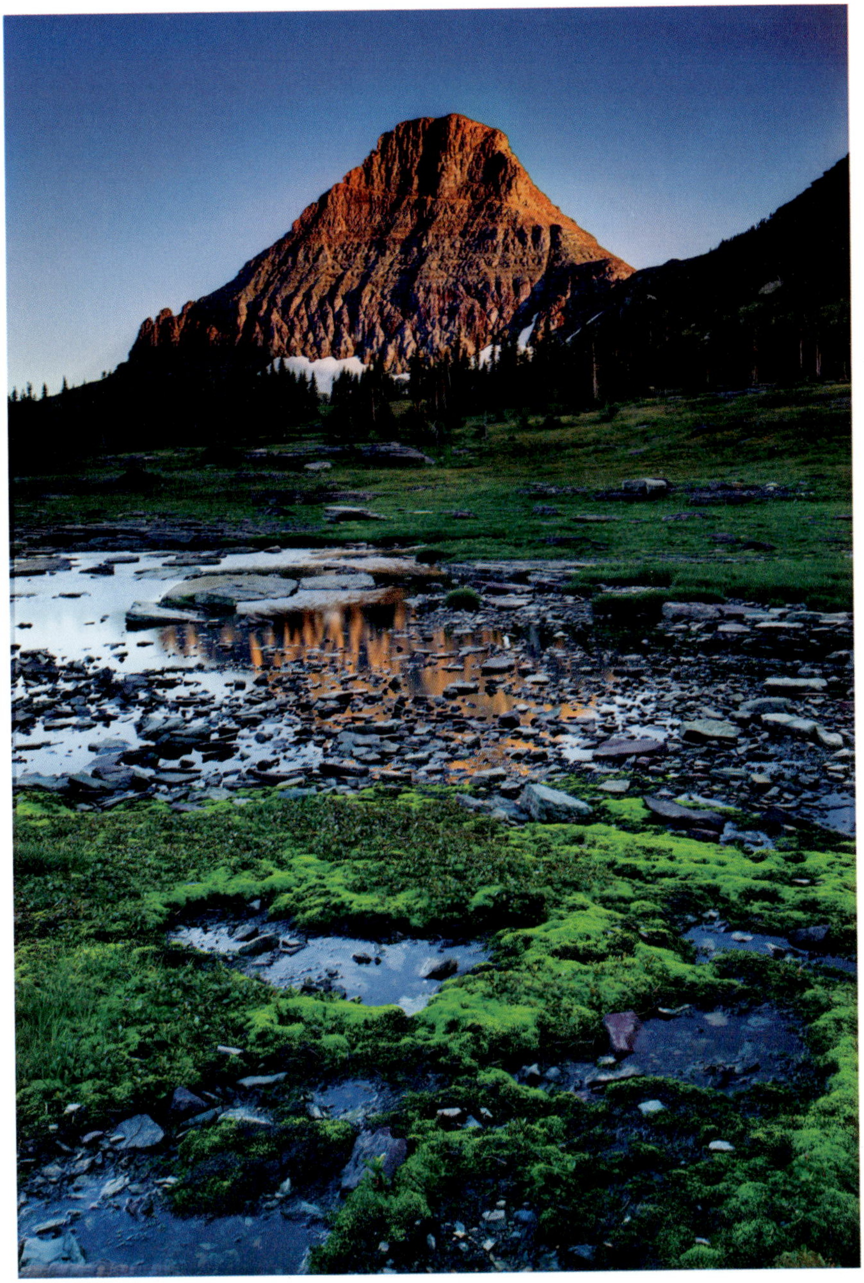

(bottom) Hiking along Hidden Lake Trail in Glacier National Park during twilight, I found Mt. Reynolds aglow from the setting sun. The blue and green colors of these small mountain tarns were enhanced by cool light.

TIME OF DAY: 8:25:25PM | FOCAL LENGTH: 32mm | ISO: 160 | APERTURE: f/16 | SHUTTER SPEED: 1 second

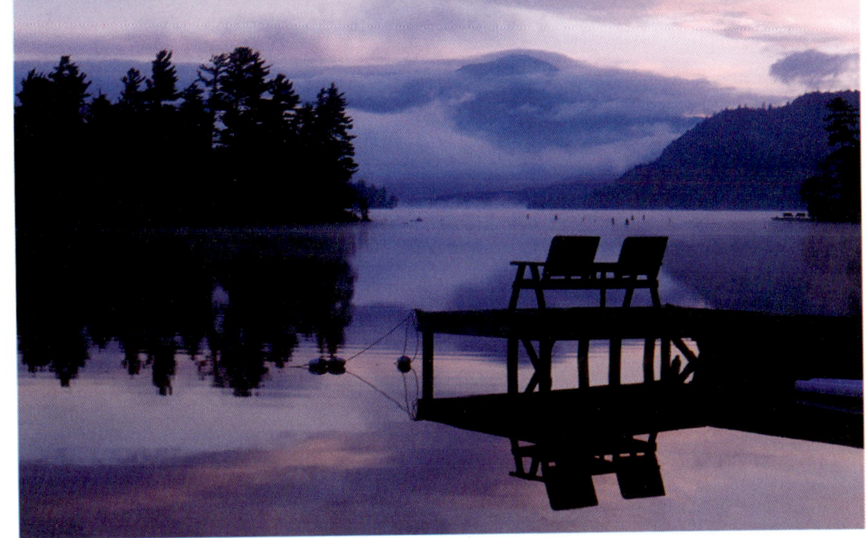

only in temperature but in color too.

Sunrises and sunsets often have a mix of light. As the sun approaches the horizon late in the day, it can give a warm glow to areas in direct sunlight, while the remaining landscape falls into shade. Hiking along Hidden Lake Trail in Glacier National Park, the last rays of sunlight hit Mt. Reynolds with a golden glow as the mountain tarn fell into open shade and cool light. Because the color of light affects the subject color, the blue and green tones of the landscape appeared very saturated in the cool blue light of twilight. Photographing cool colors in cool light will enhance their saturation.

WARM LIGHT

The warm side of the color spectrum—reds, yellows, and oranges—is the colors of fire

When you photograph during the golden hours, there is a good chance you will have warm light.

and sunsets. They visually advance and create a feeling of energy and warmth. Yellows and oranges create feelings of happiness and optimism, while red can evoke the feelings of anger and passion. As you might expect, during the golden hours (the first hour after sunrise and last hour before sunset) the light becomes warm and provides a golden glow.

When you photograph during the golden hours, there is a good chance you will have warm light. Warm colors are further enhanced when photographed in warm light. The aspen trees in Crested Butte, Colorado, are a great example of a subject that benefits from warm

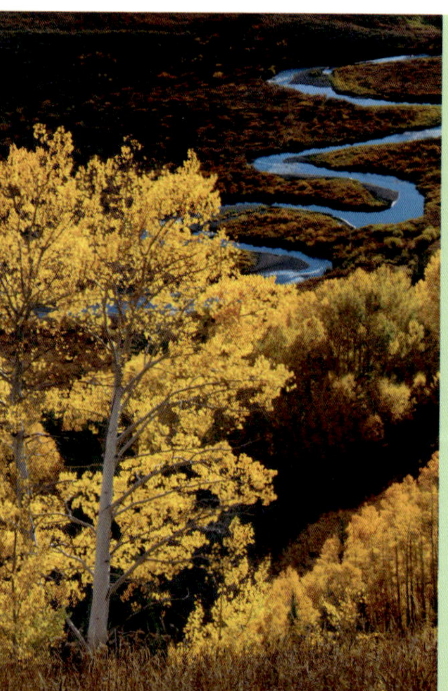

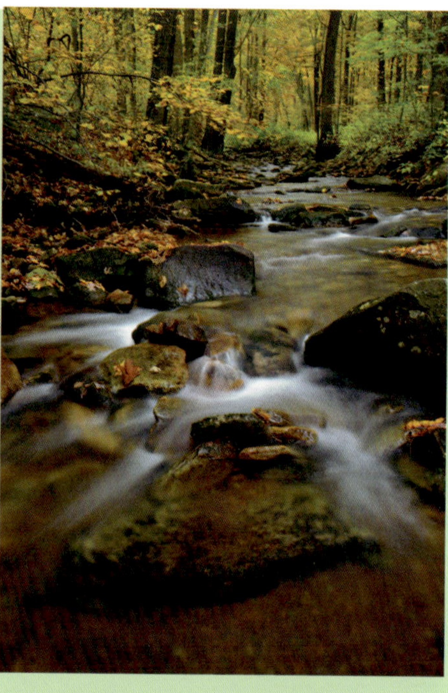

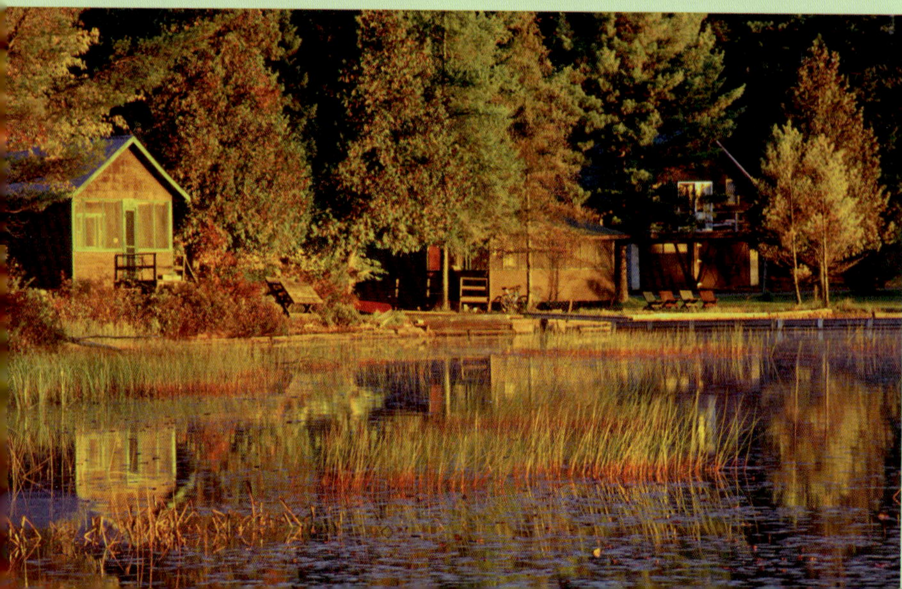

◄ (top left) Aspen trees in Crested Butte, Colorado, glisten in the warm morning light. The leaves have a translucent appearance because the sun was in front of me.

TIME: 8:31:33AM | FOCAL LENGTH: 100mm | ISO: 200 | APERTURE: f/22 SHUTTER SPEED: 1/20 second

◄ (top right) A warming polarizer reduces the glare in the water while adding the subtle effect of a warming filter. On an overcast day such as this, the Singh-Ray warming polarizer added a warm quality to the light.

FOCAL LENGTH: 30mm | ISO: 100 APERTURE: f/16 | SHUTTER SPEED: 2.5 seconds

◄ The cottages along Raquette Lake in the Adirondacks were aglow in warm golden hour light.

FOCAL LENGTH: Not available | ISO: 50 Fujichrome Velvia | APERTURE: Not available SHUTTER SPEED: Not available

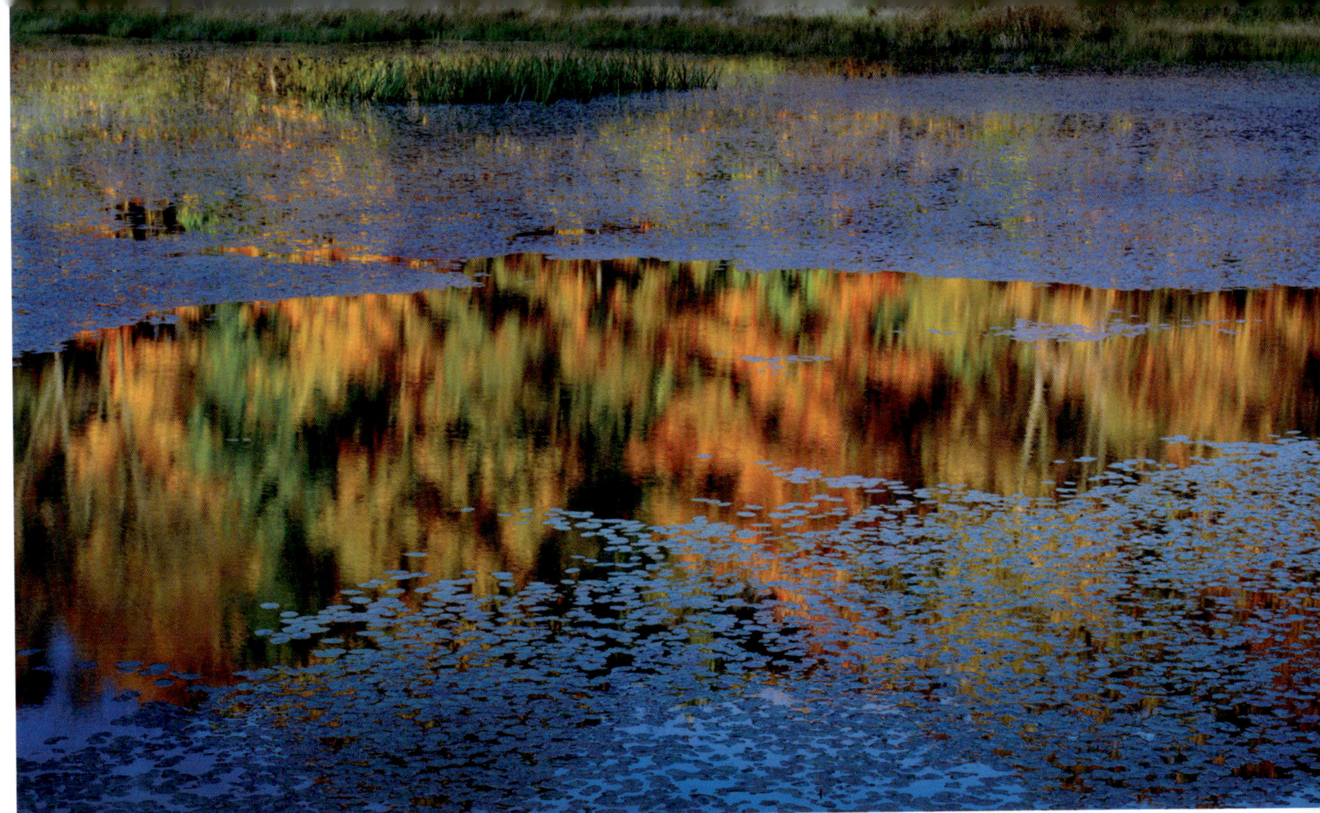

light. Their leaves turn a bright yellow (and sometimes orange) in the autumn that contrasts nicely with their white trunks. I captured the translucent effect of the leaves using back lighting as the warm early-morning light filled the valley in front of me.

The cottages along Raquette Lake were aglow on one October morning. Warm light enhanced the warm tones but also altered the green tones, making them appear more yellow. If I waited about an hour, the color of light would have been more neutral and the green would have appeared more normal, but the rich warm tones cast on the cottages and reeds would have been lost. In this case, I don't mind the green being altered because it adds to the overall warmth and moody feeling of the scene and the fall season.

The use of filters, such as an 81A or a warming polarizer, can also make a photograph appear warmer.

▲ The cool blue sky next to the warm orange created a vibrant contrast in Cranberry Lake.

FOCAL LENGTH: 86mm | ISO: 200 | APERTURE: f/18 | SHUTTER SPEED: 1/4 second

COMPLEMENTARY COLORS

Mixing cool blue skies with warm landscapes is one technique for creating dramatic and compelling images. Blue is on the cool side of the color wheel with orange directly opposite on the warm side; these colors are considered complementary. When complementary colors are used together, the contrast creates a vibrant, dramatic look.

Upon completing a commercial photo shoot in Pennsylvania, I discovered Cranberry Lake just below the wind turbines I was hired to photograph. The golden hour of evening was approaching, and the trees were at their peak autumn color around this small fishing lake. Initially, I was drawn to the reeds along

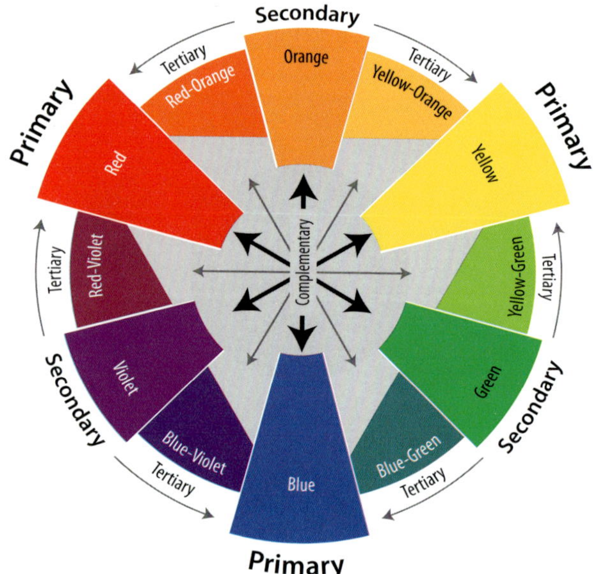

▲ The three primary colors of red, blue, and yellow provide the basic starting point of a standard color wheel. Secondary colors are created by mixing two primary colors together (e.g., when you mix blue and yellow together, you get green). Tertiary colors are created by mixing a primary color with a secondary color. Analogous colors are any three colors side by side on the color wheel. Complementary colors create maximum contrast because they are directly opposite each other on the color wheel.

> "Color evokes the greatest emotional reaction of any graphic element. Its presence significantly influences every design. More often than not, it is this aspect of a scene that induces a landscape photographer to stop and set up the camera."[10]
>
> **Tim Fitzharris**
> *Popular Photographer* columnist, renowned photographer

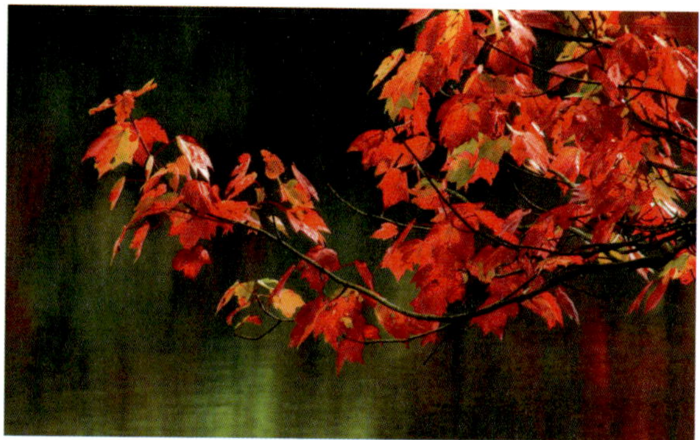

▲ The red autumn leaves appear to "pop" when contrasted with the green reflection in the background. These complementary colors are directly opposite one another on the color wheel, which means that maximum contrast results when they are used together.

FOCAL LENGTH: 210mm | ISO: 200 | APERTURE: f/13
SHUTTER SPEED: 1/30 second

the shoreline. The late-day sun gave them a golden glow that contrasted nicely against the blue water. I then moved to another spot on the lake and discovered a scene that took my breath away.

The golden light shining on the trees created a reflection in the lake that was rich in color intensity. The complementary colors of blue and orange naturally enhanced the vibrancy and saturation without the use of any special effects or post-processing. Yes, it really was that color! Complementary colors will have that amazing effect.

My evening's images were captured with a polarizer to reduce the glare on the water and a tripod for stability and sharpness. I find that using a tripod forces me to slow down and "work" the composition. Doing so was a good thing in this case, since I was so excited by the beauty of the reflection, I needed to concentrate on the scene and capture it as I remembered it.

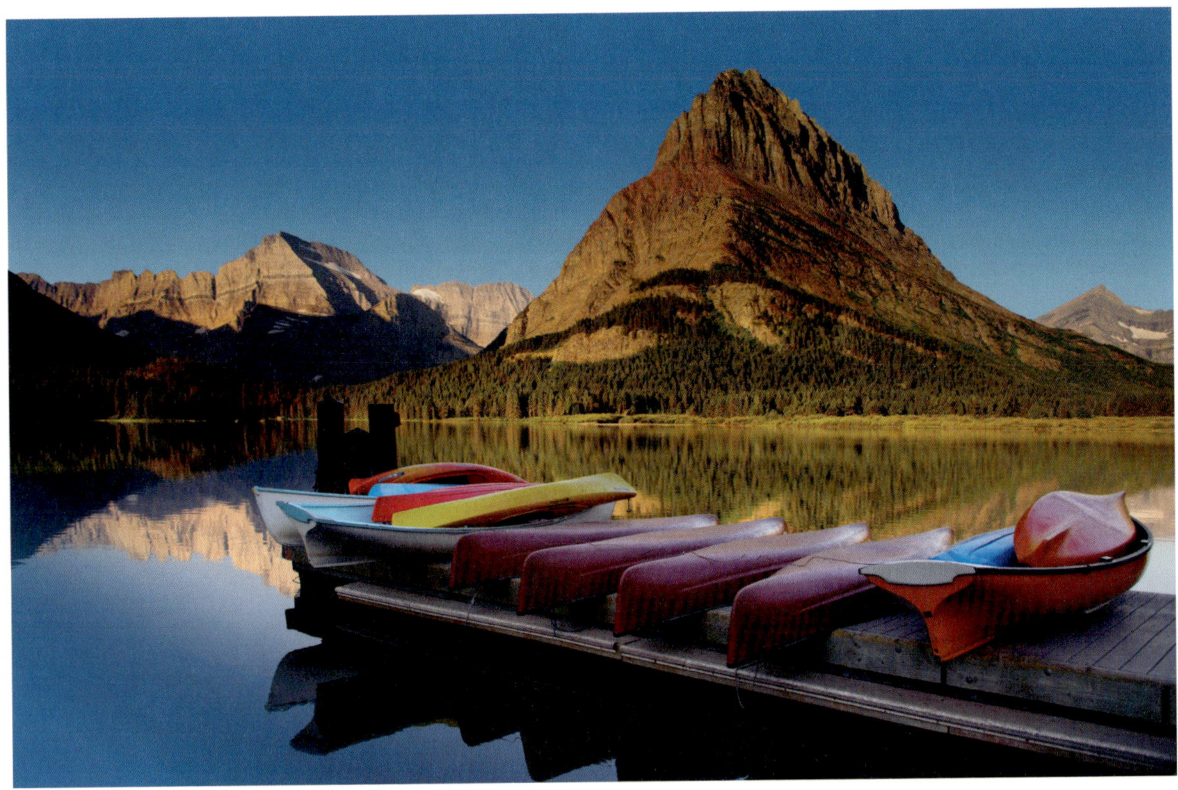

▲ Using a daylight white balance setting applied no color correction and rendered the canoes at Swiftcurrent Lake in Glacier National Park accurately and vividly.

FOCAL LENGTH: 28mm | ISO: 100 | APERTURE: f/5
SHUTTER SPEED: 1/40 second

COLOR TEMPERATURE

Light not only changes in intensity throughout the day, it also changes in color temperature. The Kelvin color temperature scale measures the color of light in Kelvin degrees. Warm colors are low in temperature, starting at 1000–2000K for candlelight, 3000–4000K during sunrise and sunset, daylight between 5000–6000K, overcast around 6500–8000K, and finally the twilight and the blue hour at 9000K–10,000K+. Fortunately, most digital SLRs provide a range of white balance presets that make it easier to record accurate color in your images. Selecting the shade preset, for example, will give you the proper white balance for a shady scene of between 7000–7500K; it effectively warms up the light by removing some of the blue cast. The daylight setting is about 5000 to 5500K and applies no color correction.

The changes in color temperature can be difficult to recognize at first because our eyes and brain auto correct for the color changes, but the camera will not adapt in the same way. The automatic white balance setting ("AWB" on Canon or "A" on Nikon) will neutralize the color to around 5500K or close to a daylight color temperature. AWB works well most of the time, except at the edges of the day when the color temperature is far from

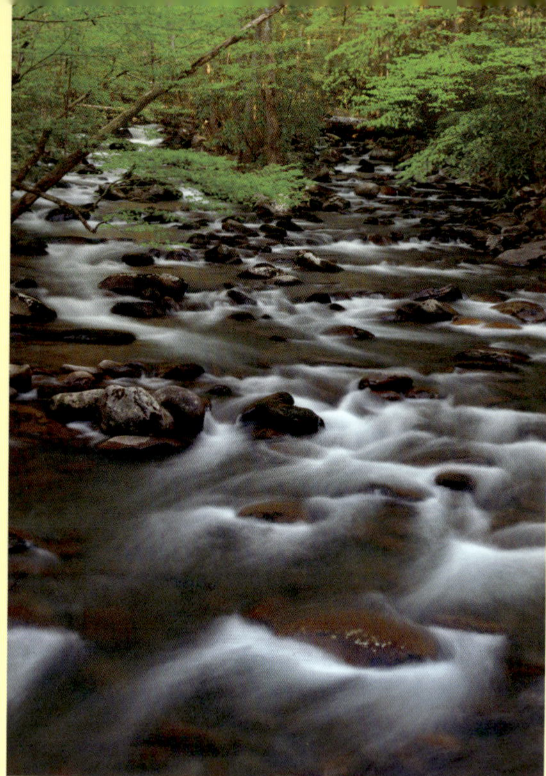

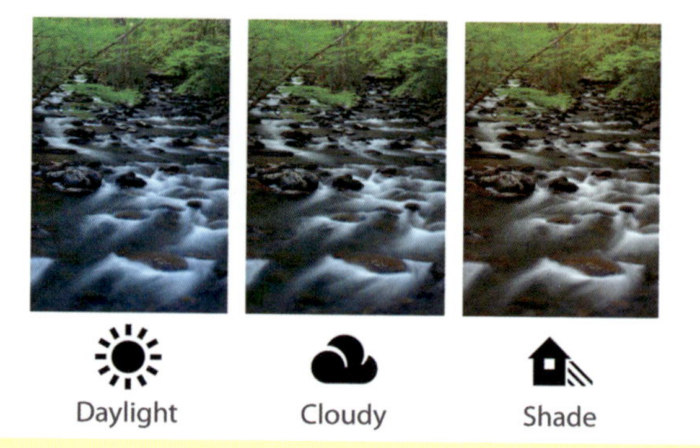

Selecting either daylight, cloudy, or shade white balance presets on my Nikon D3 produced variations in the color rendition. The scene was in shade when captured, so the shade preset produced the best results (the blue cast from the open shade was neutralized).

FOCAL LENGTH: 56mm | ISO: 100 | APERTURE: f/20 | SHUTTER SPEED: 3 seconds

the "white" of midday. The AWB setting will try to neutralize the warm light of sunrise and sunset by removing some of the orange and yellow colors.

Getting in the habit of setting the white balance manually in the camera will force you to look at the color of the light and make an appropriate selection. This is important when saving files as JPEGs because the color temperature is embedded in the file. If you are shooting in RAW, the white balance can be reset without any file degradation when post-processing. You can see an example of this in the first section of chapter 12.

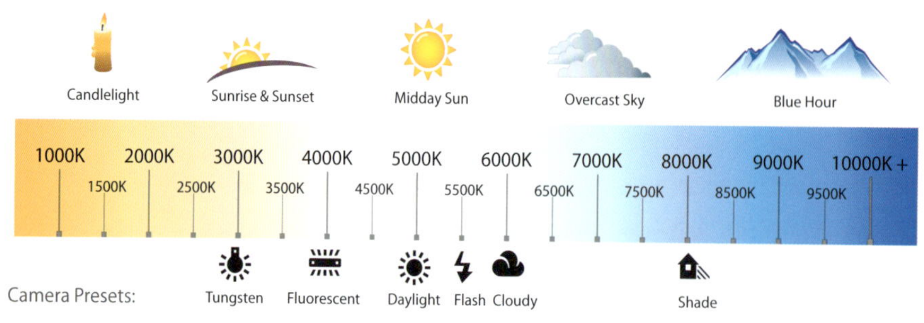

The color of light is measured in Kelvin degrees. This chart shows the color temperature of common sources.

8. WEATHER GUIDE

CHASING THE LIGHT

In sports, they say there are game-defining moments. In landscape photography, there are moments of defining light. The light may be just perfect for a second. These moments don't happen every day, but when they do, as with sports, one frame can tell the story with more visual impact than the others.

French photographer Henri Cartier-Bresson called this the "decisive moment." He said, "To take a photograph means to

▼ Chasing storm light in the Smoky Mountains was a challenge. Quick action was required to capture the defining moment of light.

TIME OF DAY: 5:30:46PM | FOCAL LENGTH: 70mm | ISO: 200
APERTURE: f/11 | SHUTTER SPEED: 1/5 second

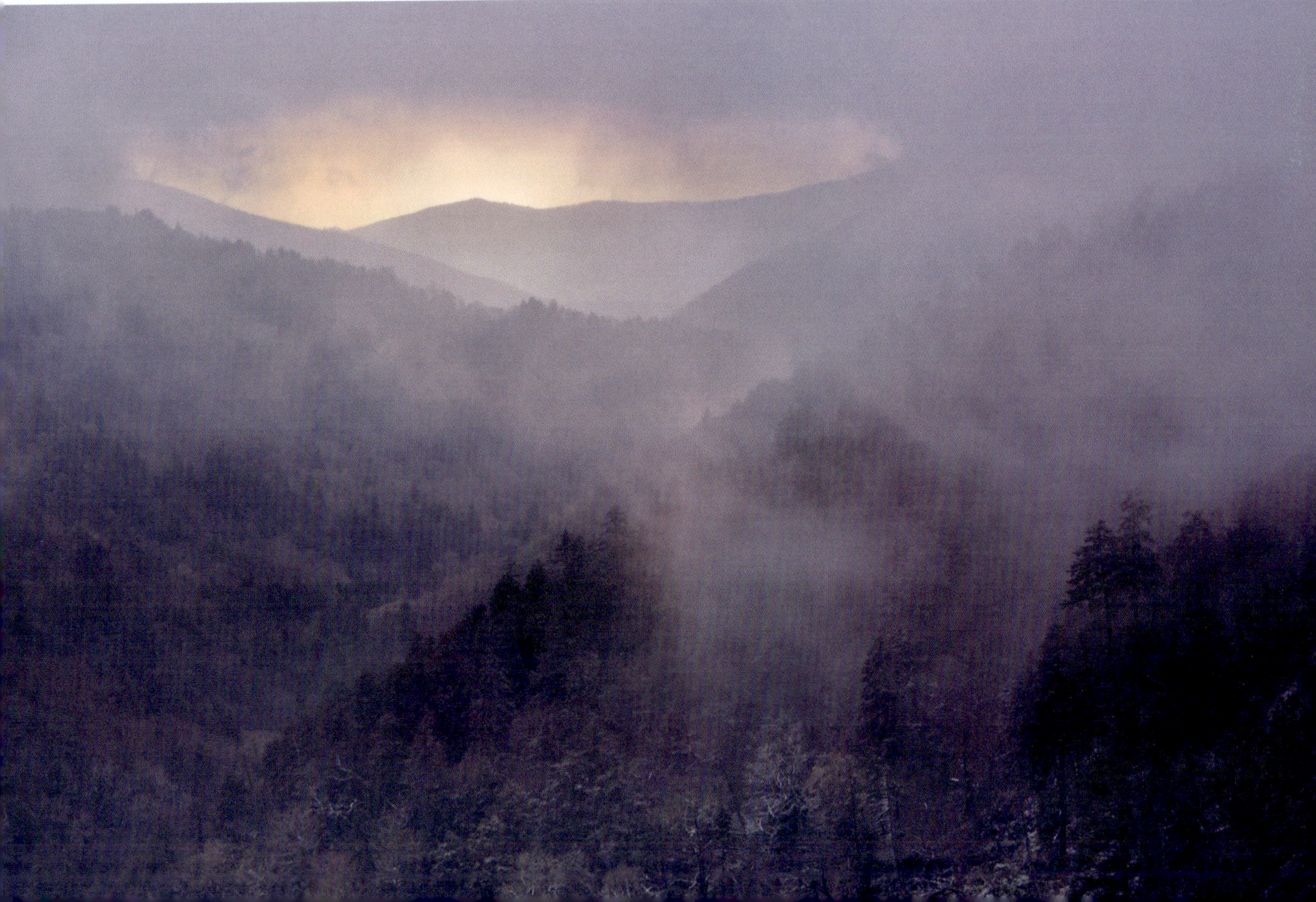

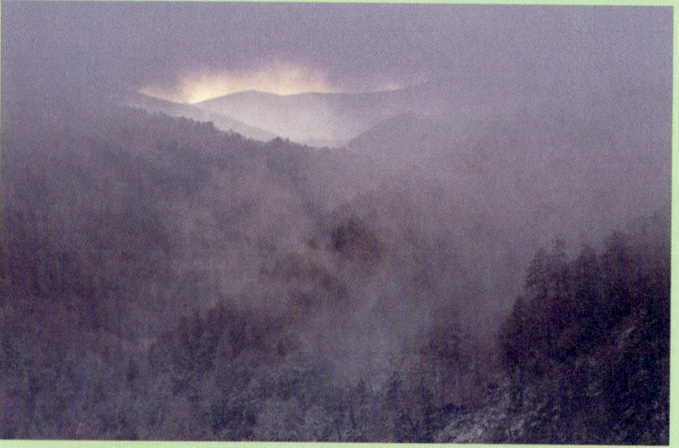

▲ At 5:29:51 PM the cloud cover was still thick and the distant peak only had a small opening of light.

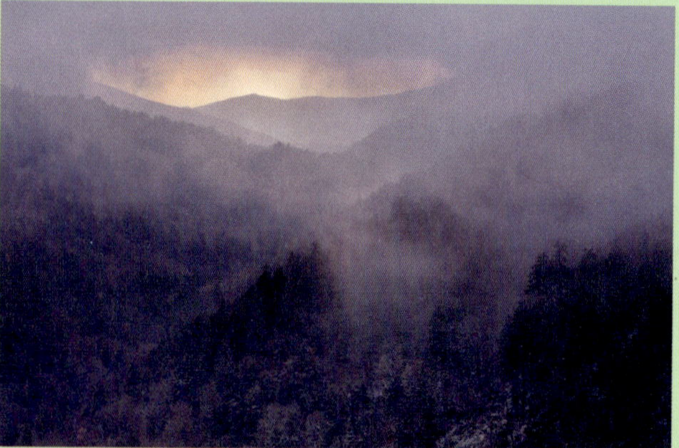

▲ 5:30:46PM. As the storm moved across the mountains 54 seconds later I pressed the shutter at the peak moment.

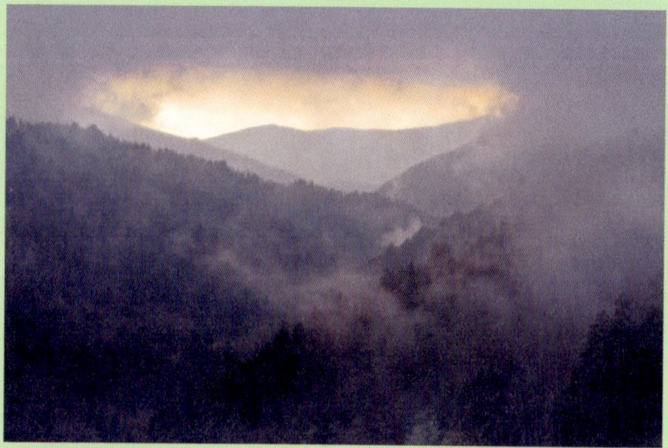

▲ At 5:31:22PM the clouds started to lift as the light spread across the distant ridge.

recognize—simultaneously and within a fraction of a second—both the fact itself and the rigorous organization of visually perceived forms that give it meaning."[11]

My trip to Great Smoky Mountains National Park began with a decisive moment of magic light. Within a matter of seconds, the light changed dramatically. This storm was moving fast, making capturing it a challenge. I set up my tripod and camera as quickly as possible to capture the striking light. At 5:30:46PM, the decisive moment came with a single frame that best captured the moment. The light changed in seconds, so knowing the basics of photography and how to work my equipment quickly was essential.

Capturing fleeting moments requires symmetry between your vision, the camera, and the light.

When chasing the light, photography needs to be "automatic" and intuitive. I'm not taking about your camera being set on "auto" (I shoot in manual mode). I'm referring to the process. Capturing fleeting moments requires symmetry between your vision, the camera, and the light. Hesitate and the moment will be lost. I'm learning in my work as a sports photographer that capturing game-defining moments happens within a second or a fraction of second. Blink and it is gone. Capturing it, on the other hand, can mean the difference between a good photo and a great one.

STORMY WEATHER

Stormy weather often paints the land with spectacular light under ominous skies, creating magic. The edges of the weather fronts tend to be dramatic; as the conditions change, so does the light. Keep an eye on the sky and look for these changes—they can be fascinating, especially just before or after a storm. Times when the skies turn deep and dark and the sun sparkles through the clouds with a special glow are magical to me. Sure, it takes a little preparation and luck to be at the right place at the right time, but when you are, you will find that your heart is pumping. Be safe and on the lookout when a storm is approaching and you just might catch theatrical, magical light—or even lightning.

Split-rail fences don't require posthole digging, making them very common in Colorado where the terrain is extremely hard and rocky. It is the Rocky Mountains, after all. As a photographer and graphic designer, I love

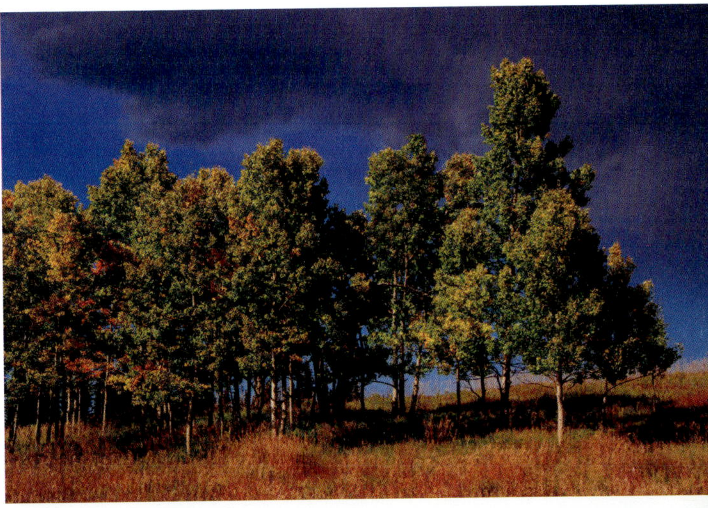

► Storm light brings dark, ominous skies with striking contrast as the sun shines through with dramatic intensity.

FOCAL LENGTH: 82mm | ISO: 200 | APERTURE: f/22 | SHUTTER SPEED: 1/20 second

▼ An approaching storm creates exceptional light in the Silver Jack Wilderness area of Colorado.

FOCAL LENGTH: 72mm | ISO: 200 | APERTURE: f/22 | SHUTTER SPEED: 1/50 second

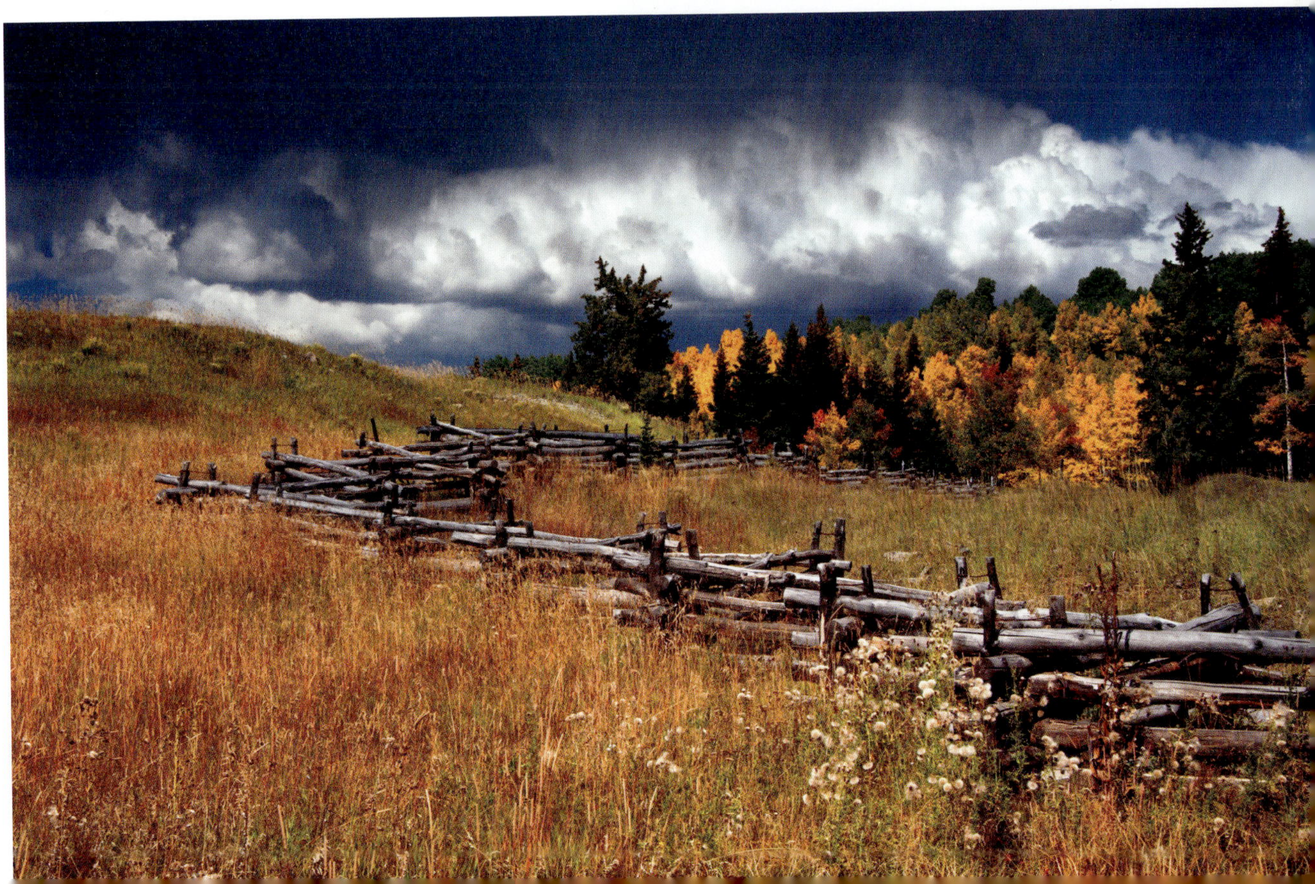

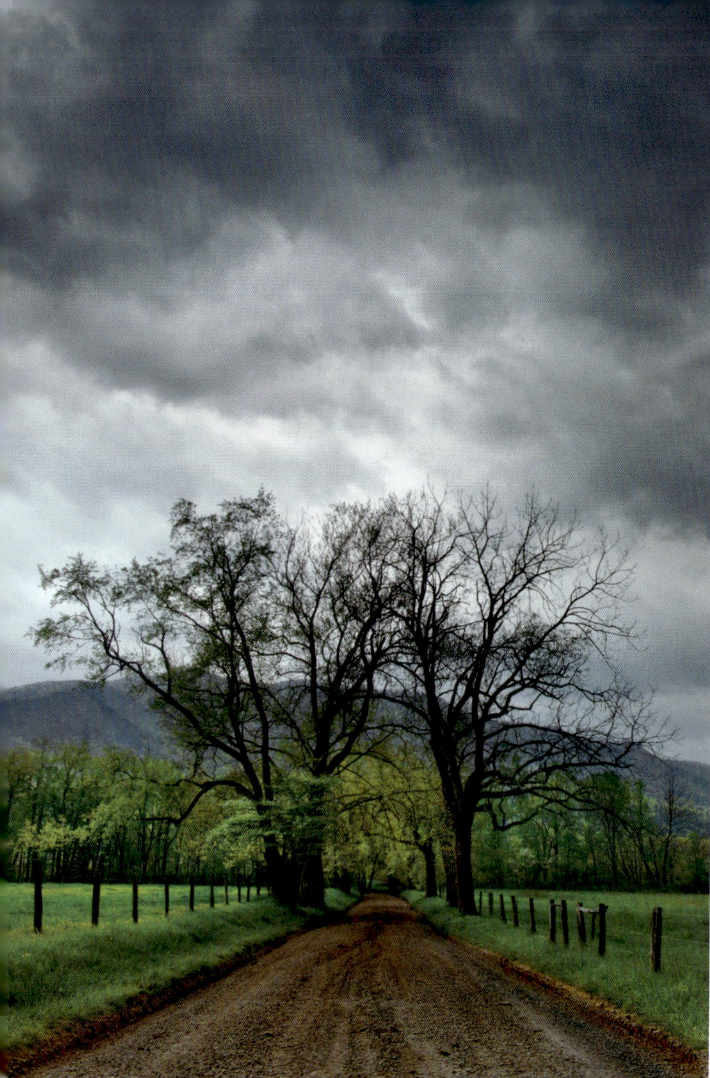

◄ Thick storm clouds passed over Cades Cove in the Great Smoky Mountains of Tennessee.

FOCAL LENGTH: 32mm | ISO: 160 | APERTURE: f/22 | SHUTTER SPEED: 1/5 second

the angles and patterns these fences create as they weave back and forth across the land. They provided the perfect leading line with an S curve to guide the viewer's eye through the image. I used the fence in the bottom two-thirds of the composition with just enough sky to tell the story of the approaching storm.

> Keep an eye on the skies during this time, as dramatic light can happen in an instant.

As the storm approached, the sky turned to dark blue/gray. The contrast of the dark sky against the sunlit trees provides a sense of drama with a unique quality to the light. The special light just before a storm can really add a nice "pop" with a three-dimensional appearance, as it did for the group of trees nearby. Keep an eye on the skies during this time, as dynamic light can happen in an instant. Shortly after putting my camera away, there were a few lightning strikes that I sadly missed.

DRAMATIC SKIES

In the mountains, storms move in and out quickly. Weather fronts often produce great cloud formations with different shapes and patterns as each hour (or minute) passes. Clouds make skies interesting, giving them texture and character. They also disperse the light to create interesting shadows on the landscape below.

At the St. Mary's entrance to Glacier National Park, the St. Mary's River flows to lower St. Mary's Lake. As the storm cleared, there was blue sky behind the moving clouds and speckled light falling onto the land. The sky was intense as the clouds gave way to sunshine. I used a two-stop graduated neutral-density filter to balance the sky with the foreground. Using a polarizer allowed me to reduce the glare in the water and darken the sky for added contrast.

Storms, fog, and cloudy skies are common in the Great Smoky Mountains, making it a popular location for several photographers. The variety of weather conditions can produce unique photo opportunities with each and every visit. This park is free to all visitors and is the most popular National Park in the United States—attracting more than nine million visitors a year. It can be challenging to "find your own space" with so many visitors to the park. Fortunately, though, most tourists are not up at the crack of dawn or out in stormy weather, which makes it easier to get around the park.

When a storm moved in on my visit, it came with thick, dark clouds that hung ominously over Cades Cove. I chose to place this compelling sky in the upper third of my frame and make it the focal point of my image. Rain saturated the landscape and turned the tall grasses a golden hue that wasn't there before the storm. With some light filtering through the clouds, these grasses shined and danced across the open plain.

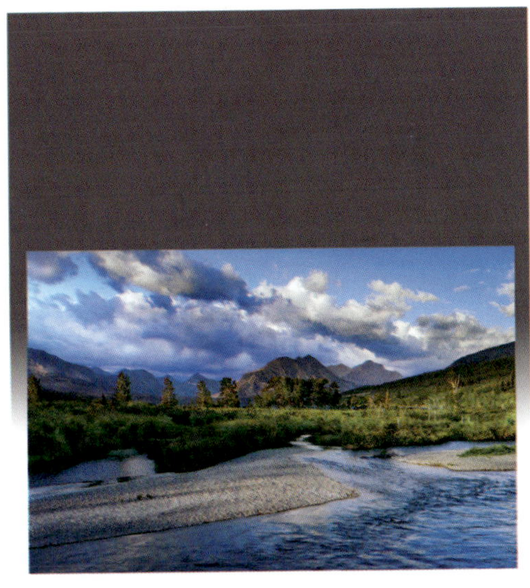

◄ A two-stop split neutral-density filter held in front of a polarizer darkened the sky and balanced the exposure. These two filters can be used together to achieve a well-exposed image.

▼ A clearing storm created a dramatic sky across the St. Mary's River in Glacier National Park.

FOCAL LENGTH: 35mm | ISO: 160 APERTURE: f/16 | SHUTTER SPEED: 1/10 second

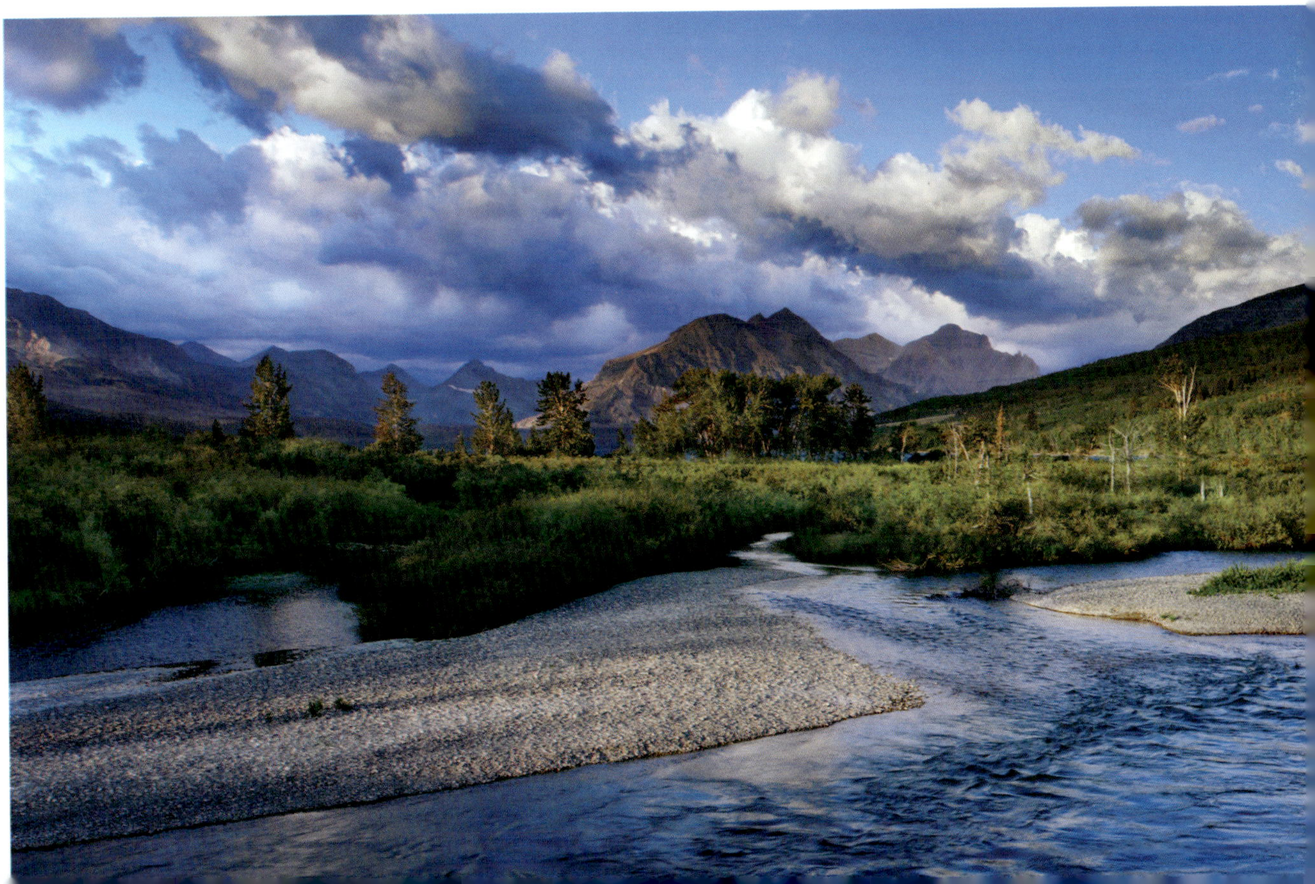

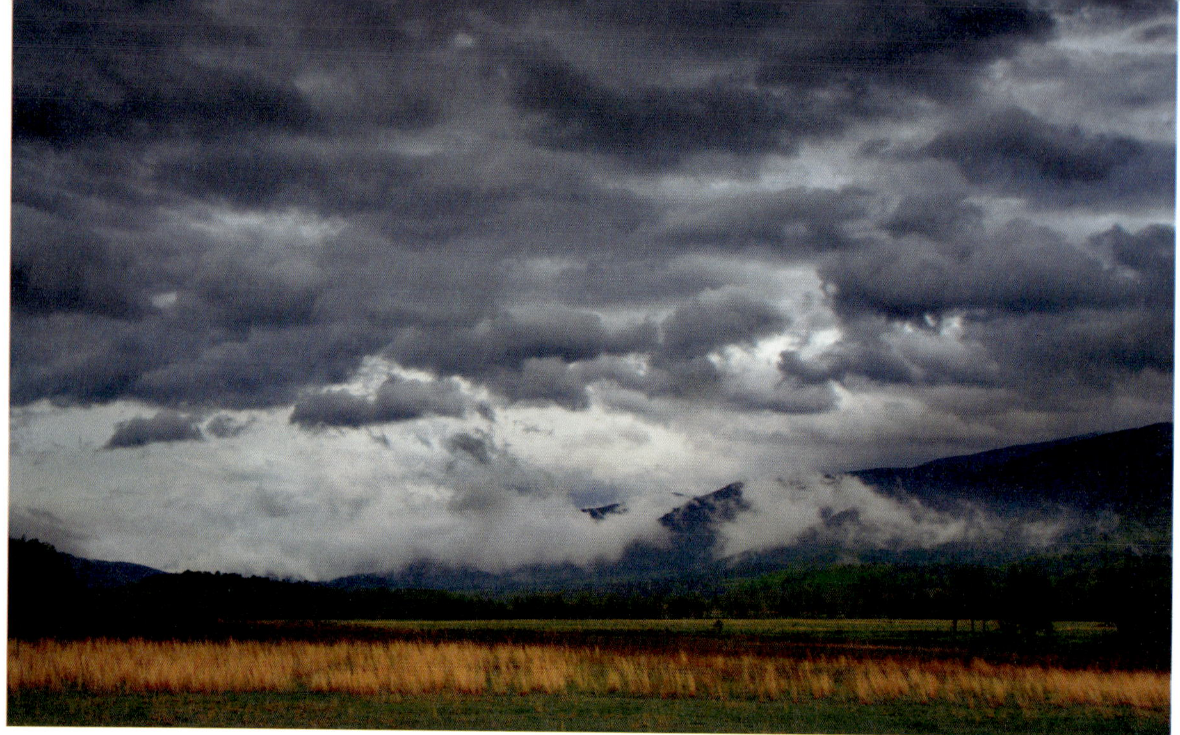

▲ Clouds and light over Cades Cove in the Great Smoky Mountains dominate the composition with a dramatic sky.

FOCAL LENGTH: 48mm | ISO: 125 | APERTURE: f/22 | SHUTTER SPEED: 1/25 second

OVERCAST SKIES

Overcast skies provide soft light by diffusing the sun with a blanket of clouds that spreads out the light and illuminates the land evenly. Overcast light doesn't have much contrast, so there are no strong shadows or bright highlights. Without strong shadows, overcast light is not intense or impressive. However, it is excellent for revealing details with a full range of tones, making overcast days great for many situations. Some subjects, such as waterfalls, actually demand overcast light to bring out the subtle details and texture.

When the light is overcast and the sky lacks interest, I tend to compose my photographs without the sky in the frame. Because overcast light brings out details, textures, and colors, it is perfect for intimate landscapes—small scenes within the large landscapes. Plus an added bonus of overcast light is you can shoot all day in this light. As long as the skies remain overcast, the light will remain constant, allowing you to fully work a location without rushing.

Soft, overcast light was perfect to capture the start of the fall color change at Linn Run State Park in Pennsylvania. On this day the skies remained overcast all day—perfect for shooting streams for hours. As you can see from these images, the exposure practically stayed the same. I wore a pair of waders to get into the water. I was then able to clean up any fallen branches and capture a different perspective. I wanted the water to be the focal point of the image. Wearing waders made all the difference. With them, I could get into the stream and use my wide-angle lens to emphasize the flowing water around the rocks.

► Getting into the water with waders allows for a low viewpoint. The vertical composition further emphasizes the foreground and the flowing water.

FOCAL LENGTH: 22mm | ISO: 100 | APERTURE: f/22 | SHUTTER SPEED: 4 seconds

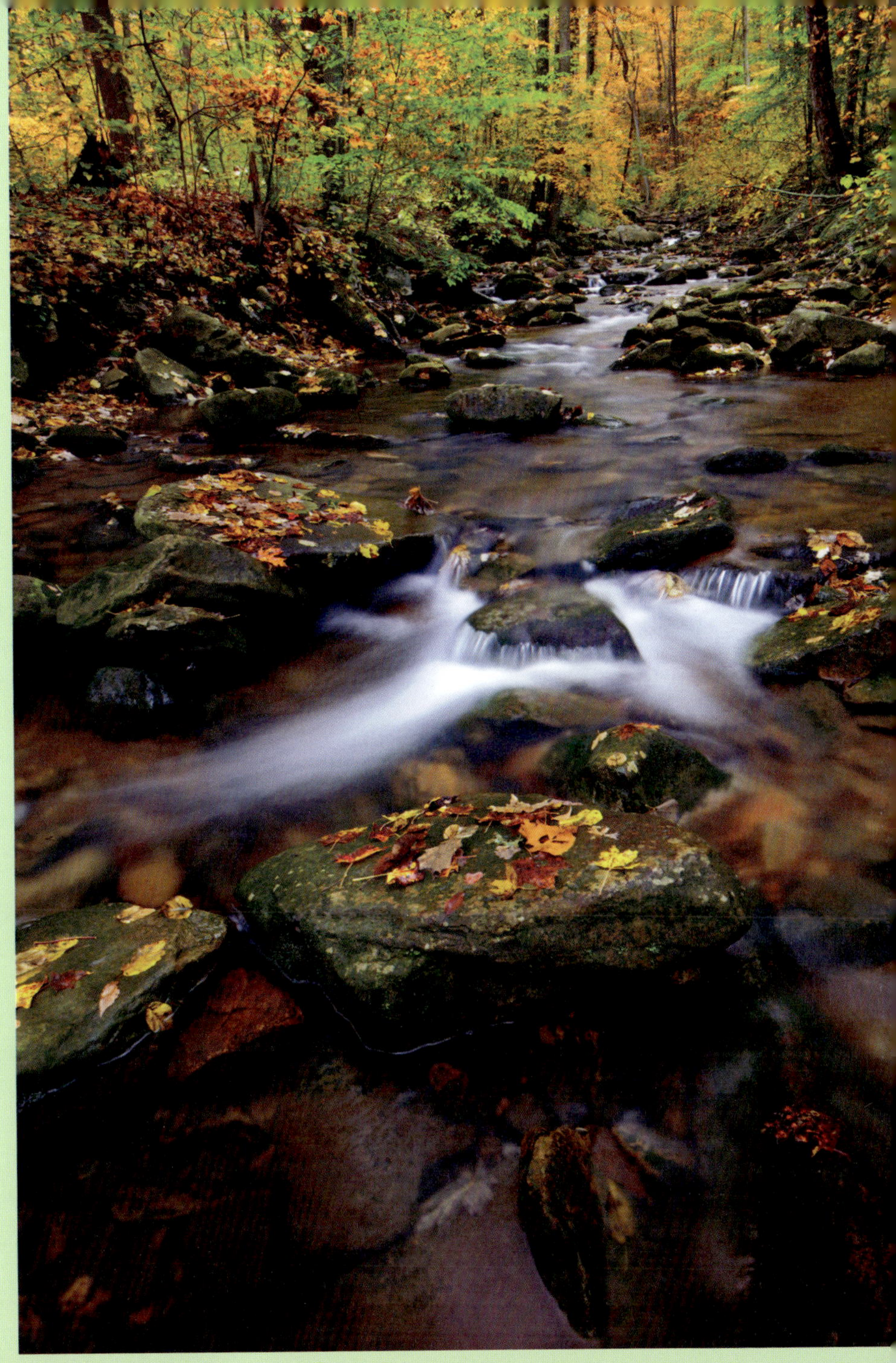

▼ (left) Without a pair of waders (or getting wet) the viewpoint from the bank is elevated and there is less emphasis on the flowing water.

FOCAL LENGTH: 19mm | ISO: 100 | APERTURE: f/22 | SHUTTER SPEED: 4 seconds

▼ (right) The light remains fairly constant in overcast situations, allowing plenty of time to fully work several horizontal and vertical compositions.

FOCAL LENGTH: 20mm | ISO: 100 | APERTURE: f/22 | SHUTTER SPEED: 3 seconds

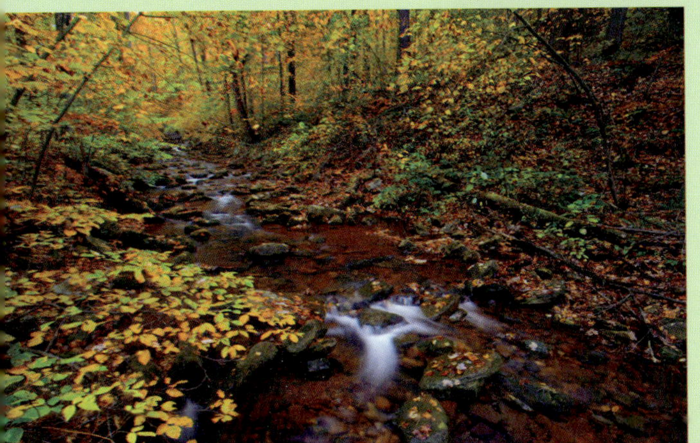

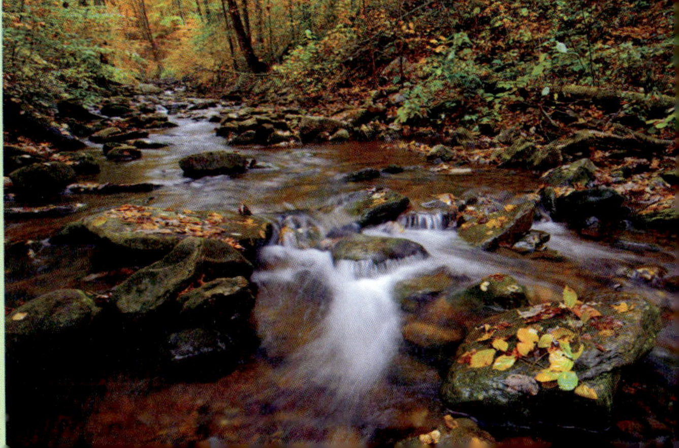

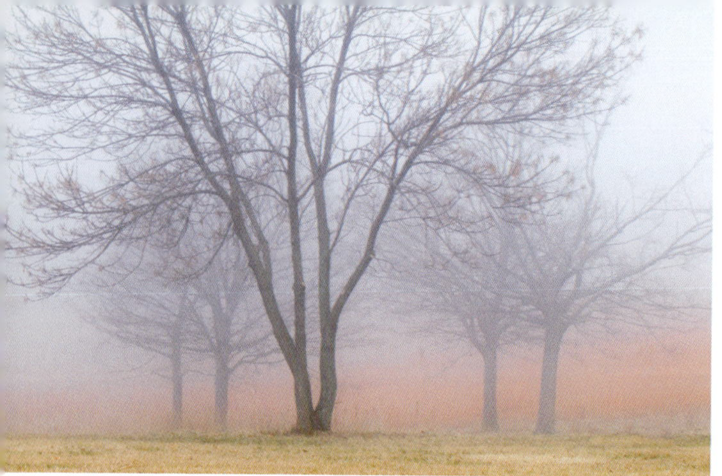

The soft light of fog is great for creating artistic images. You can control the appearance of the fog by altering your distance to the foreground subject. Choosing an 80mm focal length worked perfectly to separate this tree from the background. If I moved closer, the fog between the main tree and the others would have appeared less dense.

FOCAL LENGTH: 80mm | ISO: 200 | APERTURE: f/10 | SHUTTER SPEED: 1/80 second

FOG

Fog is fantastic for creating mood. It makes an ordinary scene appear totally different, turning a simple or drab scene into an extraordinary one. Fog simplifies compositions; nearby subjects are emphasized, while distant objects disappear into the mist. The farther away the subject is from your lens, the thicker the fog will appear. You can use this to your artistic advantage to hide and simplify busy backgrounds.

Fog, like snow, can fool your camera's meter into underexposing the subject by turning the airy white mist into shades of gray. In general, you will need to open up and slightly overexpose, usually by one stop, to capture the mystical feeling. Fog varies in density, so this is not a constant rule. Bracket exposures if you need to and check the histogram to verify the results.

One winter morning the park by my house was filled with a dense fog that lasted for a few hours. I bicycle through this park on a regular basis, and even while riding I sometimes look for photo ops. I knew there were a few trees that didn't lose their leaves in the winter along one of the mountain bike trails. I figured that was a good spot to start my day. With simple shots, such as trees in the woods, I like to break up the repetition of the pattern to add interest and give the image a focal point. The leaves on the tree branches worked to give the image some texture and color while breaking the repeating vertical pattern of the woods. Standing close to the tree I wanted to be the focal point allowed the fog to fill in behind, making the tree's color and detail stand out from the other trees.

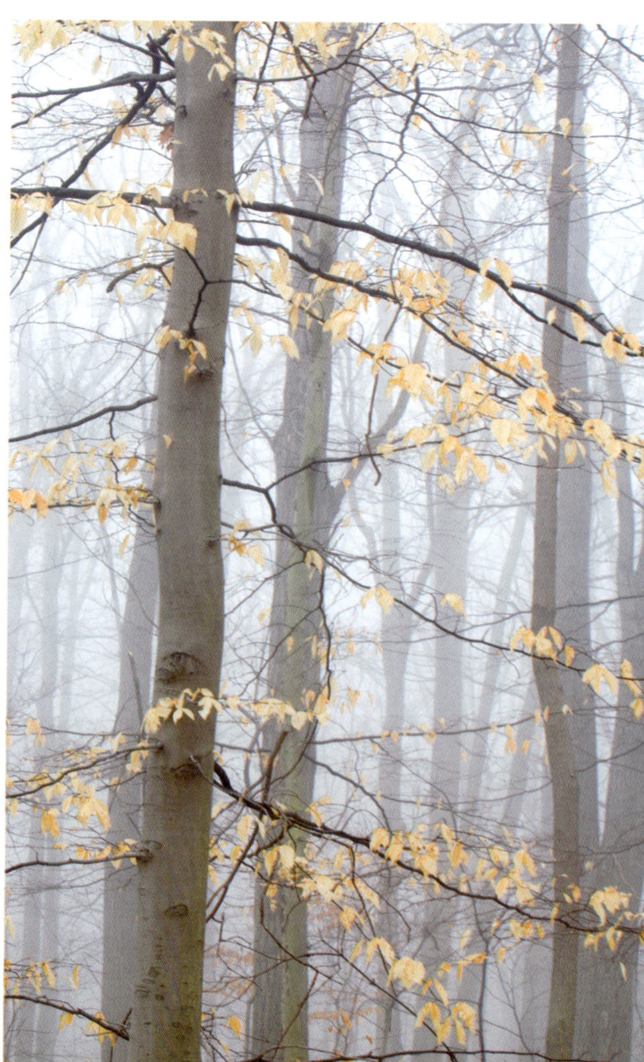

Dense fog makes this otherwise busy scene appear tranquil and mystical. Standing close to the tree with the leaves made its color and detail stand out from the background.

FOCAL LENGTH: 70mm | ISO: 200 | APERTURE: f/11 | SHUTTER SPEED: 1/20 second

RAIN

Rain is Mother Nature's version of a saturation brush—creating bold and vivid colors. Think of rocks along a lakeshore—the ones that are wet glisten with saturated color while the dry ones appear gray and dull. Ever notice how reflective wet pavement is? With deep blacks and puddles for reflection, it beats the heck out of the dry stuff.

Not every rainy day is a gem; some are gray, dark, and uninspiring. Then there are those days that are bright with a light rain that comes and goes. This is a good time to get your camera out and explore the colors and saturation that rain provides. A passing storm front can also present a fantastic opportunity for capturing dramatic light.

You don't need expensive rain gear. A shower cap or even a plastic bag works in a pinch when the rain is light. Keep a towel or lens cloth handy to wipe off the camera and lens. If you plan to shoot often in the rain, or in heavy rain, you should invest in dedicated rain gear. After all, camera equipment is expensive and it is worth the money to protect it. Watch the front of the lens and keep it clean and dry; otherwise, you will have spots on your images. A lens shade will also help to keep rain off the front element.

In addition to the added color saturation that rain brings, it is also a fun time to be creative. The selective use of shutter speed can create different effects. A shutter speed of 1/125 or faster will stop raindrops in midair and show them as tiny dots. A slow shutter speed will

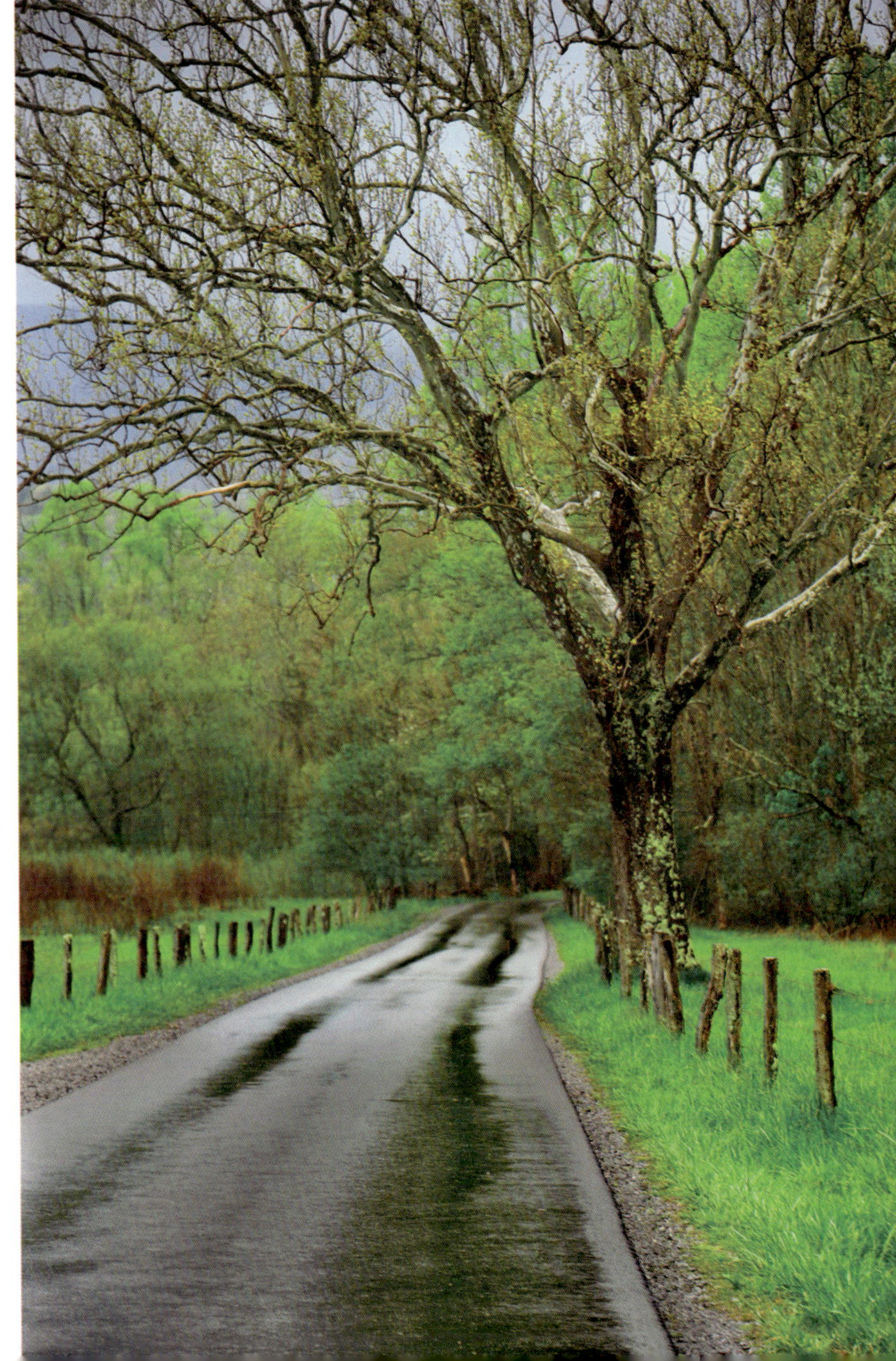

► Rain intensifies and saturates the colors of this tree and its surroundings while turning the road dark and reflective.

FOCAL LENGTH: 135mm | ISO: 125
APERTURE: f/5.6 | SHUTTER SPEED: 1/40 second

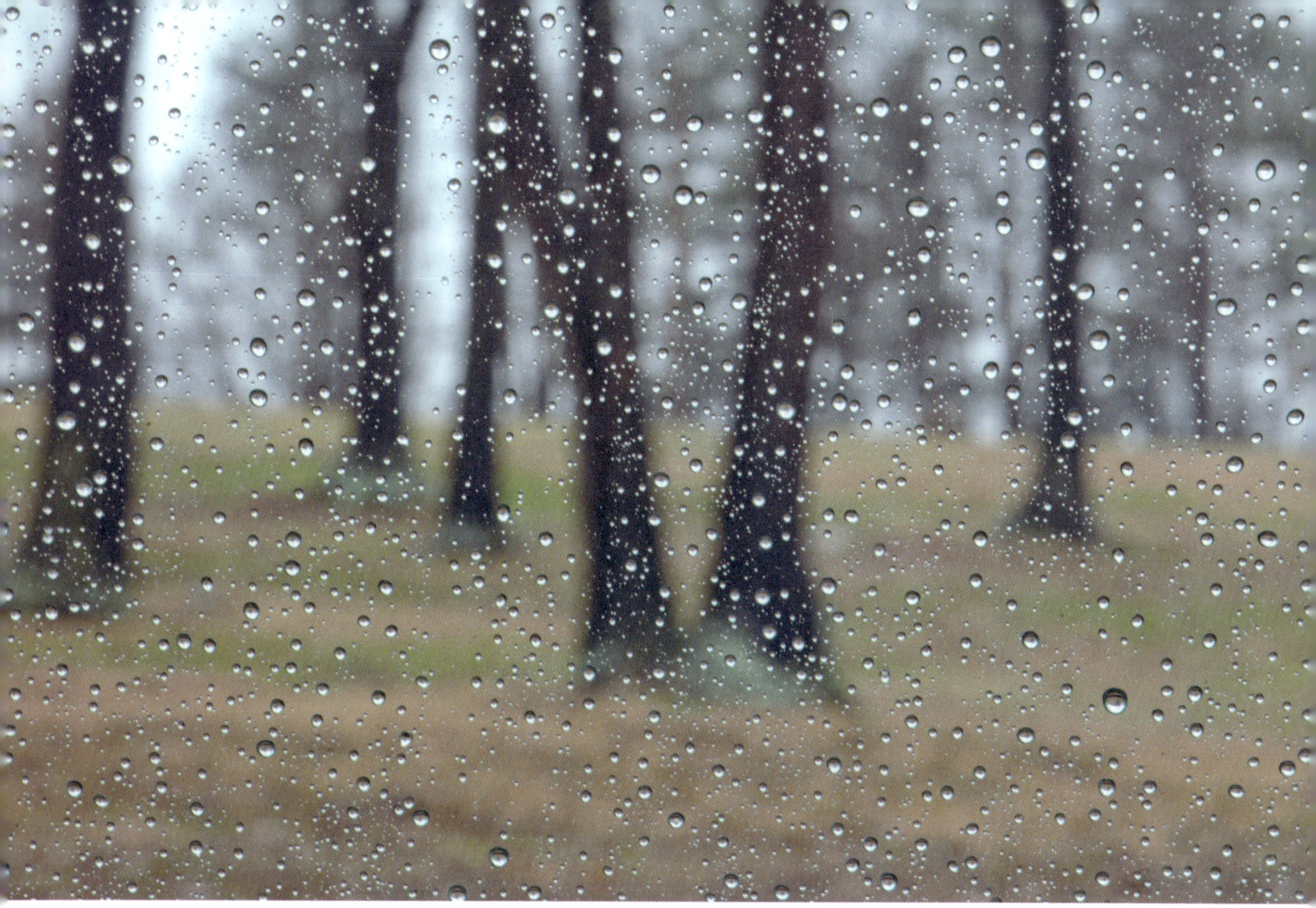

turn the falling rain into streaks. By selecting a fast shutter speed of 1/200, I was able to freeze the action of the raindrops falling onto the pavement in a shallow puddle. On another occasion, I focused on the raindrops on my car window and let the background blur. These images hint at the photographic fun you can have in the rain.

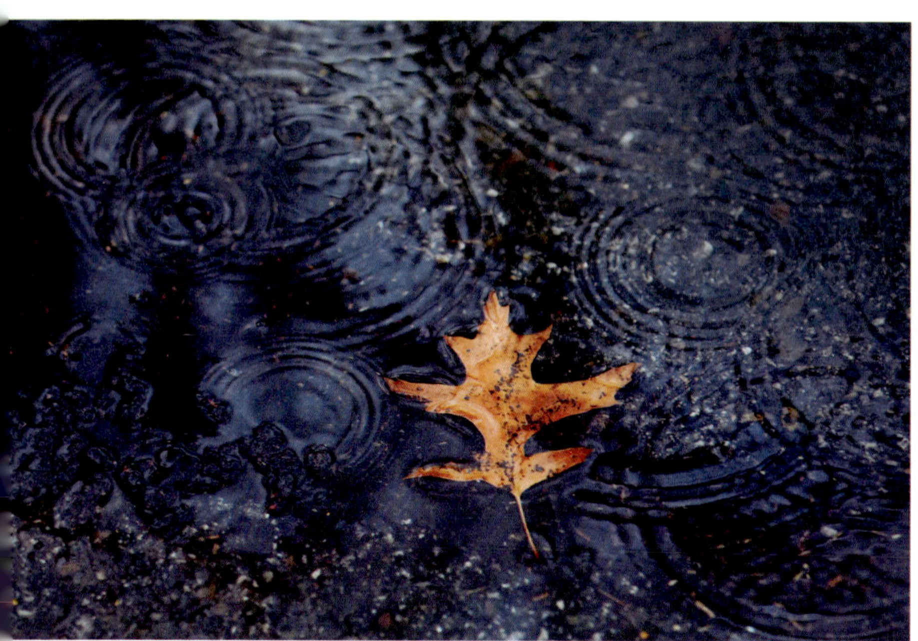

▲ There are many opportunities for creative images in the rain. This image was taken through my car window by focusing on the raindrops and experimenting with different aperture settings for varied depth-of-field effects.

FOCAL LENGTH: 105mm | ISO: 500
APERTURE: f/8 | SHUTTER SPEED: 1.3 seconds

◄ A shutter speed of 1/200 second captured the raindrops as they fell into this shallow puddle.

FOCAL LENGTH: 105mm | ISO: 5000
APERTURE: f/5.6 | SHUTTER SPEED: 1/200 second

SNOW

Snow is similar to fog—both can simplify backgrounds and trick your camera's meter into an underexposed image. Your camera is programmed to meter 18 percent gray. When you meter off grass or another mid-toned object, the recommended exposure settings will produce a correct exposure for an average scene. Fresh snow is not 18 percent gray, so you'll want to overexpose by one or two stops to photograph the snow as white.

You can show the motion of falling snow or freeze it by experimenting with shutter speeds. Depending on how hard the snow is falling, a shutter speed of 1⁄60 second may freeze the action, while at 1⁄15 second the flakes will show as streaks.

Snow, as my friend Michael says, is "boring and lacks color." When I heard the weather forecast for snow in the mountains in October, I planned a trip to Linn Run State Park, Pennsylvania. Snow on fall foliage doesn't happen often, and I wanted to capture it. To my delight, four to six inches of fresh snow lined the tree branches when I arrived at the park. Many of the fall leaves were still on the trees, providing a great opportunity to add color to the snow scene. The light was soft and overcast—perfect for snowy days. Even with the overcast sky, my polarizer reduced the glare in the water and increased the color saturation.

Be careful in the winter wonderland and remember to have a towel handy to keep your gear dry in the falling snow. The cold temperatures can drain your battery, so pack an extra one in case you need it.

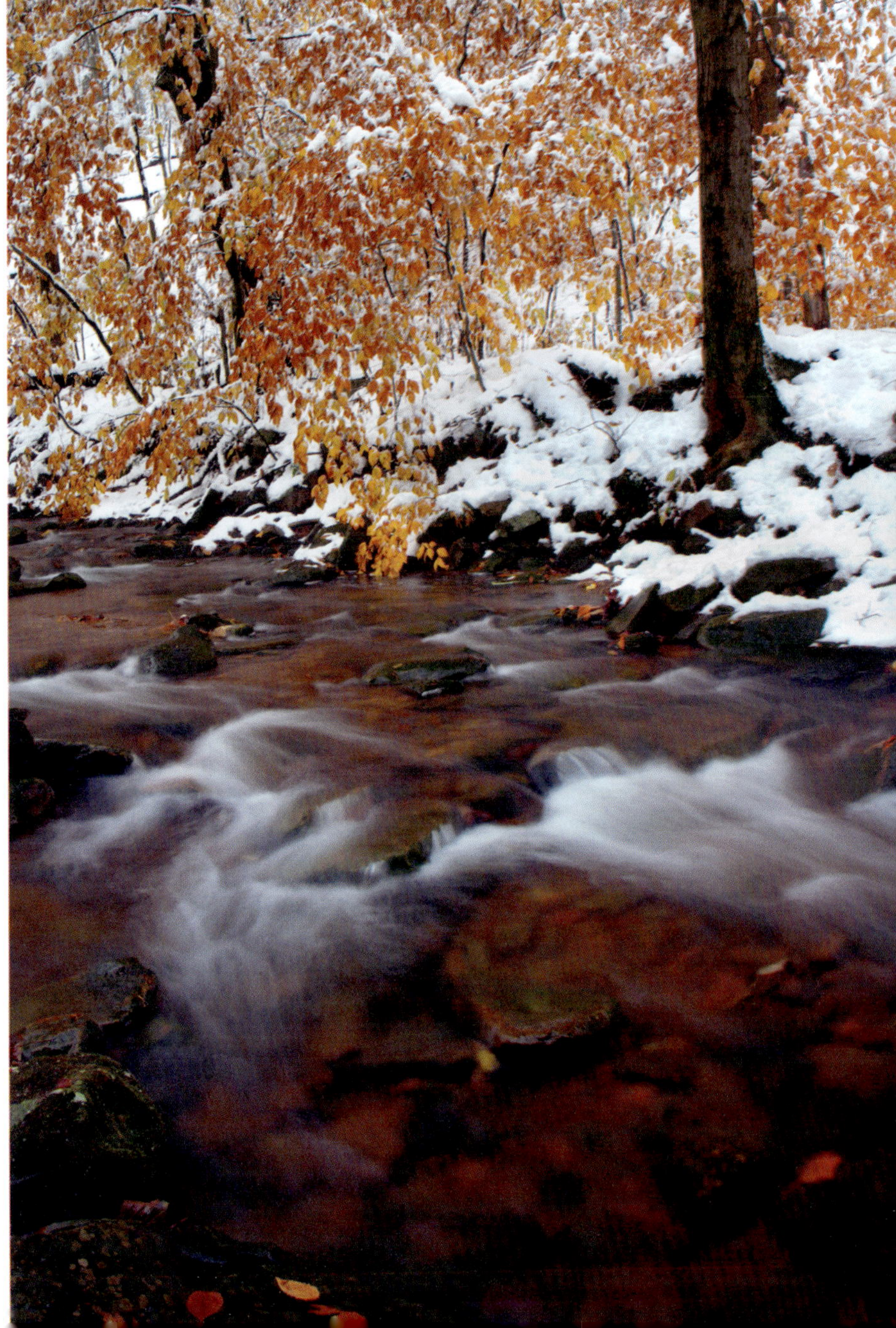

► An early snowfall landed on the autumn leaves in Linn Run State Park, Pennsylvania.

FOCAL LENGTH: 28mm | ISO: 100
APERTURE: f/20 | SHUTTER SPEED: 1.3 seconds

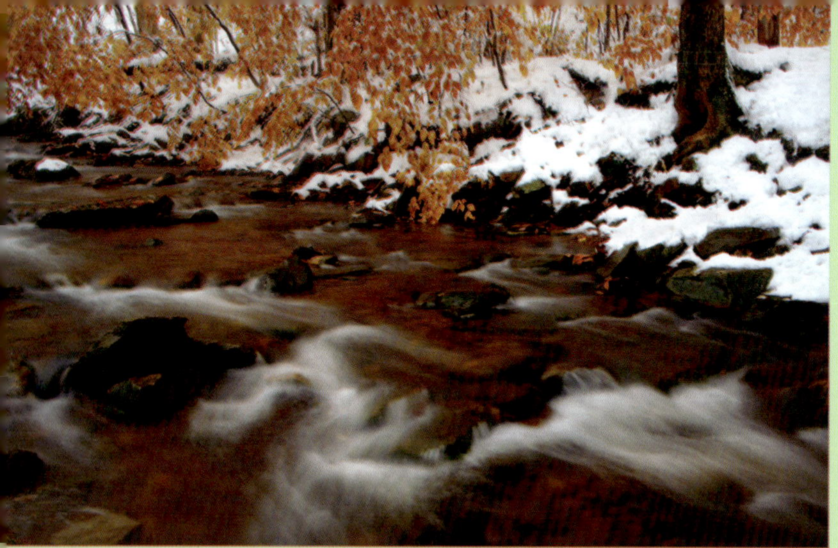

Even on snowy, overcast days a polarizer reduces the glare in water and revealing the rocks, as is evident in this image shot in Linn Run State Park in Pennsylvania.

FOCAL LENGTH: 36mm | ISO: 100 | APERTURE: f/20 | SHUTTER SPEED: 1.3 seconds

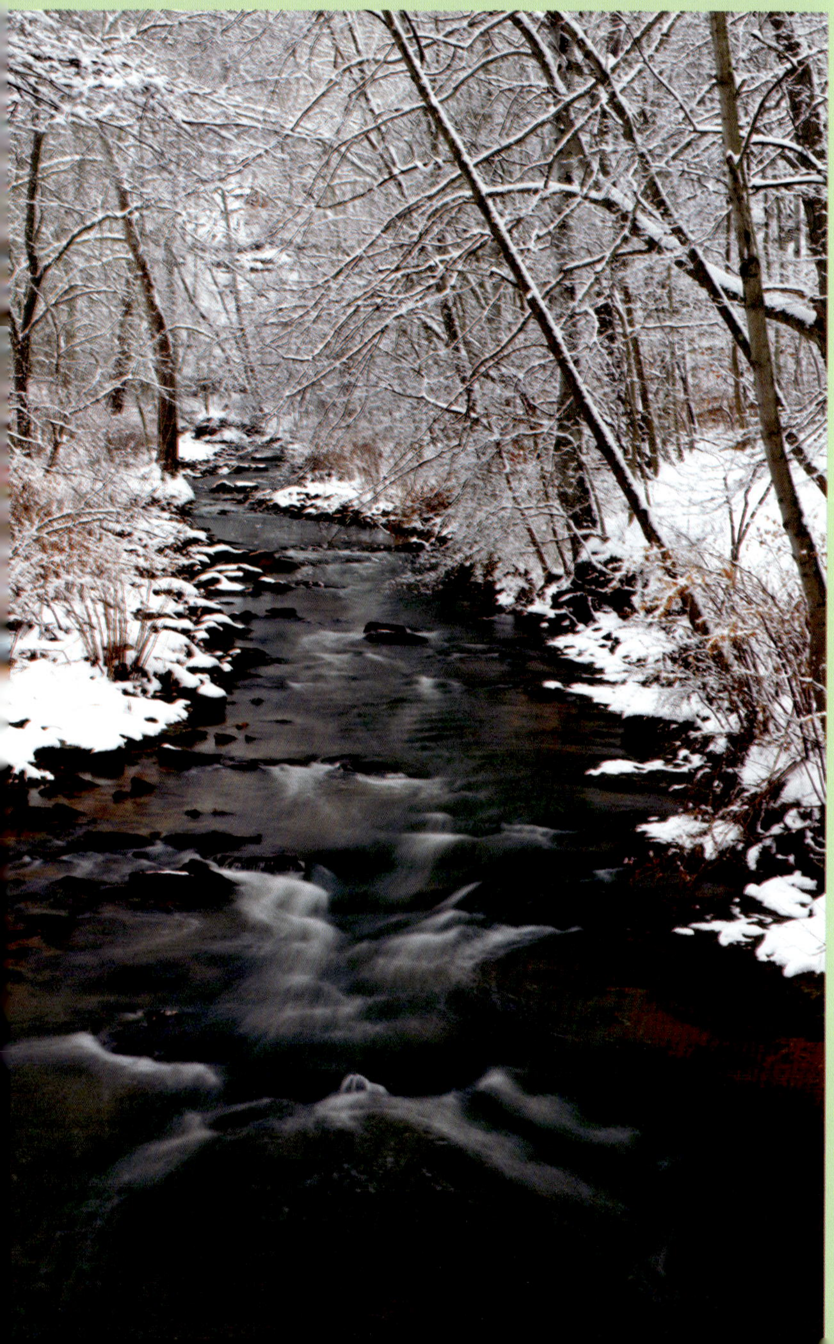

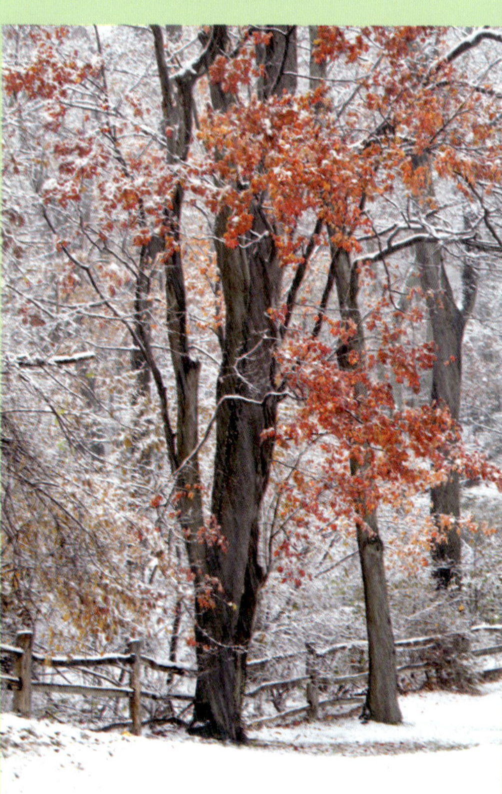

A slow shutter speed of $^{1}/_{13}$ second blurred the snow so it appears as long streaks.

FOCAL LENGTH: 100mm | ISO: 200 | APERTURE: f/16 SHUTTER SPEED: $^{1}/_{13}$ second

The gentle flowing water of Piney Fork added contrast to all the “white stuff” on a snowy winter day in Pennsylvania.

FOCAL LENGTH: 56mm | ISO: 125 | APERTURE: f/22 SHUTTER SPEED: 2 seconds

WIND

Wind can be one of the biggest challenges a photographer faces since it can't be controlled or modified easily. Yes, we can crank up the shutter speed and ISO, but this isn't always ideal. When there is a lot of movement, maybe we should go with the wind instead of fighting it. Tap into your inner artist and experiment with the motion.

Static objects such as buildings, mountains, tree trunks, and rocks don't move in the wind, so take the opportunity to capture the contrast between moving objects and static ones. The leaves on a tree will sway in the wind as the tree trunk remains still. Don't be afraid to show the motion and create painterly effects. Using different shutter speeds will create different looks, so go ahead and play.

On the last day of my trip to Colorado, I made a stop at Giberson Bay. Initially, I was drawn to this scene by the aspen leaves resting along the bay shoreline. After photographing them, I looked behind me and noticed the aspens behind me blowing in the wind and thought it would be fun to use a slow shutter speed to show their motion. With the camera still on the tripod, the stable areas would remain sharp while the blowing leaves would "brush" a soft stroke of color. A shutter speed of 1/3 second worked well to show the motion and create an artistic image. As with any subject that is moving, each frame is different, so I take a lot of images.

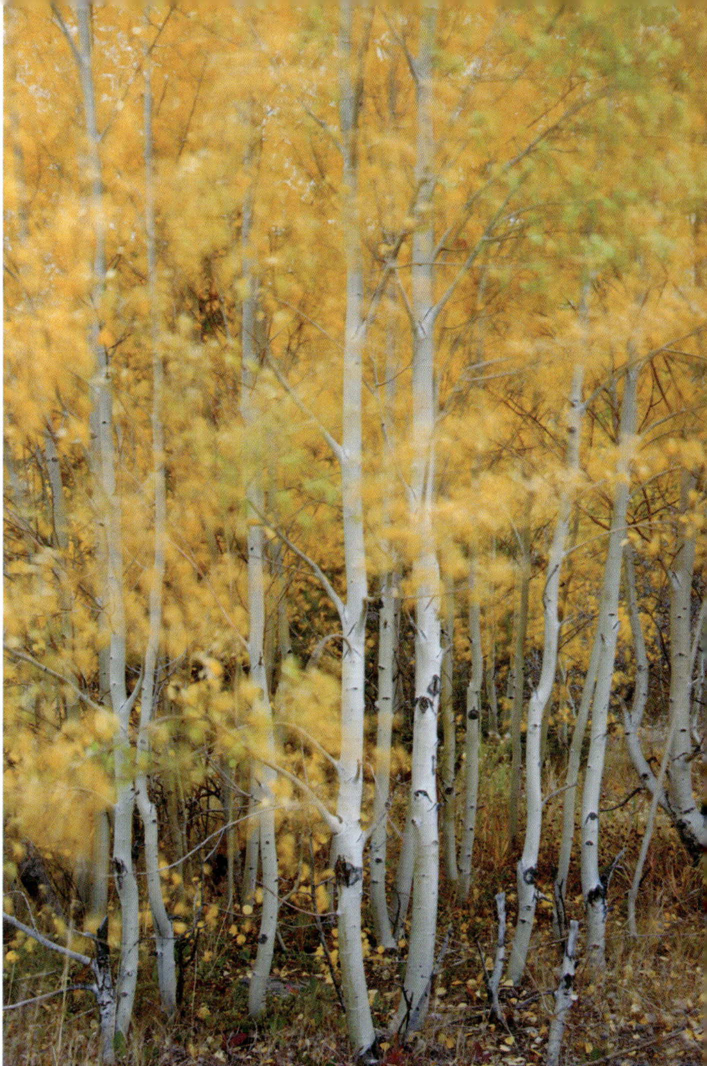

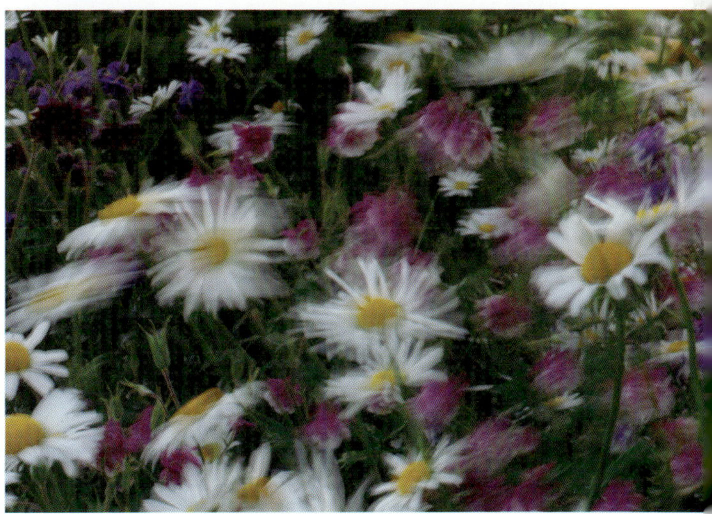

► (top) Showing the progression from the stable ground up to the blowing treetops tells the story of a windy day.

FOCAL LENGTH: 82mm | ISO: 125 | APERTURE: f/22 | SHUTTER SPEED: 1 second

► (bottom) Going with the wind and using a slow shutter speed creates an expressive, artistic image.

FOCAL LENGTH: 60mm | ISO: 200 | APERTURE: f/32 | SHUTTER SPEED: 1/3 second

9. WATER AND REFLECTIONS

IDEAL LIGHT

Photographing the grace and beauty of waterfalls and streams requires the soft light of an overcast day to bring out the subtle details and softness of the flowing water. Rain is also great for saturating the surrounding rocks and trees.

Bright sunny days produce harsh light, and more often than not, this is not a desired result. This bright, hard light casts harsh shadows with deep blacks, resulting in an image with a lot of contrast. It also will cause hot spots and glare on the water and surroundings. Hot spots lack detail, and the missing image data cannot be recovered in post-processing. Simply waiting for the light to change or revisiting a location at another time can yield better results.

Photographing along Big Creek in the Great Smoky Mountains, I captured the same scene in different light. One image was taken in hard light on my hike up the trail and another was shot on the way back when the light was considerably better. Here you can see the difference between soft light (when the clouds moved in later in the day) and the hard light of bright sun. The image shot in hard light has several hot spots that lack detail, the shadows are harsh, and the overall image has a lot of contrast. The image captured in the afternoon once the clouds moved in is full of texture, color, and detail. Notice the difference in the histogram for each image. The highlights are clipped and "blown out" in the image taken in bright sunlight. Under the soft light of cloud cover, the subtle nuances of the mossy rocks

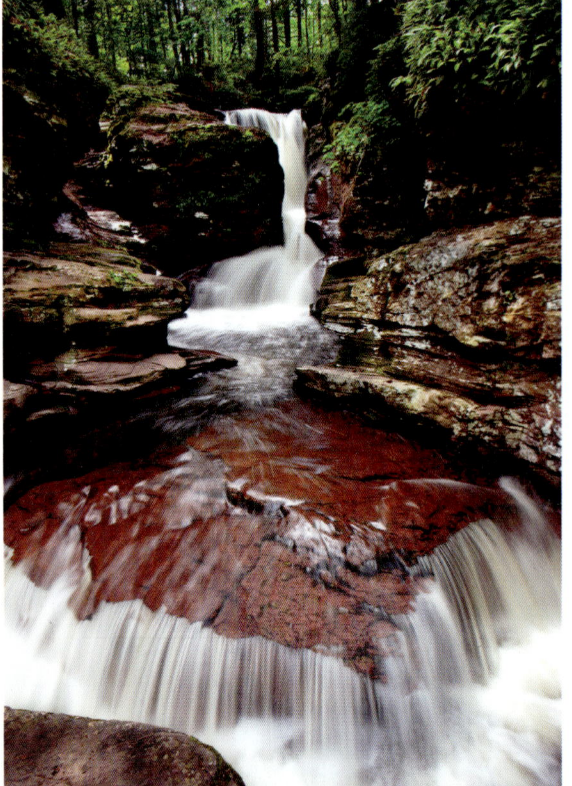

◄ Soft light was ideal to show the detail, texture, and color around Adams Falls in Ricketts Glen State Park. A slow shutter speed of 1/2 second blurred the motion of the water as it dropped 36 feet across a leaf-shaped Catskill formation rock in the foreground.

FOCAL LENGTH: 24mm | ISO: 200 | APERTURE: f/22 | SHUTTER SPEED: 1/2 second

and water are revealed. Additionally, it was not as bright, so I was able to use a slower shutter speed to show more motion in the water. To create waterfall and stream images that appear soft, saturated, and full of detail and texture, seek soft light.

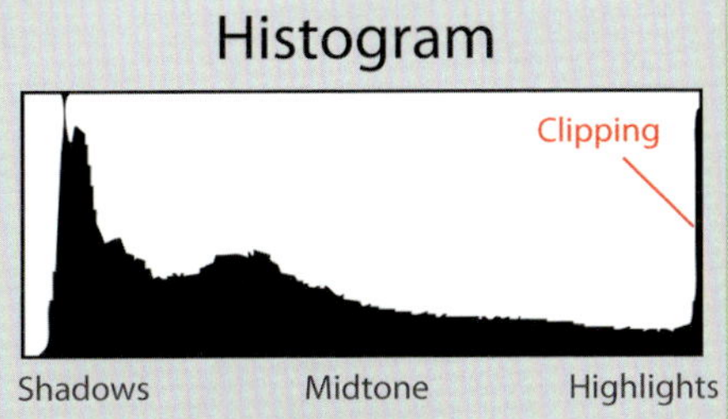

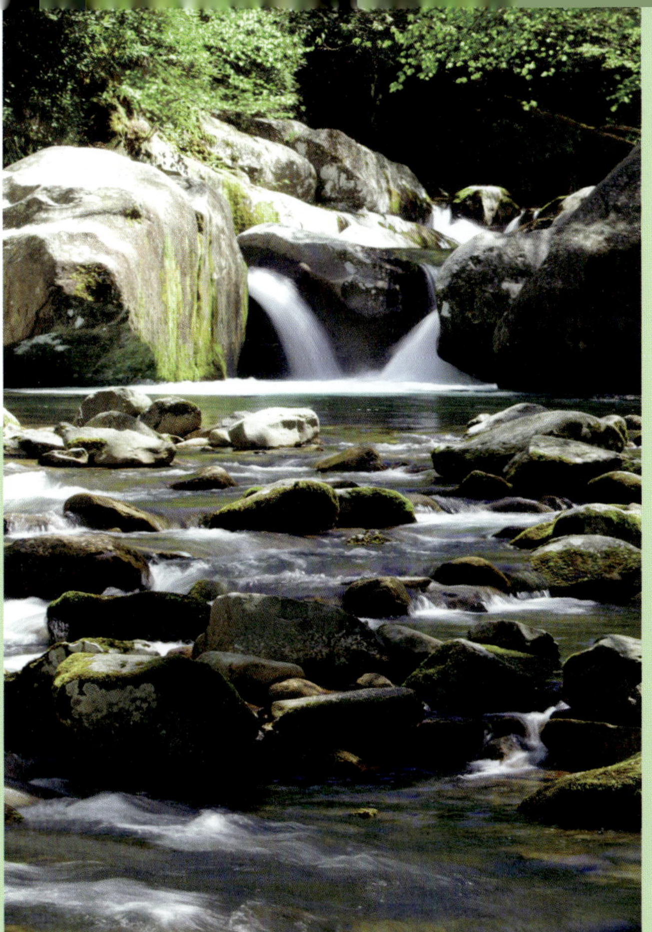

► Photographing in bright sun resulted in an image that is high in contrast with several hot spots and strong shadows. The histogram for the image shows the highlights are clipped and lack detail.

TIME OF DAY: 2:19:16PM | FOCAL LENGTH: 80mm | ISO: 200
APERTURE: f/16 | SHUTTER SPEED: 1/4 second

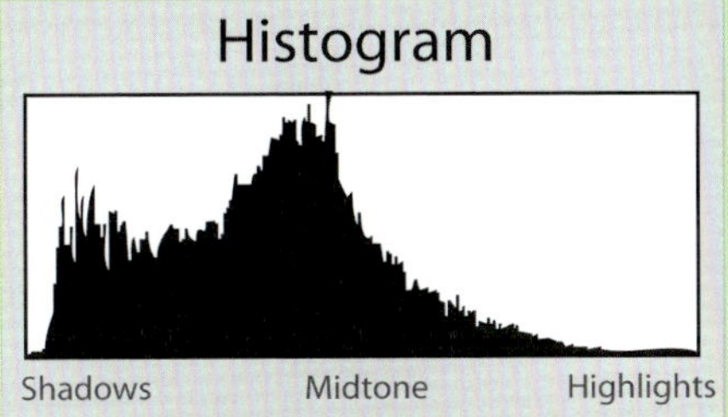

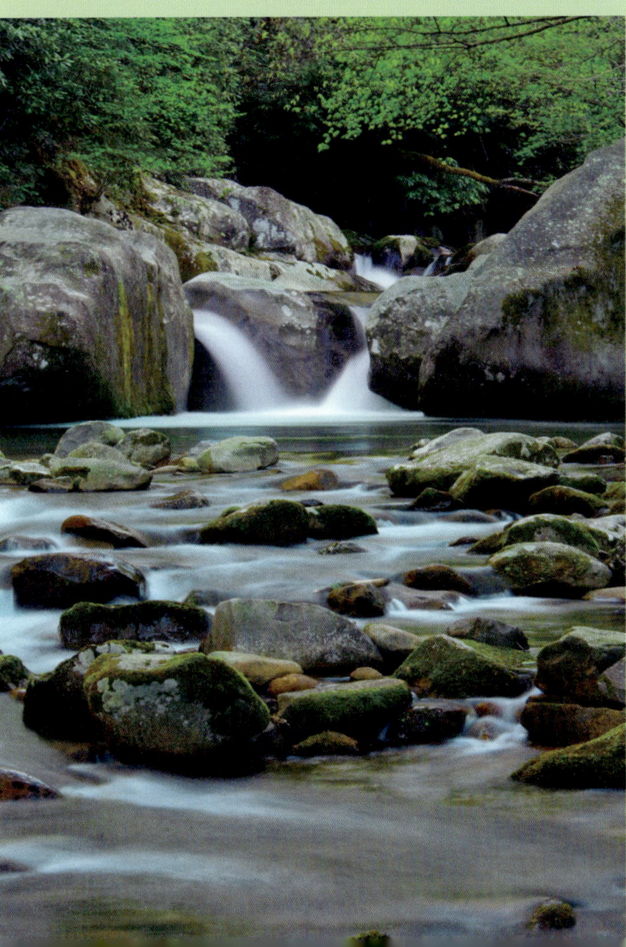

► The same scene captured under the diffused light of cloud cover is full of texture, detail, and color. Waiting for the sun to go behind a cloud softened the light and reduced the contrast to bring out the detail. The histogram for the image shows a full range of detail and tones when Big Creek is photographed in soft light. There is considerably more mid-toned data in this image than there is in the histogram of the image shot with hard light.

TIME OF DAY: 5:14:40PM | FOCAL LENGTH: 70mm | ISO: 200
APERTURE: f/22 | SHUTTER SPEED: 3 seconds

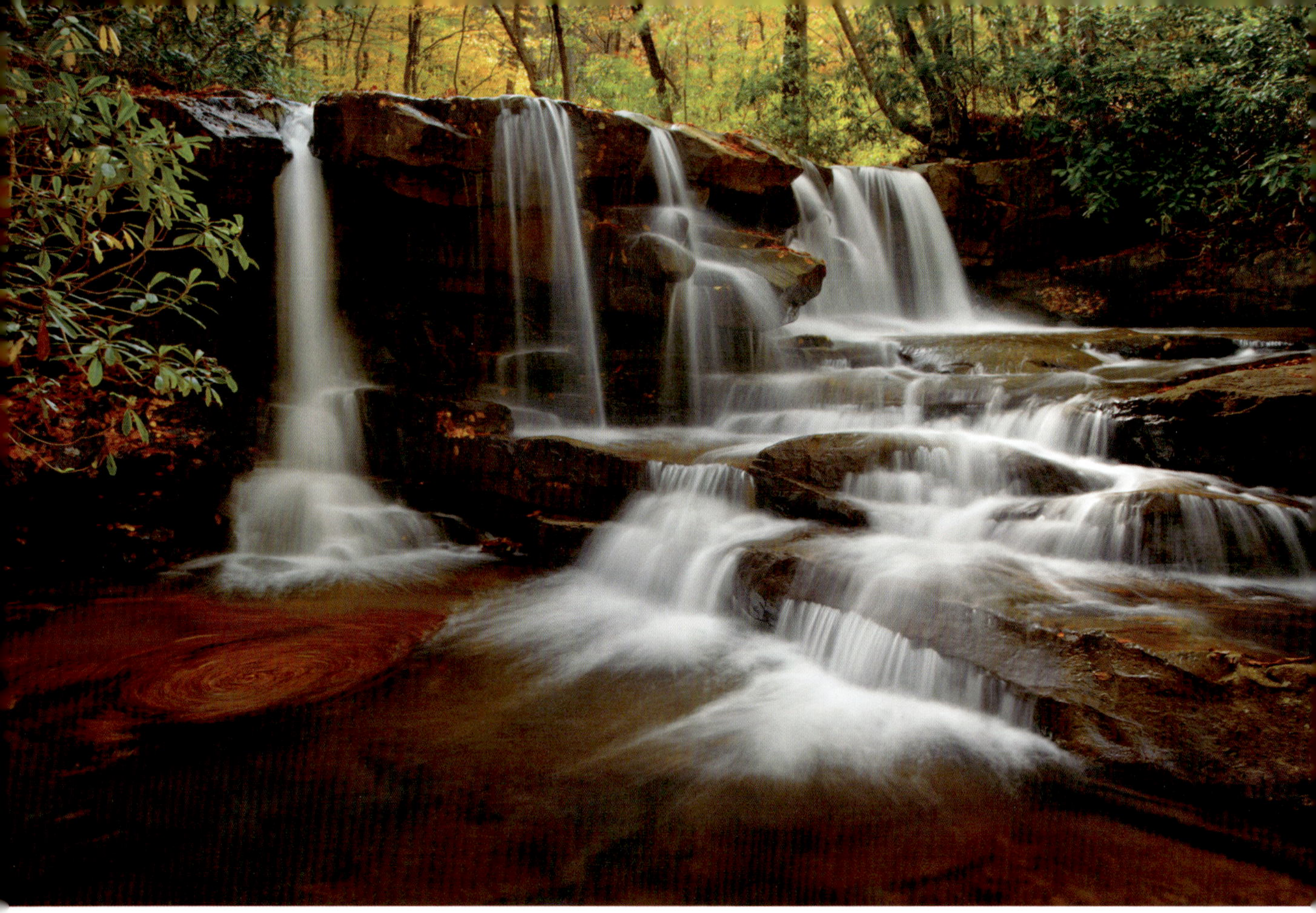

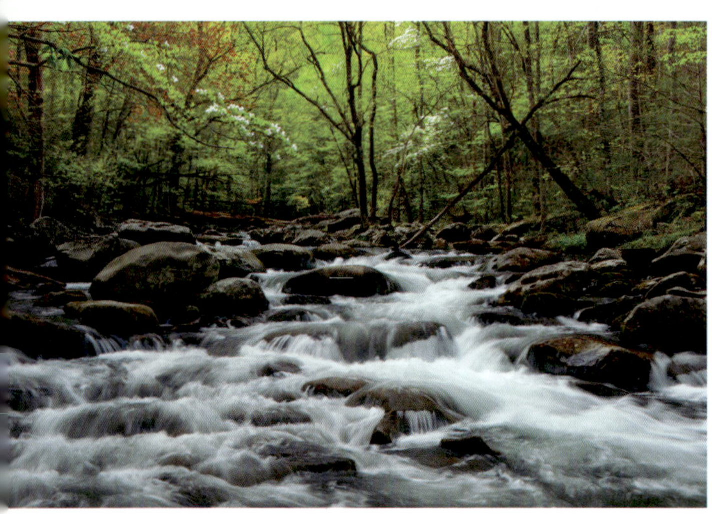

▲ Upper Jonathan Run Falls in Ohiopyle, Pennsylvania was rendered silky smooth using a slow shutter speed of 1.3 seconds.

FOCAL LENGTH: 30mm | ISO: 100 | APERTURE: f/20 | SHUTTER SPEED: 1.3 seconds

◄ This image of the Middle Prong of the Little River in the Great Smoky Mountains has a feeling of energy and a touch of softness as a result of choosing a 1/6 second shutter speed.

FOCAL LENGTH: 45mm | ISO: 100 | APERTURE: f/18 | SHUTTER SPEED: 1/6 second

WATERFALLS

Waterfalls are one of my favorite subjects to photograph. They add a dynamic element to the landscape. The choice of shutter speed, perspective, and composition all play a role in my vision for each waterfall image. As with any moving subject, various shutter speeds will impact the mood and feel of the photograph differently. The waterfall may appear soft and gentle with a sense of tranquility or powerful and strong with a lot of energy.

A slow shutter speed, usually one second or more, will soften the water so it appears velvety smooth. This can be a very effective technique for small waterfalls, cascades, and slow-moving waterfalls when the volume of water is not fast-moving or overpowering. A fast shutter speed of 1/250 second or higher (depending on the volume and rate of water) will freeze the action, showing spray and/or splashes. This can be a nice technique to emphasize large, powerful waterfalls.

The waterfall along Jonathan Run in Ohiopyle, Pennsylvania, like most waterfalls, varies in the amount of water flow from season to season. In the fall, the flow is less than in the spring when the run is rushing from snow melt and rain. I wanted the water to have a soft, velvety look as it gently flowed over the rocks. I chose a low ISO of 100, a small aperture of f/20, and a slow shutter speed of 1.3 seconds. A polarizer reduced the glare on the water and rocks. This combination achieved the dreamlike, soft, flowing waterfall I desired.

The Middle Prong of the Little River in the Great Smoky Mountains has a powerful rush

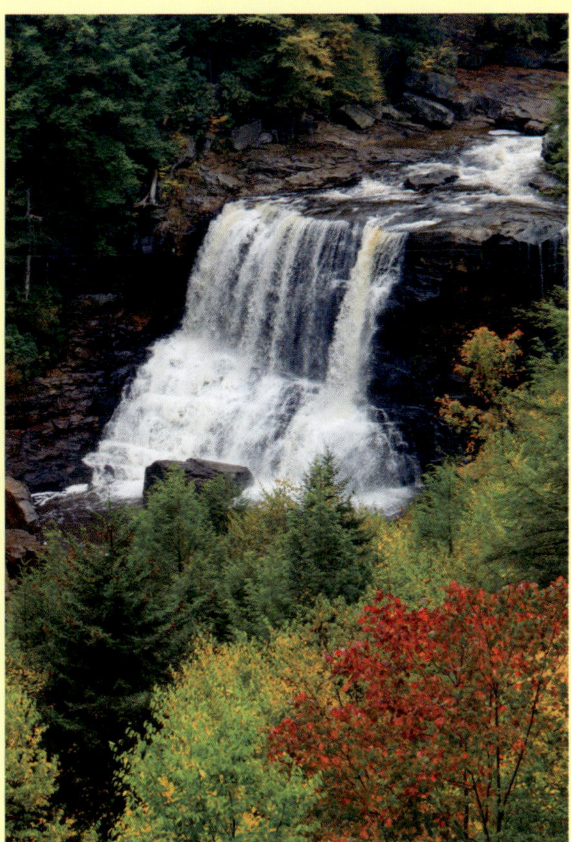

▲ A fast shutter speed of 1/400 second froze the action, showing the turbulence and power of Blackwater Falls in West Virginia.

FOCAL LENGTH: 70mm | ISO: 200 | APERTURE: f/5.6 | SHUTTER SPEED: 1/400 second

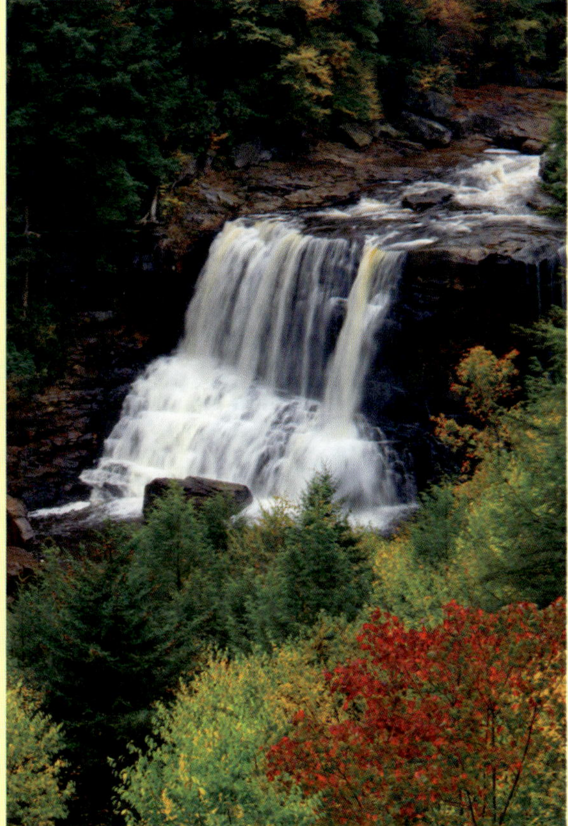

▲ A slow shutter of 1/10 second blurred the motion of the water, creating a softer and smoother look to the flowing water. Every waterfall is different, so experiment with a variety of shutter speeds to achieve your desired results.

FOCAL LENGTH: 70mm | ISO: 200 | APERTURE: f/22 | SHUTTER SPEED: 1/10 second

of water in the springtime. For this image, I wanted the water to have texture and a palpable energy. Because there was a large volume of water flowing rapidly, the shutter speed didn't need to be very long. A setting of $^1/_6$ second worked to achieve the results I wanted—a mix of power and energy with a touch of softness.

Go ahead and experiment. Bracket your shutter speed when photographing water. The volume and rate of water will alter the effect of the shutter speed. For each location or time of year, you may want a different look and feel to the flowing water.

FLOWING REFLECTIONS

Moving water is a very versatile subject for the creative photographer. We can make water appear silky smooth, hard and choppy, swirling, and so on, depending on the selected shutter

▼ Spring-green color is reflected in the flowing water of the Middle Prong in the Greenbrier area of the Smoky Mountains.

FOCAL LENGTH: 200mm | ISO: 100 | APERTURE: f/20
SHUTTER SPEED: 2.5 seconds

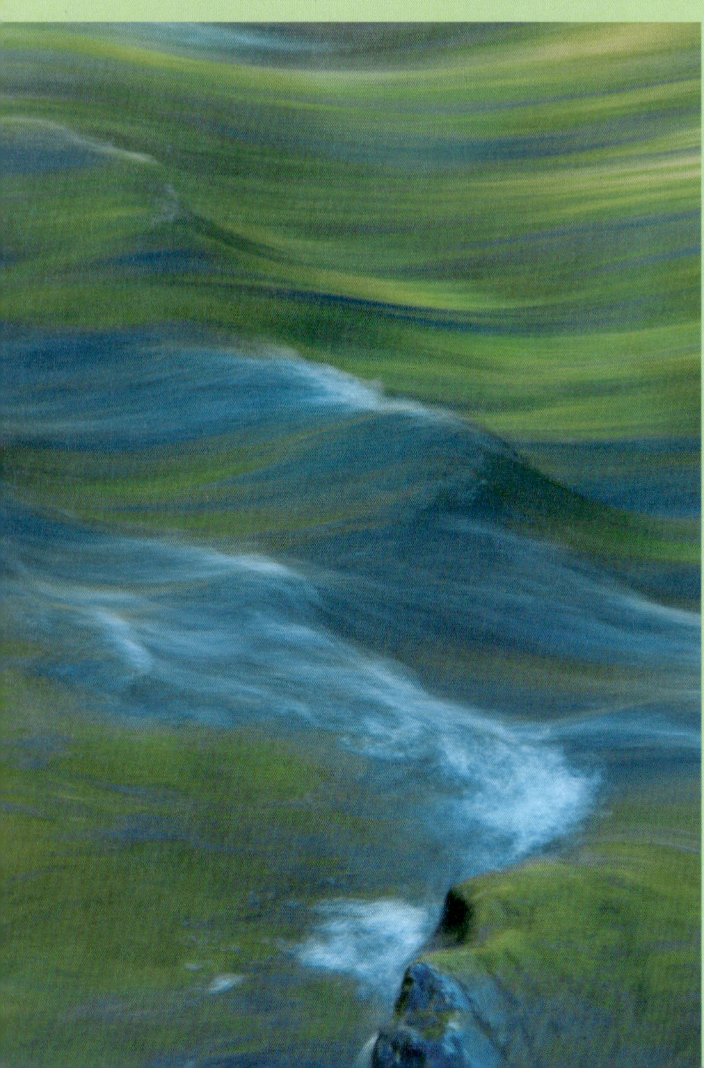

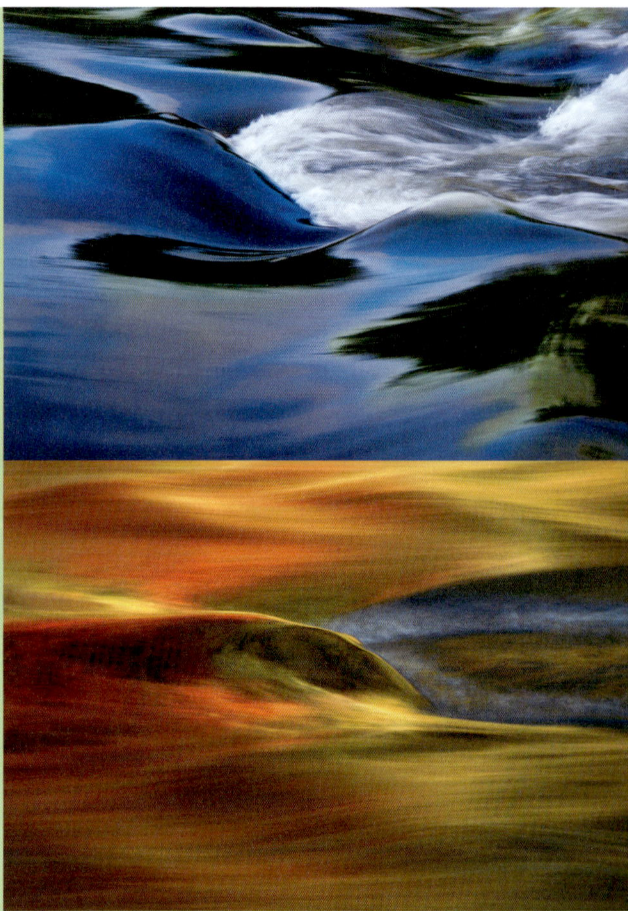

▲ (top) A slow shutter speed of $^1/_{10}$ second swirls the blue and green reflections on the water. The image was shot in summertime.

FOCAL LENGTH: 116mm | ISO: 200 | APERTURE: f/13 | SHUTTER SPEED: $^1/_{10}$ second

▲ (bottom) Isolating one ripple in the river creates a simple composition with energy and movement.

FOCAL LENGTH: 200mm | ISO: 100 | APERTURE: f/22 | SHUTTER SPEED: $^1/_{1.3}$ second

▶ A twist of the polarizer revealed the colorful rocks at the bottom of Two Medicine Lake in Glacier National Park. Wind, boats, or swimmers can quickly disturb a reflection and causes it to blur and vibrate.

FOCAL LENGTH: 32mm | ISO: 100 | APERTURE: f/16 | SHUTTER SPEED: 1/10 second

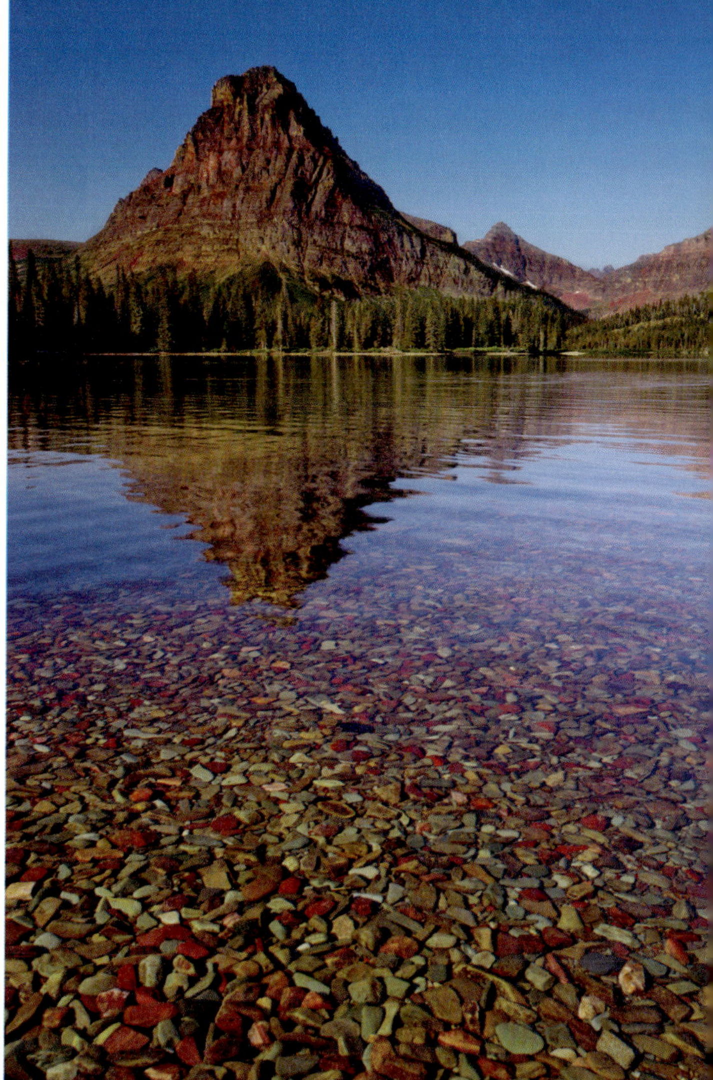

speed. Color from reflections can also add emotion and mood to the palette. The possibilities are endless.

When photographing flowing water, I look for a river or stream with strong currents or ripples of movement. I will study the flow for interesting shapes or sections, thinking about how it will look when blurred. Our eyes "stop" the motion, but a long exposure will create a swirl and brush-stroke effect to the water. Reflected color will appear as if a color dye was dropped in the water, flowing and moving with the currents. Of course, the paint colors are determined by the season and the color of the object being reflected.

In the springtime with blue skies overhead and lush green trees on the shore, the Greenbrier area of the Smoky Mountains had smooth movement and flowing curves along the white-capped water. I positioned my camera and tripod to capture the reflection, knowing the movement of the water would create an interesting S shape in the frame. Sometimes it takes several attempts to capture the movement at just the right moment. I shot several frames this afternoon, and each capture was different from the next. Fortunately, one of the many benefits of digital photography is it doesn't cost extra to shoot until you find the one you like.

MIRROR REFLECTIONS

A perfect mirror image as it reflects in a body of water is probably one of the most common types of reflection associated with landscape photography. When the water is absolutely still, it creates a perfect mirror reflection. Finding a perfectly calm lake can be a bit of a challenge. Just a small amount of wind or disruption can result in ripples and motion. Ripples tend to occur as the sun rises and the air temperature differs from the water temperature, making the odds of finding a mirror reflection best in the very early morning. Also, large bodies of water are more likely than small

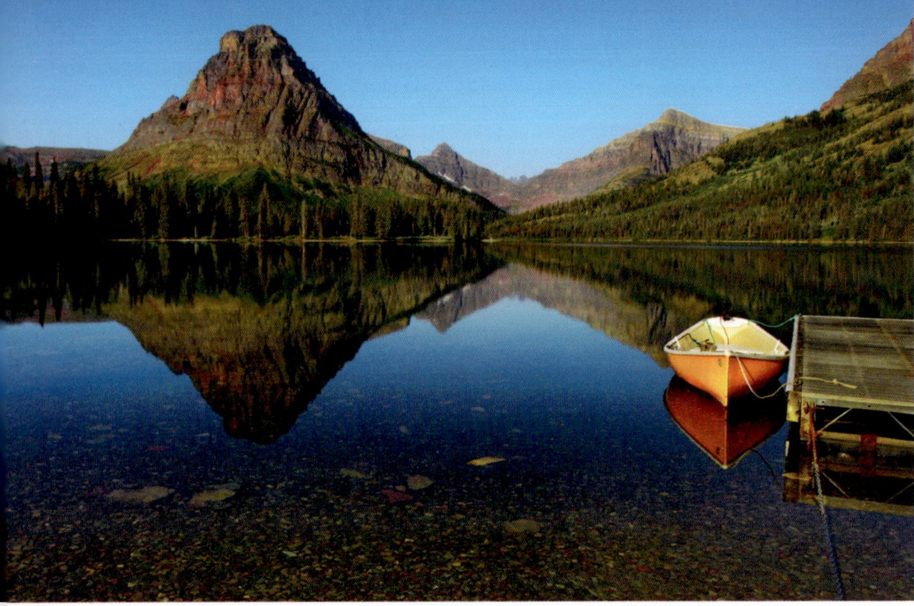

◄ In the morning when the air is still, mirror reflections are more common at Two Medicine Lake in Glacier National Park.

FOCAL LENGTH: 32mm | ISO: 100
APERTURE: f/16 | SHUTTER SPEED: 1/25 second

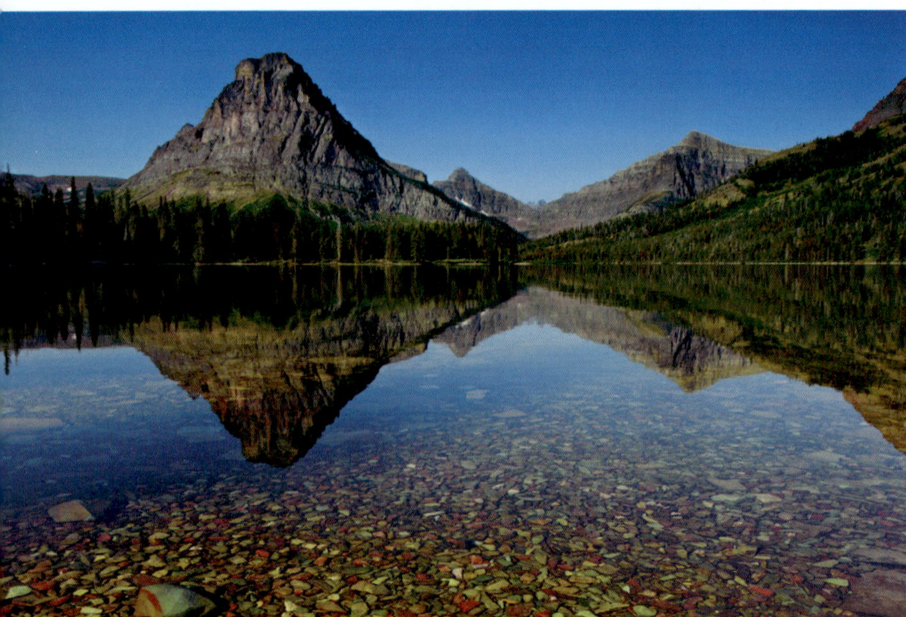

◄ Positioning Sinopah Mountain toward the top of the frame allows the mirror reflection and colorful rocks to dominate the image.

FOCAL LENGTH: 32mm | ISO: 100
APERTURE: f/16 | SHUTTER SPEED: 1/10 second

bodies to "catch" the wind, leading to ripples on the surface. (Of course, skipping a stone could produce ripples in a small pond.)

The colors in reflections are bolder, stronger, and more saturated than the actual subject above the water. As a result, reflections can be one or two stops darker. This creates an imbalance in the exposure that can be corrected with a graduated neutral density filter. A polarizer will control the amount of glare in the water and reveal the rocks below the surface. For my images at Two Medicine Lake in Glacier National Park, I turned the polarizer until the maximum number of colorful rocks were showing under the water.

As always, a tripod and cable release helped me to keep the camera steady; this is especially important when using a large depth of field and a slow shutter speed. For mirror reflections, I want both the subject and its reflection to be in focus. There was a little bit of motion in the reflection in the featured image, but I don't mind it because the foreground rocks are clear and undisturbed.

LEAF SWIRLS

The circular motion of swirling leaves adds interest to waterfall images with a spinning blur of color. These swirls happen in autumn when trees drop their leaves onto the ground and into the flowing water. It doesn't take a lot of water movement to produce a swirl, and of course, the more leaves that are in the water, the more noticeable the spin and color will be.

Part of the trick to capturing swirling leaves is seeing them spinning in the water.

Part of the trick to capturing swirling leaves is seeing them spinning in the water. Because the human eye moves with the motion and the brain processes the action quickly, it can be difficult at first to see the slow swirl of leaves. A still camera, however, has the ability to record a span of several seconds (or even minutes) with slow shutter speeds. Fortunately for us, digital cameras also allow us to see the results instantly by looking at the LCD on the back of the camera. This instant feedback is a great visual aid for seeing the swirl and the effect of a slow shutter speed.

"The camera enables us to see and do things creatively that are beyond the capability of the human eye. It expands our range of seeing and gives us new options. Fast shutter speeds can freeze a moment in time that is too quick for the eye to see, and slow shutter speeds allow us to capture motion in a way we cannot experience."[12]

Art Wolfe
Internationally renowned nature and cultural photographer

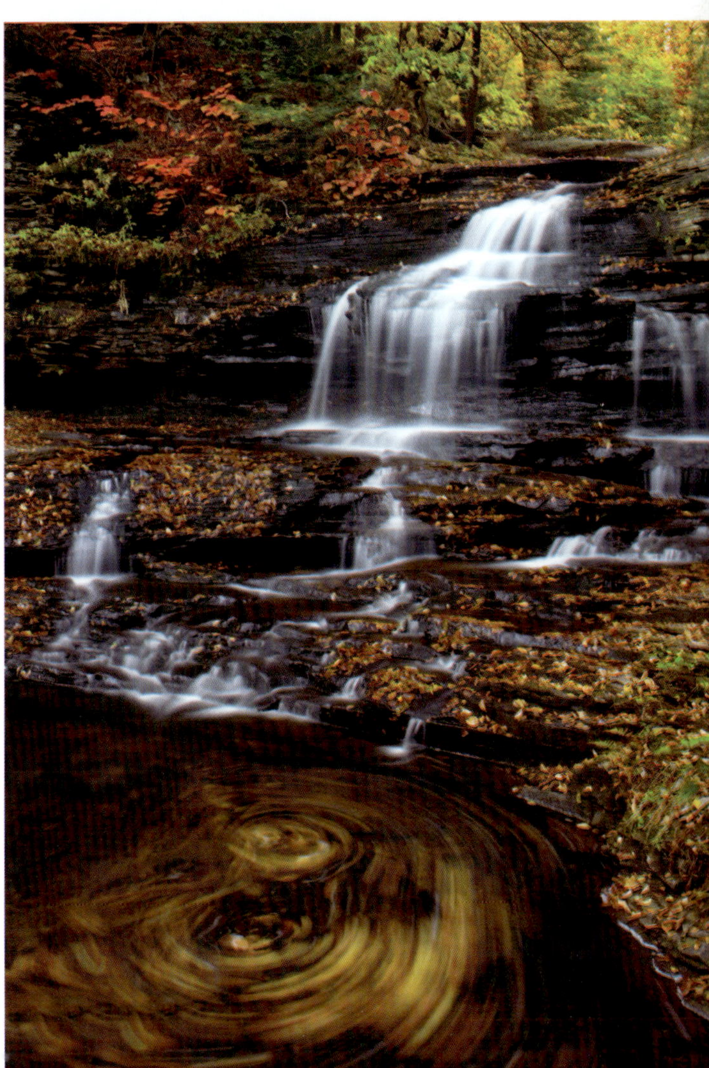

► The instant feedback from a digital camera is a fabulous way to see the effect of a slow shutter speed and swirling leaves.

FOCAL LENGTH: 27mm | ISO: 100 | APERTURE: f/22 | SHUTTER SPEED: 20 seconds

Onondaga Falls in Ricketts Glen State Park is a 15-foot cascade waterfall located on the Glen Leigh section of the trail. There are twenty-four named waterfalls in the park, making it a wonderful location for waterfall photography. Visiting the park late in the fall season offered several opportunities for swirling-leaf images. On this day, Onondaga had plenty of fallen leaves around the waterfall and in the stream. I wanted the slowest shutter speed possible to make the water appear soft and smooth, so I chose a small aperture of f/22. This resulted in a 20-second exposure with silky smooth water and swirling leaves.

I wanted the slowest shutter speed possible to make the water appear soft and smooth . . .

A longer shutter speed is most effective to show the swirl; short speeds may not capture a full circle of motion. A tripod is a requirement to hold the camera steady over this long time period. Set up the composition with room for the swirl, ensure your exposure settings are accurate, use a polarizer to reduce the water glare, and you are on your way to adding leaf swirls to your images.

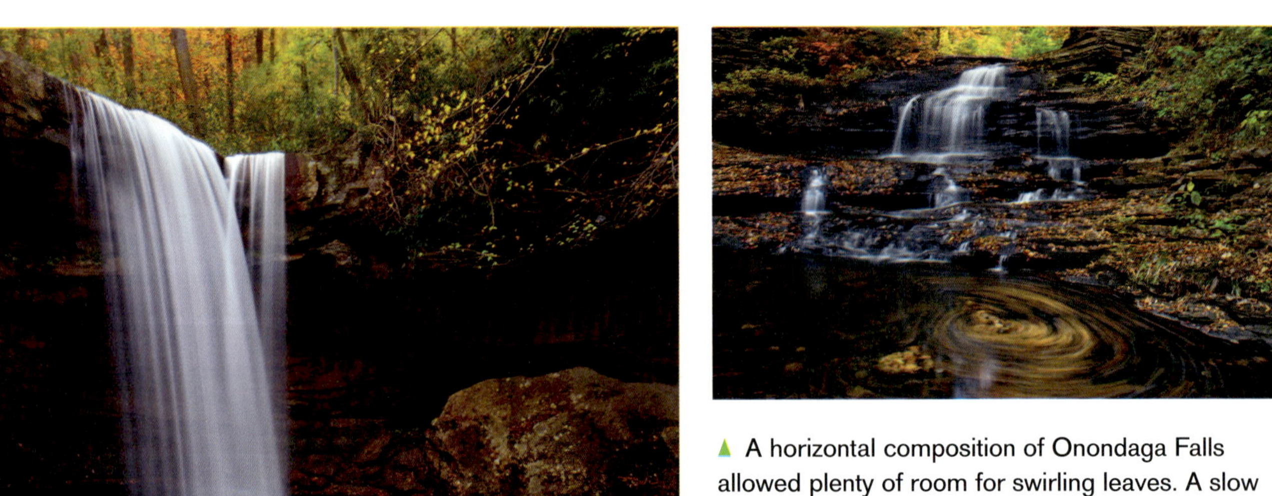

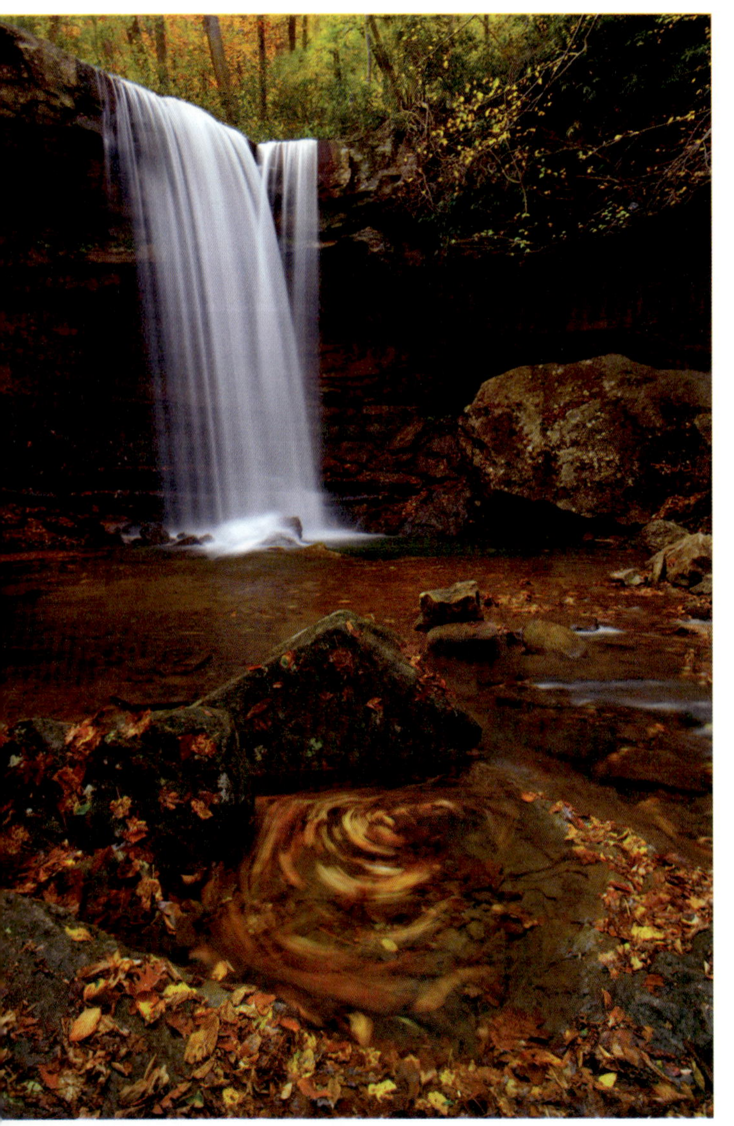

▲ A horizontal composition of Onondaga Falls allowed plenty of room for swirling leaves. A slow shutter speed of 20 seconds effectively showed the swirl.

FOCAL LENGTH: 18mm | ISO: 100 | APERTURE: f/22 | SHUTTER SPEED: 20 seconds

◄ Adding leaves to the water created a spinning blur of color and foreground interest to Cucumber Falls in Ohiopyle, Pennsylvania.

FOCAL LENGTH: 24mm | ISO: 100 | APERTURE: f/20 | SHUTTER SPEED: 2.5 seconds

LIGHT PAINTING

Reflections are my way of painting with light. As the light changes direction, so does the angle of the reflection, resulting in different colors reflected into the scene. I can "paint" a different reflected color into my frame just by moving my tripod.

Autumn is my preferred season to paint with reflected light. The fall spectrum of colors creates a full palette to "mix" my paints. Fallen leaves along waterways can be found in many locations at this time of year. Mixing the colors of the reflected light with orange and red leaves tells the story of the changing season.

One fall morning in New Hampshire, I began my painting by finding a location with great reflections, interesting rocks along a stream, and a few fallen leaves. I set up my tripod and 105mm Macro lens low to the ground so I could sit comfortably and work with the light and composition. I used a shallow depth of field to emphasize the leaf and let the reflections be a soft wash of color. A polarizer was effective to reduce the glare and increase the color saturation.

Throughout the morning, the blue sky reflected a brilliant accent color. The trees on the opposite shoreline were a range of colors from green to orange to red, providing a great palette to paint the light with subtle composition tweaks. Starting with a single orange sugar-maple leaf resting on the wet rocks, a green maple tree provided the reflection in the water. I worked the composition and painted with the light as the background color changed according to the tree color reflected onto the water. A few hours later, I had a series of light paintings.

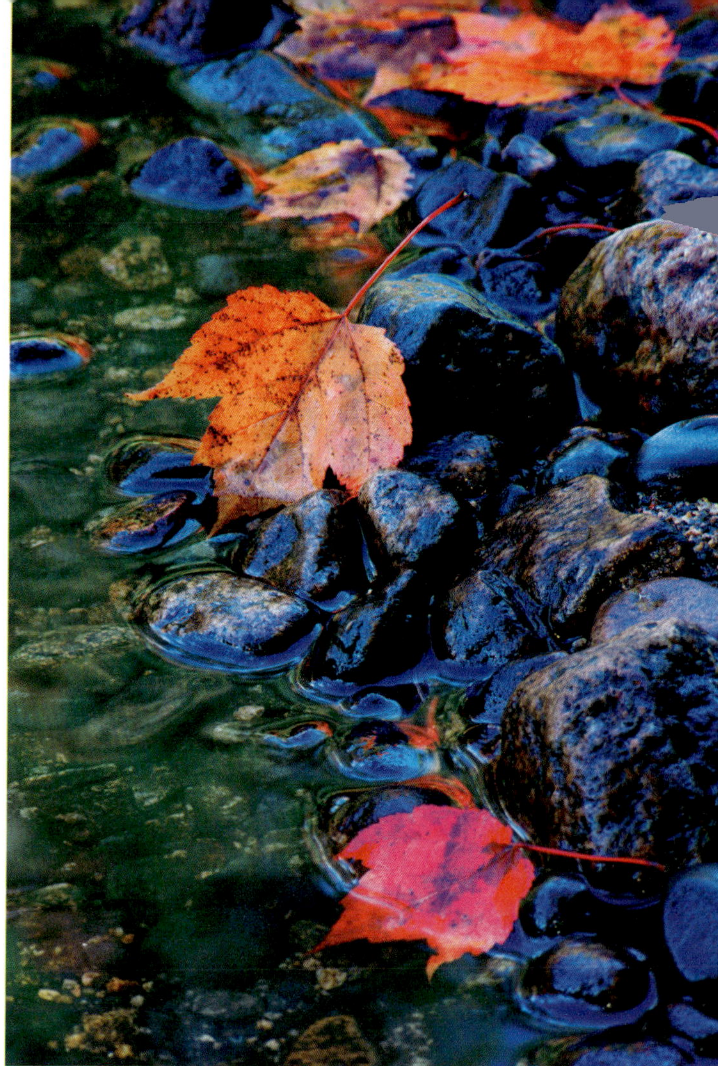

▲ A green tree and blue sky reflect around an orange sugar maple resting on the shore.

FOCAL LENGTH: 105mm Macro | ISO: 50 Fujichrome Velvia
APERTURE: Not available | SHUTTER SPEED: Not available

I can "paint" a different reflected color into my frame just by moving my tripod.

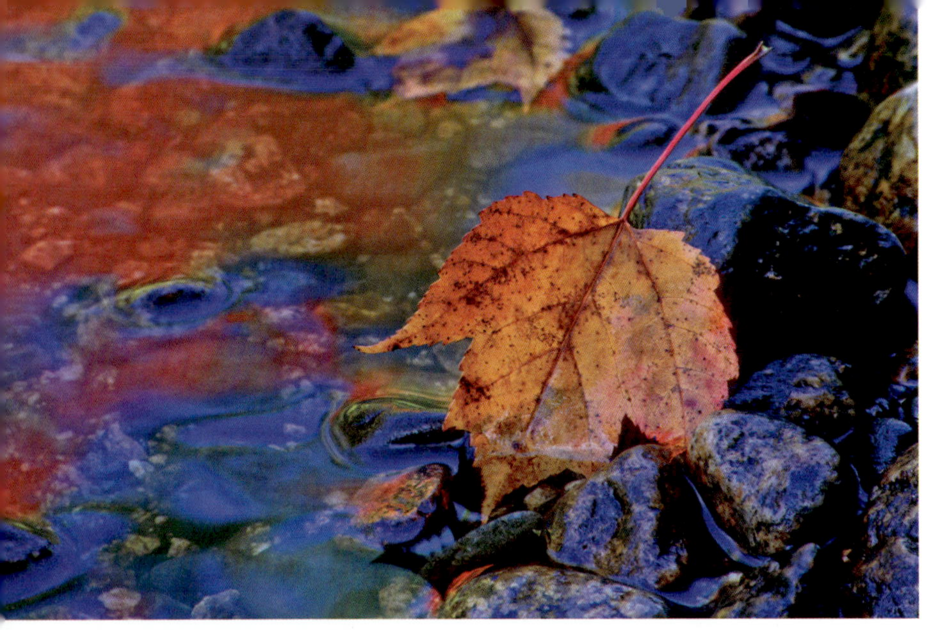

A horizontal composition and slight repositioning of my camera painted more red reflection onto the water.

FOCAL LENGTH: 105mm Macro | ISO: 50 Fujichrome Velvia | APERTURE: Not available SHUTTER SPEED: Not available

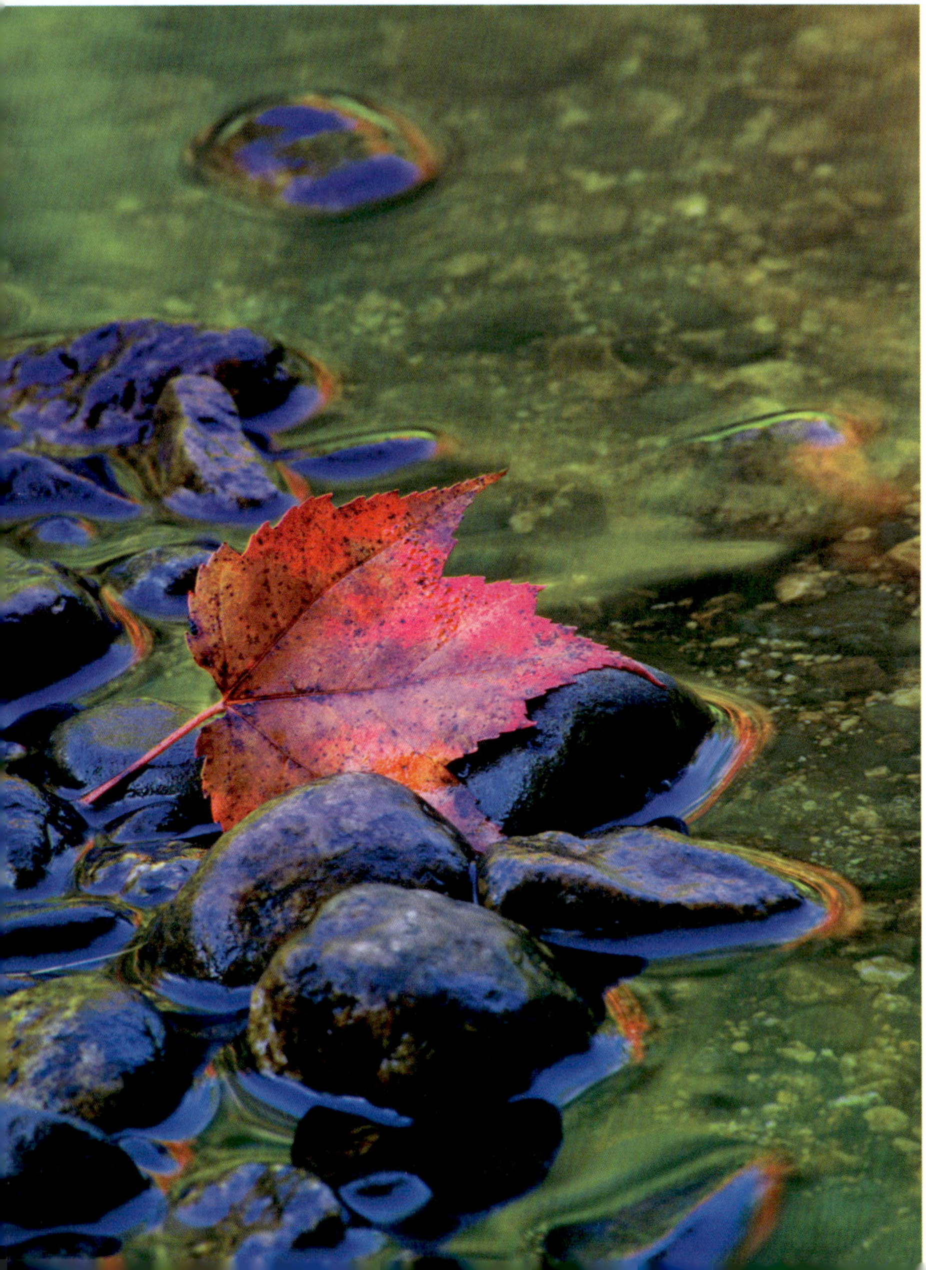

A new angle and composition painted a green reflection around another maple leaf. The red and green (complementary colors) added contrast and vibrancy.

FOCAL LENGTH: 105mm Macro ISO: 50 | Fujichrome Velvia | APERTURE: Not available | SHUTTER SPEED: Not available

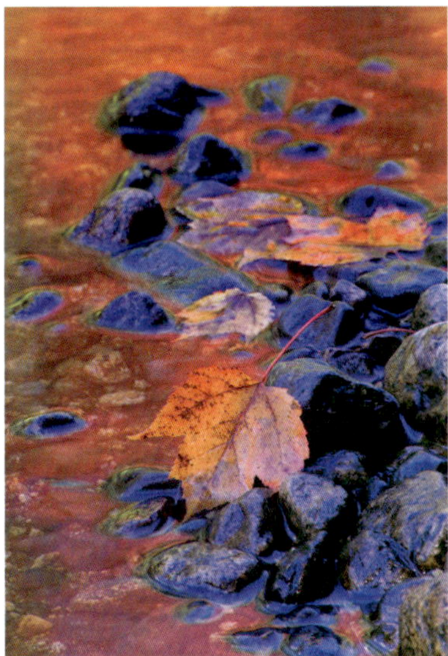

Red reflected light was painted around the same maple leaf as I worked the composition and the angle of the light changed throughout the morning.

FOCAL LENGTH: 105mm Macro | ISO: 50 Fujichrome Velvia | APERTURE: Not available SHUTTER SPEED: Not available

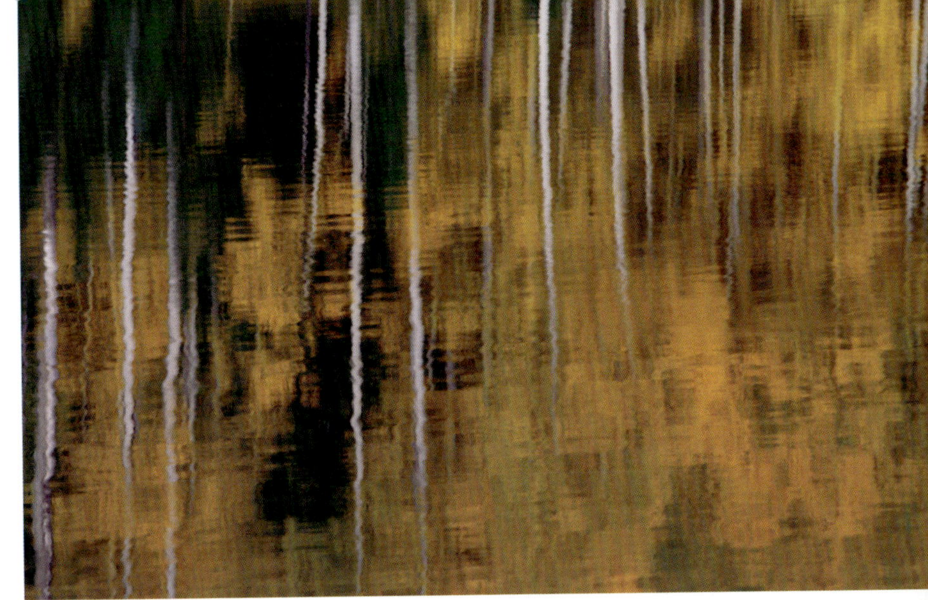

► Aspens reflected into Woods Lake during autumn in Colorado. Wind on the water created a vibration and texture in the reflections.

FOCAL LENGTH: 200mm | ISO: 100
APERTURE: f/20 | SHUTTER SPEED: 1/6 second

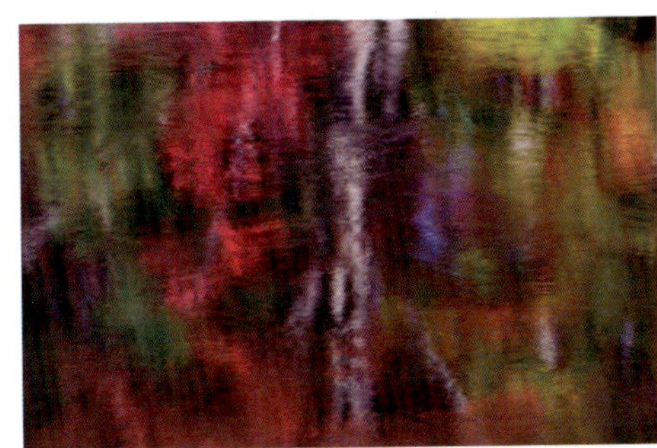

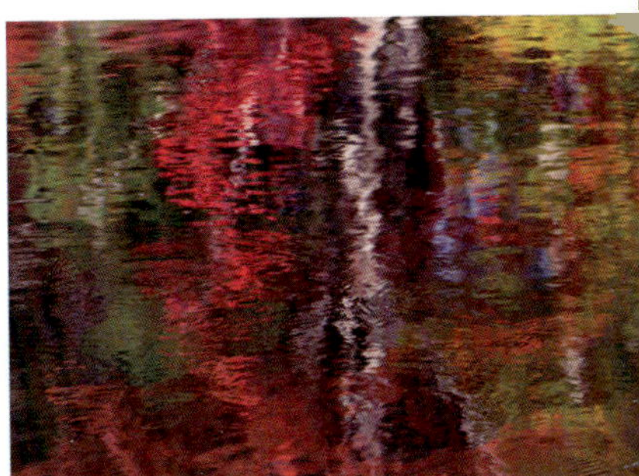

► (bottom left) A soft, smooth look was produced with a small aperture of f/22 and slow shutter speed of 1/3 second.

FOCAL LENGTH: 140mm | ISO: 100
APERTURE: f/22 | SHUTTER SPEED: 1/3 second

► (bottom right) Increasing the shutter speed to 1/30 second and opening up to f/6.3 created more of a brush-stroke effect.

FOCAL LENGTH: 140mm | ISO: 100
APERTURE: f/6.3 | SHUTTER SPEED: 1/30 second

IMPRESSIONIST LIGHT

Isolating colors and shapes in reflections creates abstract images. Color alone can be the subject and a fun way to explore your creativity. Autumn is the optimal time to find colorful abstract reflections. I love this season for the full palette of colors, from the last remains of summer greens to the peak foliage of reds and yellows.

Perfectly still water reflects in a mirrorlike way with an exact repetition of the land above. Add movement to the water and you will see texture or "brush strokes" in your image. Varying the shutter speed will change the appearance of movement and texture in the water.

Late in the morning, when the sun hits the autumn trees and reflects into the water with brilliant colors, is a great time to create vivid photographs. One fall day, I set my camera and tripod to compose for a series of abstract reflections along the Raquette River in the Adirondack Mountains. I used the white trunks of the birch trees to add an interesting graphic design element to the artistic

Perfectly still water reflects in a mirrorlike way with an exact repetition of the land above.

impression. A different texture and feeling happens when the shutter speed and aperture are changed. A soft, smooth look is produced with a small aperture of f/22 and slow shutter speed of 1⁄3 second. Increasing the shutter speed to 1⁄30 second and opening up to f/6.3 created a brush-stroke look. There are no hard rules in these situations. I encourage you to experiment in the field and try different combinations.

ARTISTIC CHOICES

Wherever there are water reflections, the artistic choices are diverse and plentiful for the creative photographer. There is a choice between including the whole scene, part of the scene, or just the reflection. Then there are countless ways to capture the image using different combinations of shutter speed, aperture, focal length, and composition. The conditions of the water also play a part in your artistic choices. How large or small is the body of water? Is it calm or flowing? Does it have texture with leaves or rocks at the surface? What is the quality of light? Is there a story to be told within the reflection? These are all choices we make as photographers.

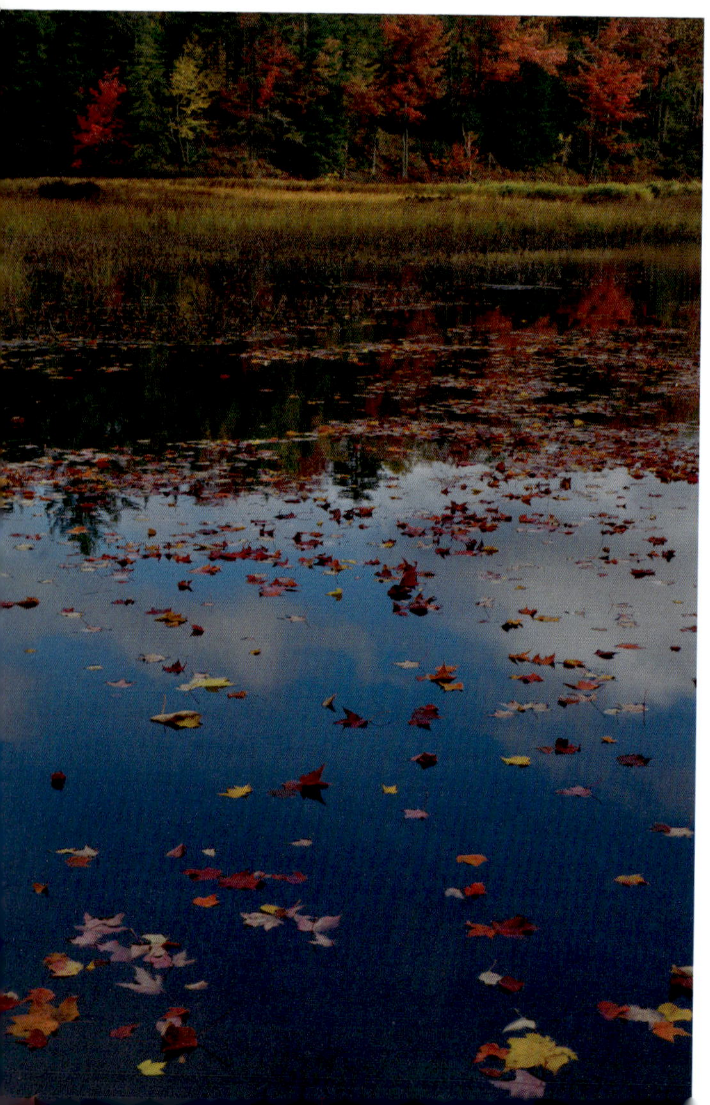

Reflections can also be very effective at giving the suggestion of other surrounding elements. Plus, reflected color is darker than the actual subject; this makes the image appear more intense and saturated. Using reflections can be a creative way to add color with an interpretive view the surroundings—albeit an upsidedown view.

Your viewpoint plays a huge role in reflections. When you move a little, the reflection can change considerably. A higher vantage point will show less reflection, while a lower vantage point will show more with a longer reflection. Getting down low or into the water will make the reflected scene the dominant part of the frame. This is especially true with wide-angle lenses because they are fantastic at putting the emphasis on the foreground.

The suggestion of blue sky is captured in a reflection on the leaf-filled Middle Branch Moose River in the Adirondack Mountains. For this image, I didn't need to include the actual sky in the frame to tell the story of the blue sky. I let the reflection do it.

◄ The combination of a vertical composition with a low viewpoint and a wide-angle lens made the water and reflection prominent in the frame.

FOCAL LENGTH: 40mm | ISO: 100 | APERTURE: f/11 SHUTTER SPEED: 1/80 second

The mineral-laden water of Zion National Park produced texture-filled reflections enhanced by the copper-colored canyon and blue sky. This popular location and time of year were key factors in my artistic choice to show the location in a unique way with a reflective story.

FOCAL LENGTH: 105mm | ISO: 50 Fujichrome Velvia | APERTURE: Not available | SHUTTER SPEED: Not available

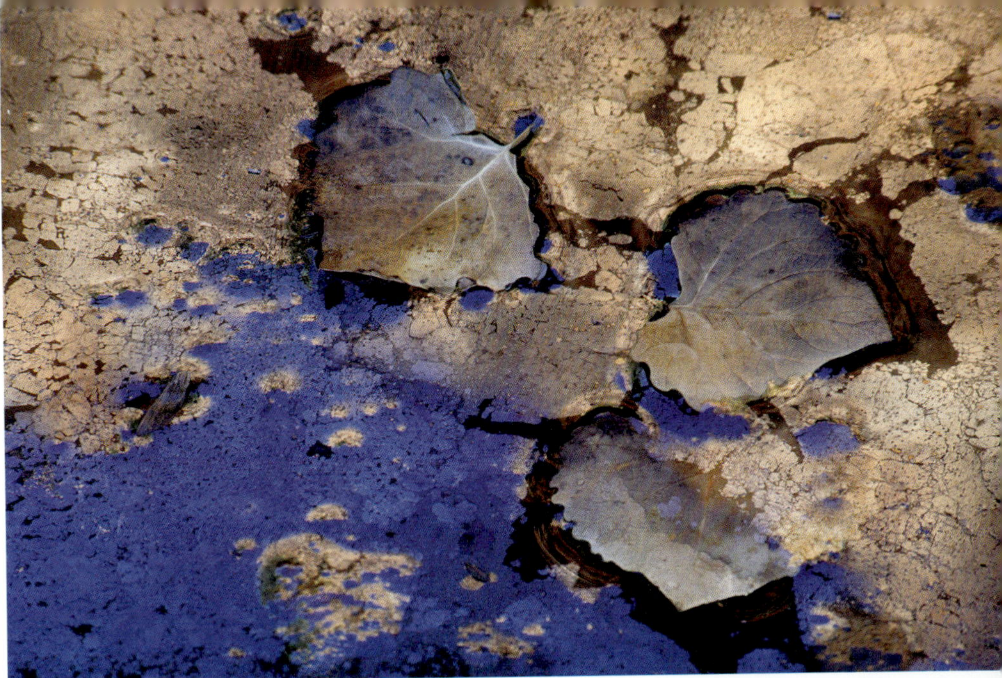

A hint of blue sky and autumn maple trees was reflected into the water at Rickets Glenn State Park in Pennsylvania.

FOCAL LENGTH: 105mm | ISO: 100 APERTURE: f/8 | SHUTTER SPEED: 1/2.5 second

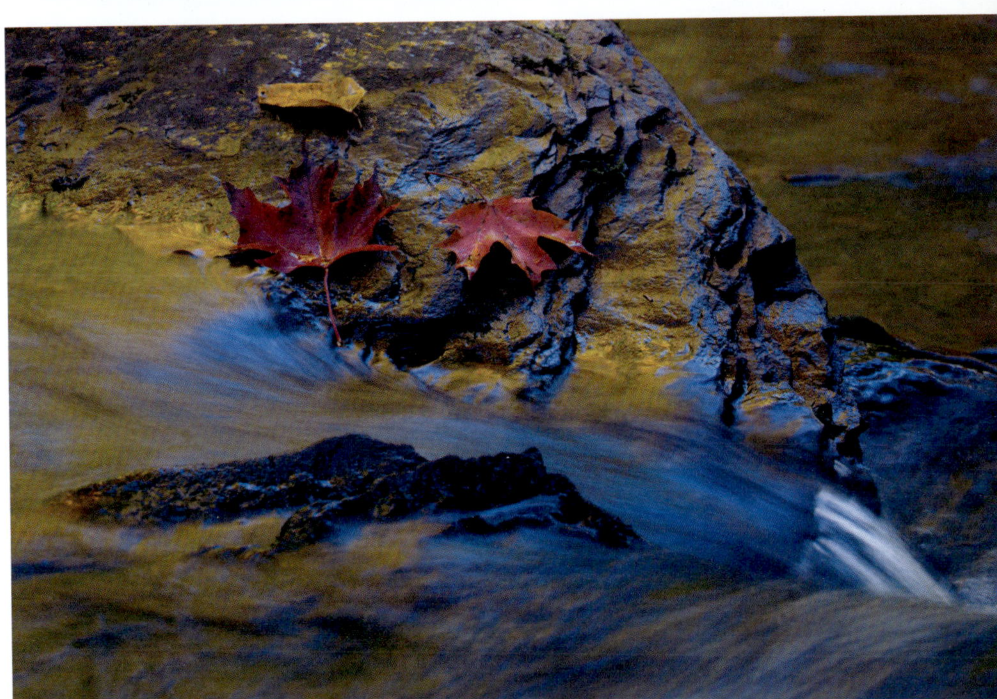

SENSE OF PLACE

Waterfalls make great subjects and provide a dynamic center of interest, even when they are small in the frame. The elements around a waterfall can set the stage to tell the story of the waterfall and its location. Framing a waterfall with surrounding trees gives the viewer a sense of approaching the falls through the woods.

Elakala Falls in Blackwater State Park, West Virginia, is a difficult location to get near because the falls are located at the bottom of a steep gorge with many large boulders along the way. The boulders are covered with moss, which makes them slick. There is no trail down to the falls—you must carve your own path. I highly recommend that you travel in pairs for safety.

My tendency when photographing waterfalls is to get close and make the flowing water the focal point of the image. This can create a dramatic image but may not give a sense of the place or location. Hiking to Elakala Falls

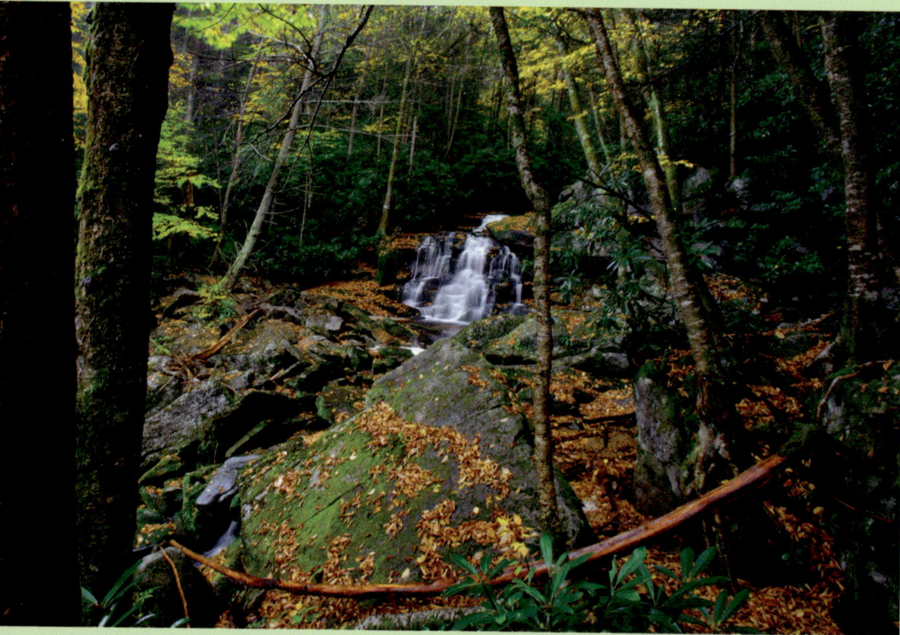

◄ When the surroundings are included in the frame, it is better to have attractive elements and exclude fallen trees or logs. Here, the fallen tree in the foreground distracts from the waterfall.

FOCAL LENGTH: 17mm | ISO: 100
APERTURE: f/22 | SHUTTER SPEED: 6 seconds

▼ The fallen leaves resting on the large boulders around Elakala Falls provided a sense of place for this waterfall located deep in the woods.

FOCAL LENGTH: 22mm | ISO: 100
APERTURE: f/22 | SHUTTER SPEED: 6 seconds

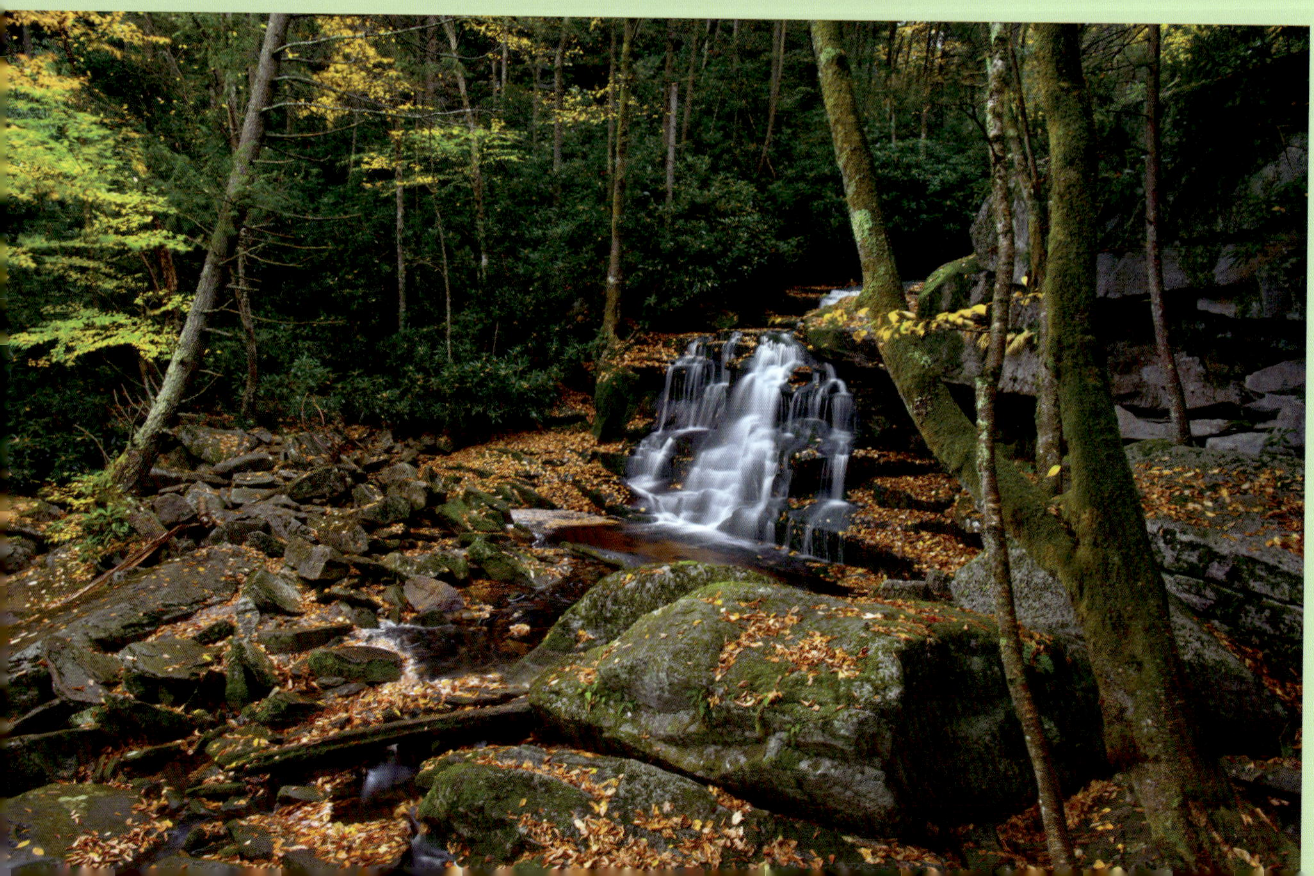

during autumn was not exactly easy; with the steep terrain and slick boulders, I was not able to get close to the falls. Instead, I positioned my camera at a distance so the entire falls were in clear view. There were plenty of surrounding elements to fill the frame.

To create a sense of place, I had to ensure that the details in the surroundings would appear sharp. I used a tripod and a small aperture of f/22 to ensure there would be sufficient depth of field. A 4-second exposure gave the

To create a sense of place, I had to ensure that the details in the surroundings would appear sharp.

waterfall a velvety smooth appearance. A light rain was falling, making all the rocks and leaves appear saturated with color. My polarizer revealed the texture and details in the rocks as it removed the glare. Even in the rain, a polarizer is effective when photographing water and shiny surfaces.

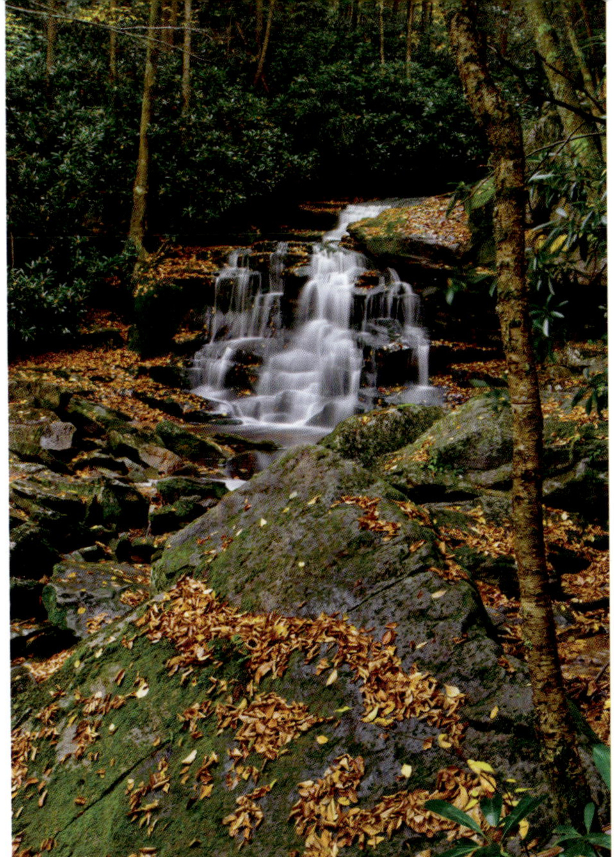

▲ A vertical composition excluded the downed tree and provided a different feel to the setting. Note that there is more emphasis on the foreground boulder.

FOCAL LENGTH: 35mm | ISO: 100 | APERTURE: f/22 | SHUTTER SPEED: 4 seconds

PERSPECTIVE

Get your waders or waterproof boots on—we're going in the water.

Perspective is the visual depth created by the relationship between the apparent size of foreground elements versus background elements. Changing your perspective can add impact to your images. In this case, I left the trailside and got into the water. This enhanced the perspective and resulted in a more dynamic image. Streams and waterfalls, when the water flows toward the viewer, can be very dramatic. The use of a wide-angle lens close to the foreground will make it appear prominent in the frame.

The flowing water along this section of Ricketts Glen State Park was easily accessible from the trail. With the help of another photographer, I carefully made my way into the water. The rock bed at the bottom was smooth and slick and the rushing water was intimidating, but it was all worth it for the dynamic perspective.

Once in the water, I moved cautiously to keep my gear and myself upright and dry. I carefully positioned my tripod close to the

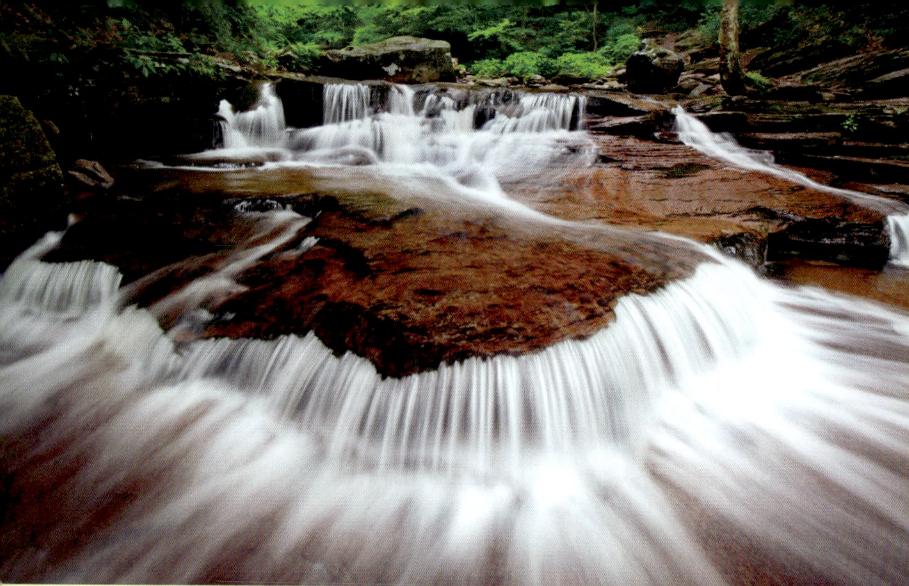

◄ Getting in the water showed the water rushing toward the viewer with energy and impact. Making the effort (and taking the risk) creates a more dramatic image than shooting trailside.

FOCAL LENGTH: 22mm | ISO: 500 APERTURE: f/20 | SHUTTER SPEED: $^{1}/_{1.7}$ second

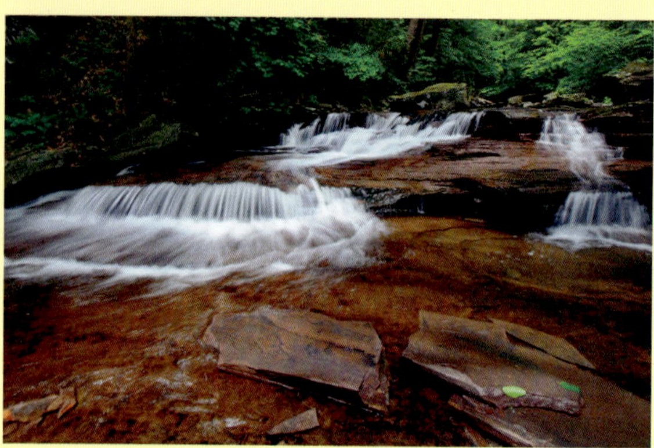

▲ The viewpoint from the trail before getting in the water offered a different perspective, as the flow moved sideways without the energy of the water rushing toward the viewer.

FOCAL LENGTH: 19mm | ISO: 500 | APERTURE: f/18 | SHUTTER SPEED: $^{1}/_{3}$ second

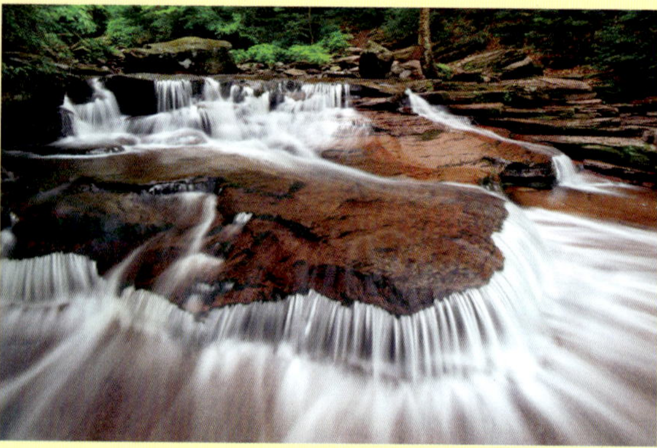

▲ Changing the tripod and camera angle showed the trail in the upper-right corner of the frame. When using a super wide-angle lens, a slight change in position can make a big difference in the impact of the image.

FOCAL LENGTH: 24mm | ISO: 500 | APERTURE: f/22 | SHUTTER SPEED: 1.3 seconds

foreground rock and low to the water. Rushing water can spray drops onto the front of the lens, so keep an eye on it and dry it off when needed. Using a low perspective with a wide-angle lens made the foreground dominant and put the emphasis on the rushing water. A slow shutter speed further accented the rushing water with long streaks of motion. A polarizer was necessary to remove the glare and show the rock texture under the water.

Always use caution when getting into flowing water and streams, as the rocks can be slick. Use your best judgment and, again, travel in pairs so that there's always someone who can lend a helping hand should the need arise.

10. DESIGN

INTIMATE LANDSCAPES

Grand vistas and large landscapes show a view that can include multiple elements and extra "data." Intimate landscapes, on the other hand, focus on the details, smaller sections, and essential elements of the grand landscape. Focusing on the details can be a fantastic way to show colors, textures, shape, and form in a unique way. These small scenes within the larger scope of the landscape can simplify a composition down to the "nuts and bolts."

Instead of trying to squeeze everything into the frame, focus only on the core elements needed to tell the story of the place. My friend Nancy called this "capturing the essence." Exploring a subject intimately will uncover only the relevant information, and with practice, you can do this in an artistic and imaginative way. If you are tired of seeing the same picture of a popular location, then get intimate with your subject and do something different from everyone else. One of the masters of the intimate landscape, Guy Tal, points out "[When] exploring a subject deliberately, up close, in earnest, with no preconception, an endless array of graceful lines, patterns, subtle variations of color and tone, and any number of unique traits will be revealed. Intimate landscapes readily lend themselves to original creative

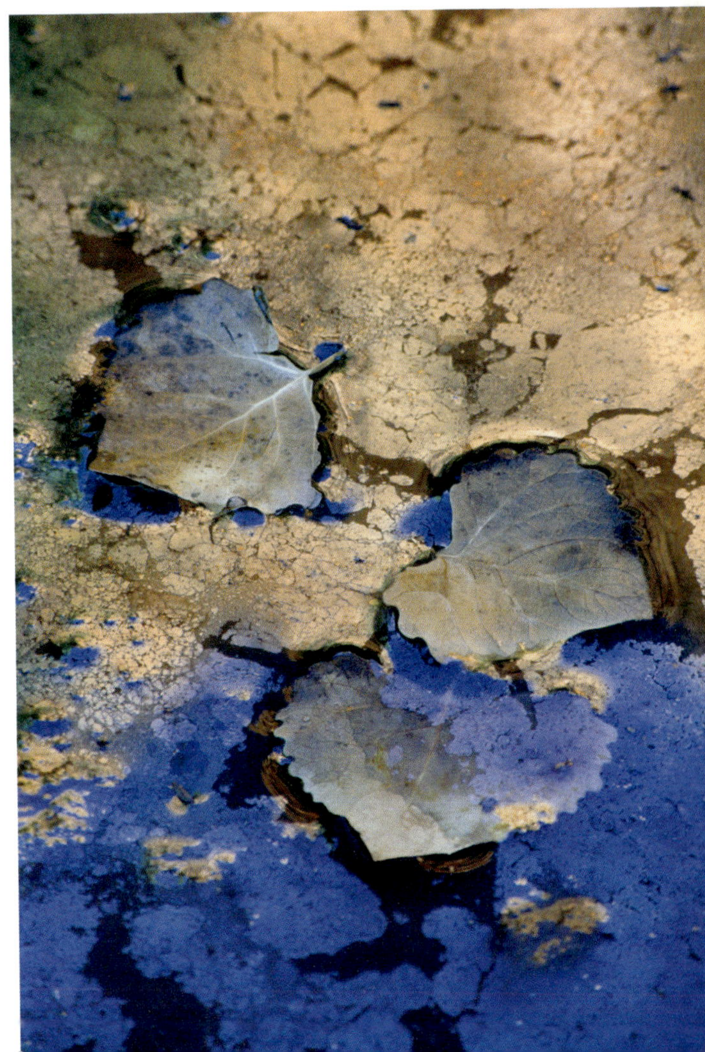

► The Narrows in Zion National Park, along with the high plateaus, copper canyons, and Virgin River, make this a popular destination for photographers. I chose to only include the cottonwood leaves resting in the mineral-laden water within the frame for a unique and intimate landscape.

ISO: 50 Fujichrome Velvia | APERTURE: Not available | SHUTTER SPEED: Not available work and to the much-desired development of the artist's personal vision and style."[13]

Intimate landscapes can be found anywhere. The simple act of looking down at our feet can unveil a new composition. Using a telephoto lens and zooming in on a section of landscape can isolate interesting shapes and patterns. A macro lens is another way to concentrate on the small details.

The cottonwood leaves resting in the mineral-laden water is a good example of getting intimate with a subject. Using a 105mm macro lens, I was able to explore the textures and colors in the small puddle. My artistic decision to not include everything in the frame allowed me to go home with a unique image from Zion National Park.

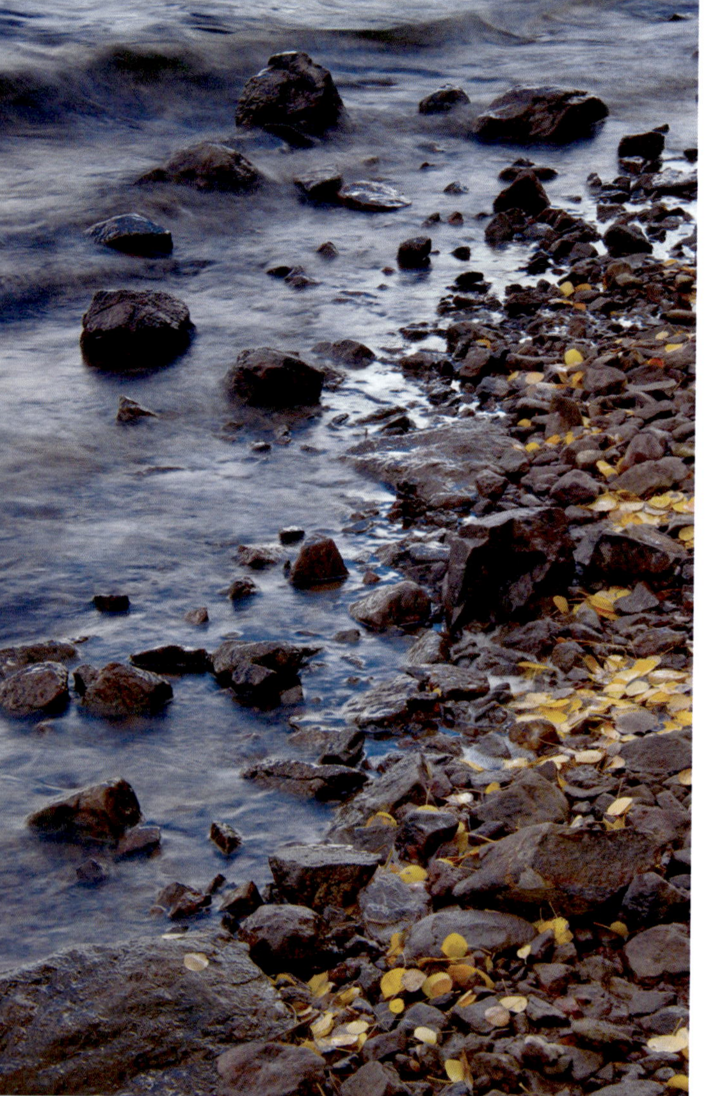

Zooming in on a section of landscape can isolate interesting shapes and patterns.

◄ (top) The fallen aspen leaves along Giberson Bay, Colorado tell a simple story of autumn in Colorado. Although the bay is very beautiful, I didn't feel that I needed to include it all in the frame to tell its story.

FOCAL LENGTH: 100mm | ISO: 100 | APERTURE: f/25 | SHUTTER SPEED: 1/3 second

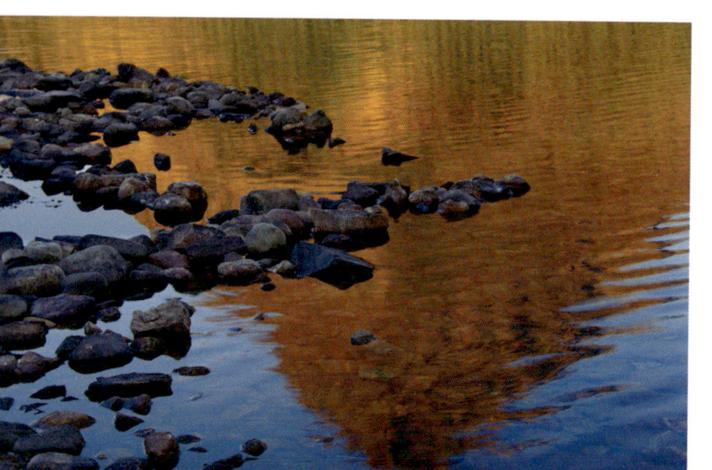

◄ (bottom) Creating intimate landscapes is a great way to create an original image at a popular location that has been photographed a million times before. Here, Grinnel Point is reflected into Swiftcurrent Lake in Glacier National Park.

FOCAL LENGTH: 78mm | ISO: 100 | APERTURE: f/11 | SHUTTER SPEED: 1/8 second

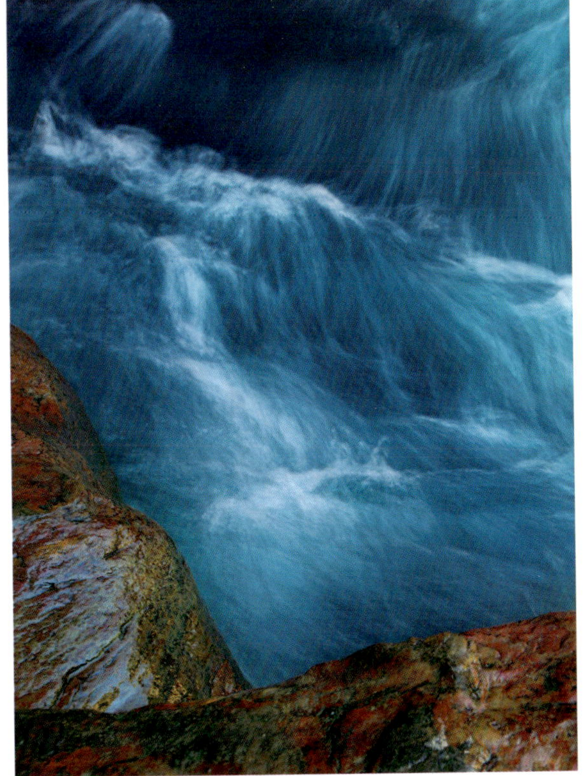

Abstract landscapes are open to personal expression and creativity. It is up to the artist to determine the unique characteristics and how to portray them.

FOCAL LENGTH: 35mm | ISO: 100 | APERTURE: f/7.1 | SHUTTER SPEED: 1/4 second

ABSTRACTS

Abstract images rely on color, shape, form, and texture. Exploring the relationship between these elements is open to interpretation with no limits on creativity. No clear subject needs to be defined; it can be unimportant and ambiguous, allowing for a high level of artistic expression. Abstract images are often very graphic, using patterns and lines as design elements. In addition to composition and selective framing, photographers can use techniques such as soft focus, limited depth of field, or motion blur when creating abstract images.

As I photographed St. Mary's Falls in Glacier National Park, the waterfall drew me in with brilliant blue water and colorful rocks. The sedimentary rocks are full of color and they are especially vibrant when wet. Fine particles floating in the water, known as "rock flour," are formed when rocks grind together under a glacier. When sunlight hits the water, the rock flour absorbs other colors in the spectrum and leaves behind brilliant blue water.

These two elements—the brilliant water and the vibrant rocks—were unique characteristics of this location. To capture their essence, I excluded other elements, creating a simple and abstract image that focuses only on the

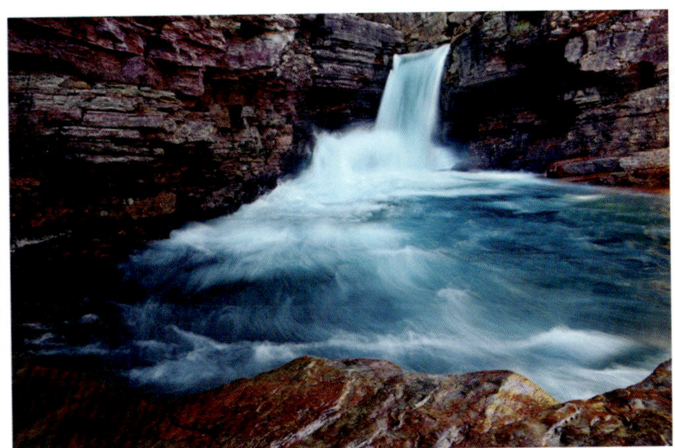

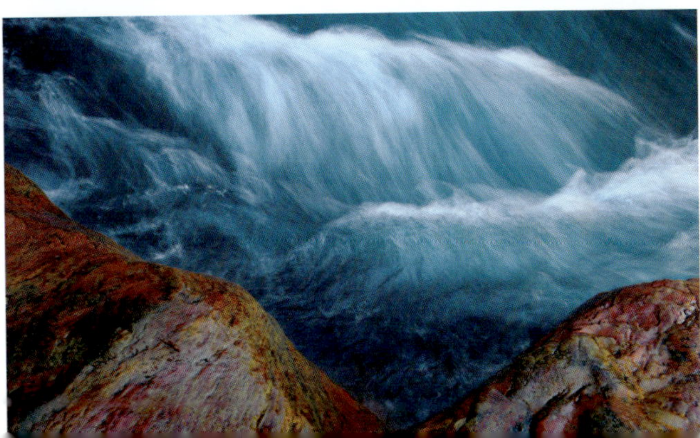

(top) Here is the overall view of St. Mary's Falls before I focused on the vibrant rocks and blue water to create an abstract interpretation in an intimate landscape.

FOCAL LENGTH: 28mm | ISO: 100 | APERTURE: f/10 | SHUTTER SPEED: 1/2.5 second

(bottom) By focusing on the details in the foreground of St. Mary's Falls, I was a able to show color, texture, and form in an abstract way.

FOCAL LENGTH: 35mm | ISO: 100 | APERTURE: f/7.1 | SHUTTER SPEED: 1/4 second

color and texture. The flowing water creates a brush-stroke effect with a slower shutter speed. In this example, a 1/4 second shutter speed achieved the artistic effect of moving water with accent streaks. A selective turn of the polarizer reduced the shine on the wet rocks. Rotating the polarizer will control the amount of the polarizing effect. Don't overdo it and remove all the reflection.

LINES

Scouting—the process of looking for the convergence of the "right" light and a dramatic landscape, whether it is via car, plane, bike, canoe, or foot—can take a lot of time. In Colorado, there are aspen trees growing tall along the edge of many of the back roads. After several days of watching them out the Jeep window, I found the right mix of light,

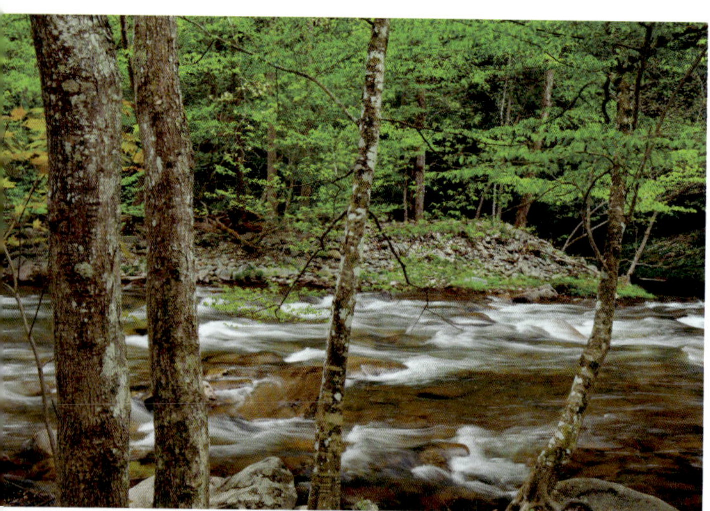

◄ The foreground trees provided vertical lines that draw the viewer's eye across the image with the fast-flowing Little River in the Great Smoky Mountains.

FOCAL LENGTH: 42mm | ISO: 125 | APERTURE: f/20 | SHUTTER SPEED: 1/4 second

▼ The repeating vertical lines of the aspen trees that appear across the frame draw the eye across the image and through the scene to Mt. Sneffles in the distance.

FOCAL LENGTH: 48mm | ISO: 160 | APERTURE: f/25 | SHUTTER SPEED: 1/2 second

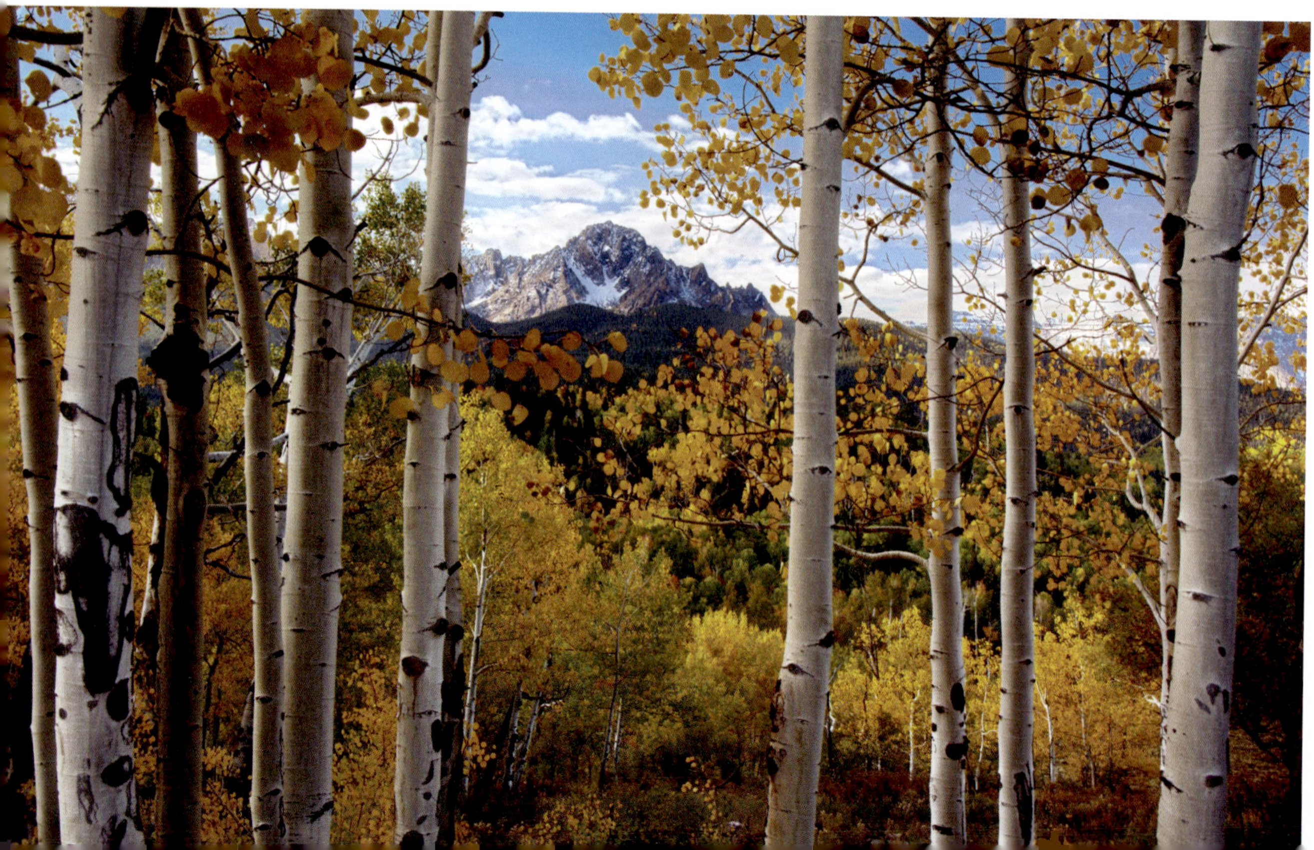

foreground trees, and a distant mountain peak to make the image I wanted.

The white bark of birch and aspen trees is very appealing to me. I love their texture and how they stand out against the foliage and background. Aspens grow in clonal colonies from a single seedling to form multiple trees in one location. These aspen groves are great for patterns with repeating vertical lines.

Vertical lines can be a strong compositional element, implying strength and power. Horizontal lines imply calm and stability. Repeating the vertical lines across a horizontal frame draws the eye across the image. As with any pattern, a strong composition results when there is a break in the pattern.

In my image of Mt. Sneffles through the aspen trees, I purposely placed the mountain peak in between the gap in the trees. I worked the composition diligently, paying attention to the small details—in particular, the small tree branches above and below Mt. Sneffles so they aligned and echoed the shape of the mountain.

Each composition was bracketed by 5 stops, even though the far ends of the exposure (-2 and +2) were not needed for the final blended exposure. Shooting these extra exposures in the field didn't cost any more. That's one of the many reasons to love digital photography.

▲ (top) Placing the horizon in the bottom third of the frame created stability and accented the width of the moving clouds above.

FOCAL LENGTH: 135mm | ISO: 200 | APERTURE: f/20 | SHUTTER SPEED: 1.3 seconds

► (bottom) Using a vertical composition for horizontal elements can be dramatic because the eye travels a shorter path across the image. This placed all of the emphasis on the moving clouds.

FOCAL LENGTH: 135mm | ISO: 200 | APERTURE: f/20 | SHUTTER SPEED: 1.3 seconds

S CURVES AND LEADING LINES

A favorite compositional technique for photographers, painters, and designers alike is the use of an S curve that leads the eye from the foreground to background along a winding path or line. An S curve is one type of leading line. This shape provides a sense of depth with rhythm and flowing movement from side to side through the image. Some of the common places to see S curves in nature are in the bends of a river, sand dunes, beach shorelines, and farm fields. They can also be subtle, formed by light and shade falling on the landscape.

Leading lines use foreground elements to direct the viewer into the image and toward a focal point. Fences, rocks, logs, roads, and

▼ (top) An S curve can be subtle, as it is here, with a visual path to Mt. Clements through the fallen rocks.
FOCAL LENGTH: 20mm | ISO: 100 | APERTURE: f/20 | SHUTTER SPEED: 1/8 second

▼ (bottom) Foreground rocks provided a leading line as the flowing stream created a subtle S curve for the viewer's eye to follow through the image.
FOCAL LENGTH: 20mm | ISO: 100 | APERTURE: f/22 | SHUTTER SPEED: 2 seconds

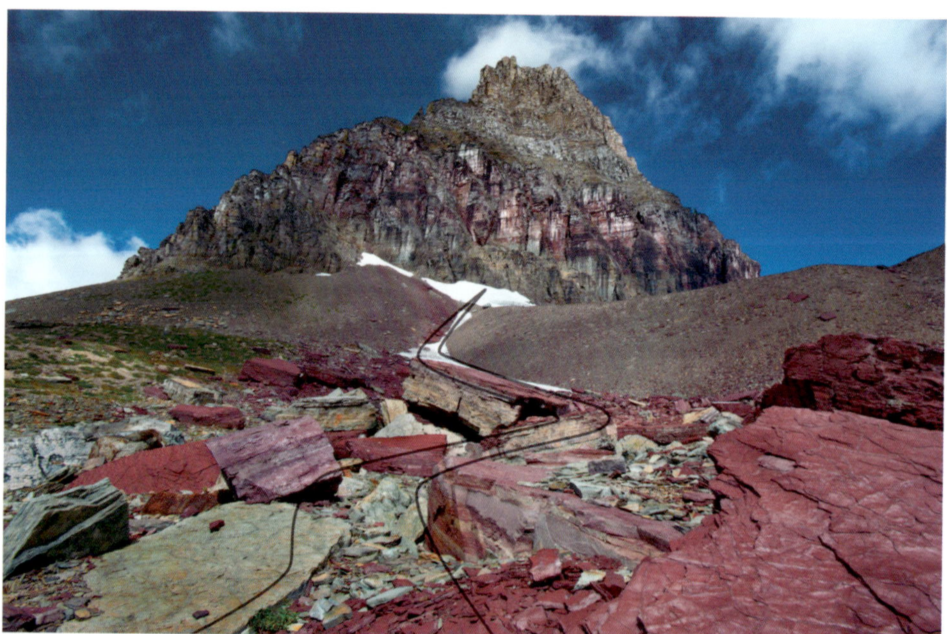

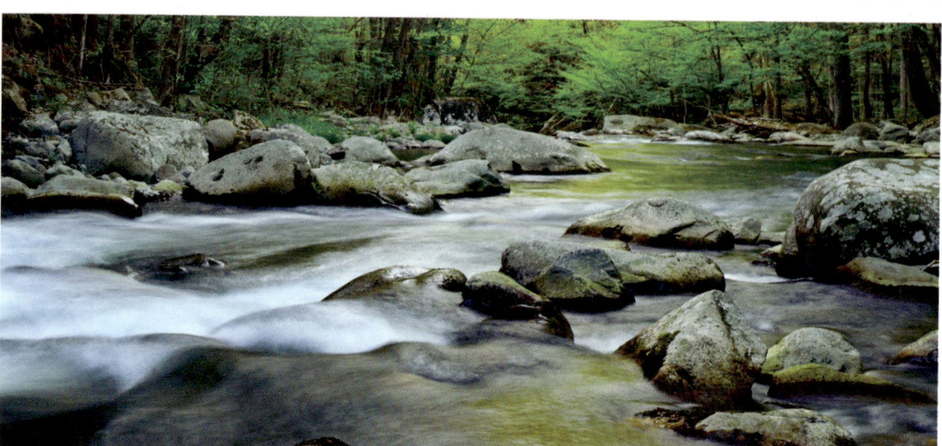

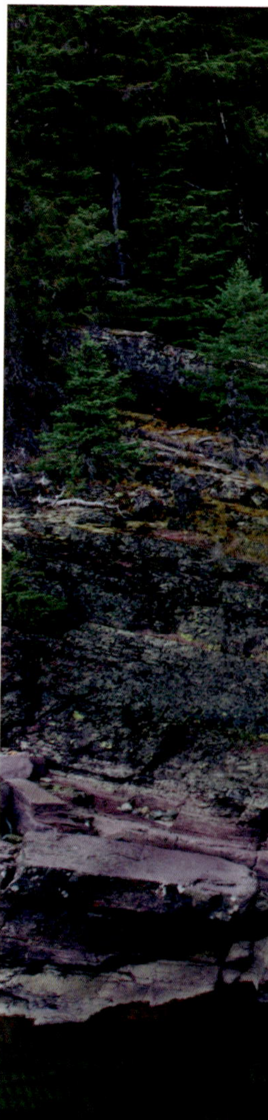

railroad tracks (or any straight or diagonal object) can be effective at leading the viewer into an image and adding perspective. Leading lines usually start at the bottom of the frame and extend into the middle or to a focal point. When composing your image, be careful that the line or implied line doesn't divide the image or direct the viewer's gaze out of the frame.

McDonald Creek in Glacier National Park presented a perfect opportunity to use an S curve in my composition. When you look at the image, note that the visual path into the image starts in the lower-left corner and draws the eye along the water and through the image to the background trees. S curves are great for taking the viewer through all parts of the scene as they weave back and forth across the frame. In this image, it was important to have enough of the rocks visible on the right side to keep the S shape (and the eye) within the frame.

▼ Light rain saturated the rock formations along McDonald Creek, forming an S curve that leads the eye into and through the frame.

FOCAL LENGTH: 32mm | ISO: 100 | APERTURE: f/14 | SHUTTER SPEED: 1/4 second

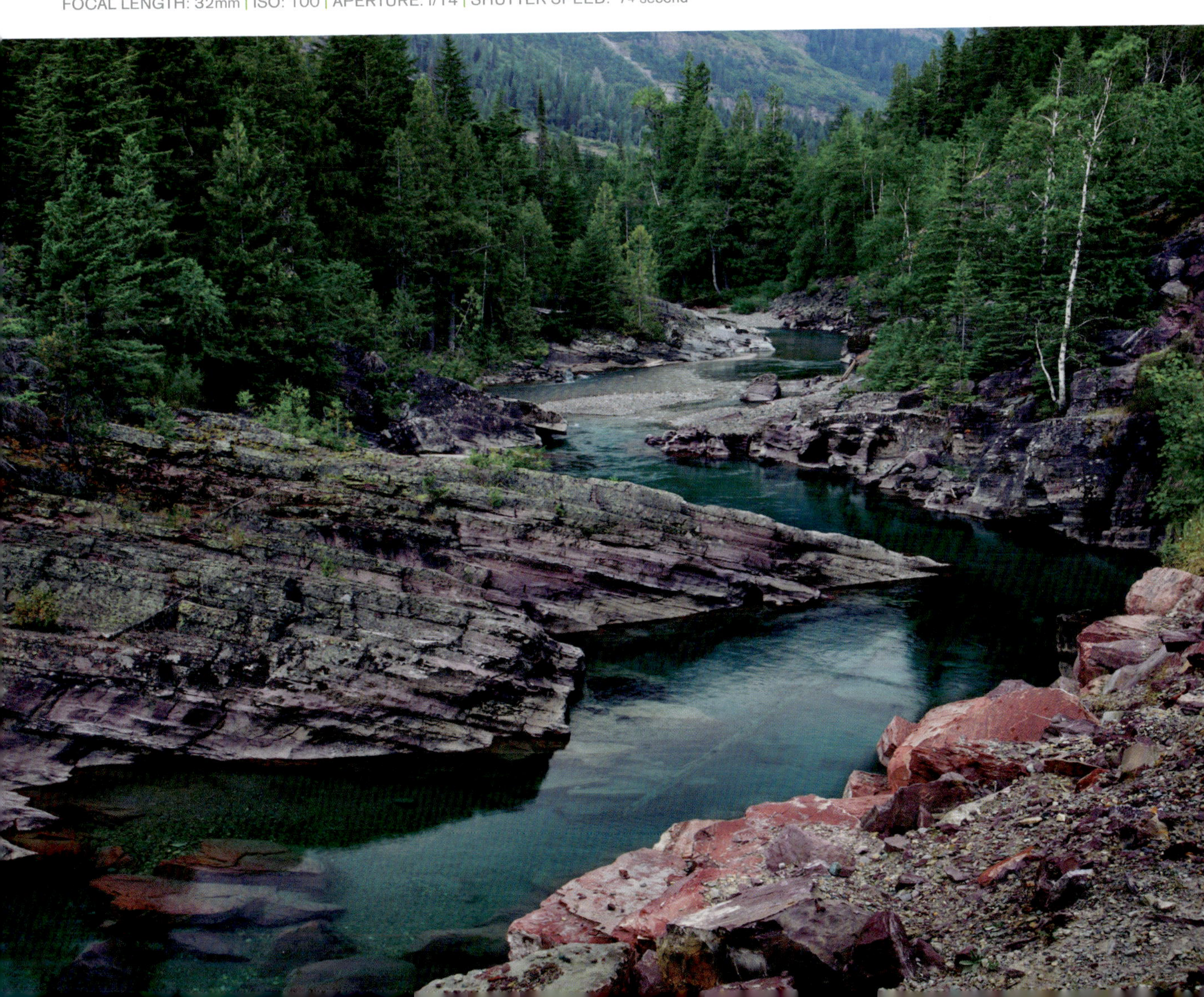

11. FILTERS

CIRCULAR POLARIZERS

With all the advances in digital software, many lens-mounted filters are not as necessary as they used to be. However, polarizers and neutral-density filters are the exception. Photoshop can't duplicate the effect of a polarizer.

Circular polarizers are an essential tool for landscape photography. They can be used to remove glare on wet rocks, reveal details underwater, darken blue skies, increase cloud contrast, reduce atmospheric haze, and boost color saturation. A polarizer has two pieces of glass; the bottom ring screws onto the lens and the front ring turns to change the strength of the polarization. Light waves scatter in all directions. A polarizer works by filtering out

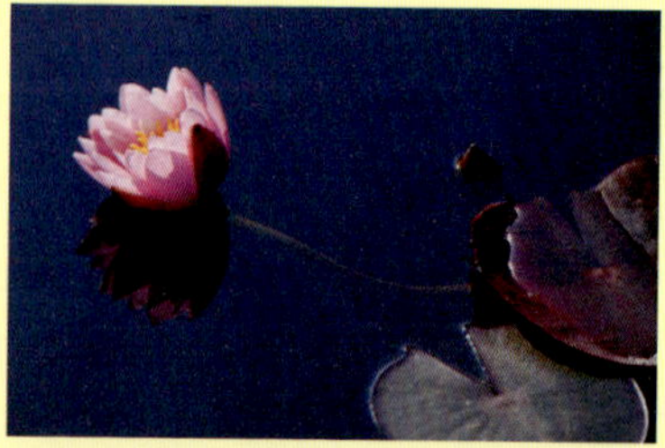

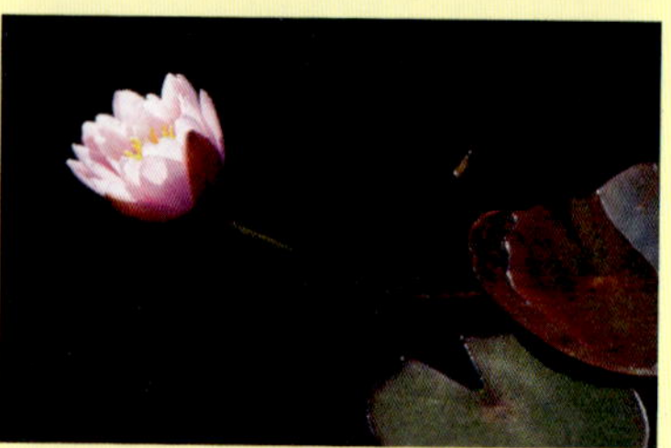

▲ (top) Blue sky is revealed with the polarizer, but there is glare on the bottom of the lily pad.

▲ (bottom) Turning the polarizer in the opposite direction removed the glare on the lily pad and revealed the black bottom of the water tank.

▼ This image is the result of blending two images in Photoshop. The circular polarizer was turned at a different angle for each capture of the water lily.

FOCAL LENGTH: 210mm | ISO: 200 | APERTURE: f/7.1 | SHUTTER SPEED: 1/125 second

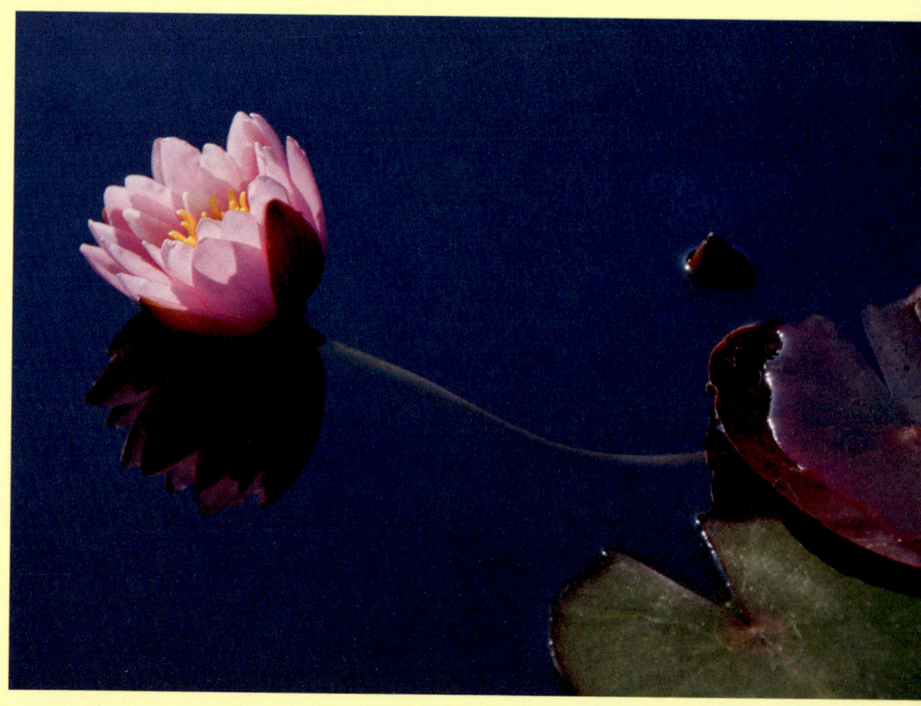

some of those rays to varying degrees relative to the sun's angle and the amount the polarizer is rotated. It effectively blocks some of the polarized light rays while allowing other rays to be transmitted. The amount of rotation will control the strength of the effect—it is not an all-or-nothing effect. Simply turn the filter until the effect is to your liking. Remember to readjust if you change your camera's orientation.

A polarizer is most effective when used at a right angle to the sun to deepen the sky and improve cloud contrast. It can, however, create an uneven variation in the sky, making one side darker than the other. The effect is amplified at high altitudes, and very dark or almost black skies can result.

Polarizers are not just for skies. They are also very effective at reducing glare in water and uncovering details. A turn of the polarizer can reveal rocks below the water surface, for example. While the effect is subtle, they can also reduce glare and boost saturation in low light, under overcast conditions, and in the rain.

Note that polarizers reduce the amount of light by 1.5 to 2 stops, so you must compensate for the loss of light when determining the exposure.

SOLID NEUTRAL-DENSITY FILTERS

Another useful filter for the landscape photographer is the *neutral-density (ND) filter*. There are three basic types of neutral-density filters: solid, variable, and graduated (sometimes called *grads* or *split ND filters*). They are available in a variety of densities comparable to stops of light, starting with a one-stop (.3), one-and-a-half-stop (.45), two-stop (.6), three-stop (.9), and so on, up to 10 with the

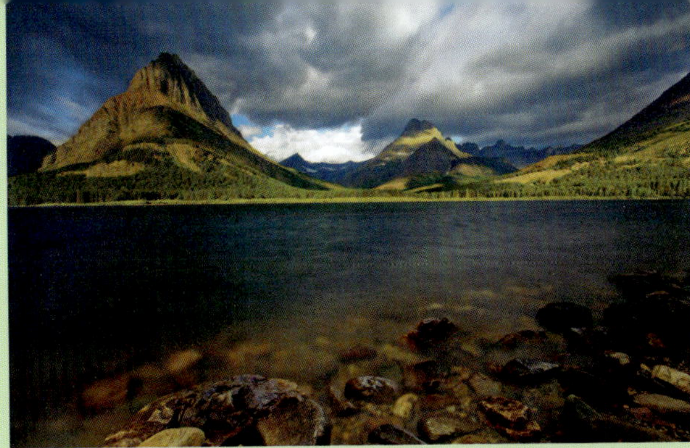

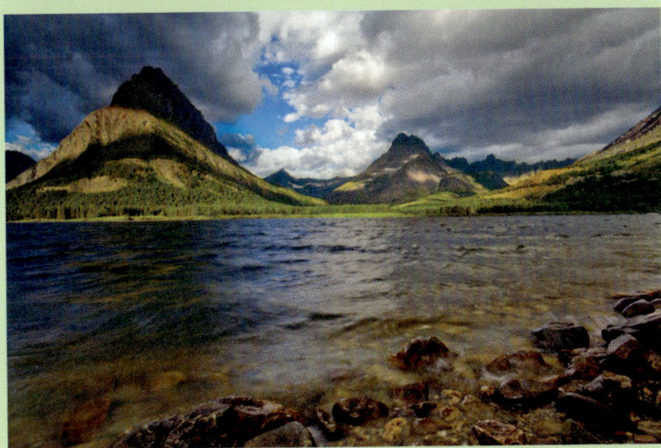

▲ (top) Using a Singh-Ray Vari-Duo filter reduced the light reaching the sensor by 2¾ stops, so a 5-second exposure was necessary. The increased exposure time blurred the motion in the water and clouds, changing the feel and look of the image.

FOCAL LENGTH: 19mm | ISO: 100 | APERTURE: f/22
SHUTTER SPEED: 5 seconds

▲ (bottom) Without the ND filter, the slowest shutter speed possible was ⅓ second. This revealed the texture in the water and clouds.

FOCAL LENGTH: 20mm | ISO: 100 | APERTURE: f/22
SHUTTER SPEED: ⅓ second

Lee "Big Stopper." And, Singh-Ray recently released a whopping 15-stop Mor-Slo ND filter.

Variable ND filters are similar to their solid counterparts except they rotate, allowing you to dial down the amount of light passing

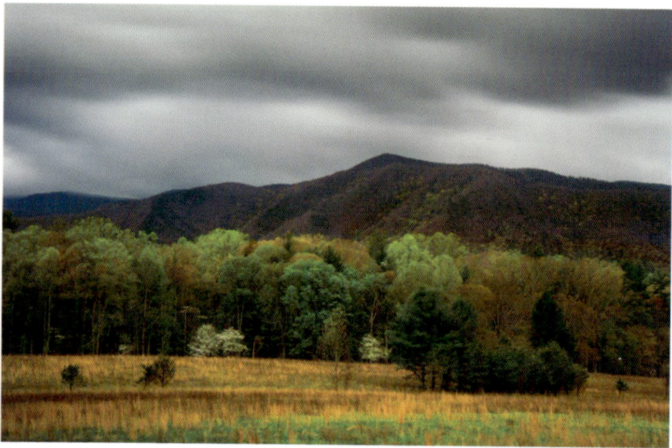

▲ A variable ND filter slowed for an exposure of 20 seconds, giving the moving clouds a soft brush-stroke effect.

FOCAL LENGTH: 70mm | ISO: 100 | APERTURE: f/22 | SHUTTER SPEED: 20 seconds

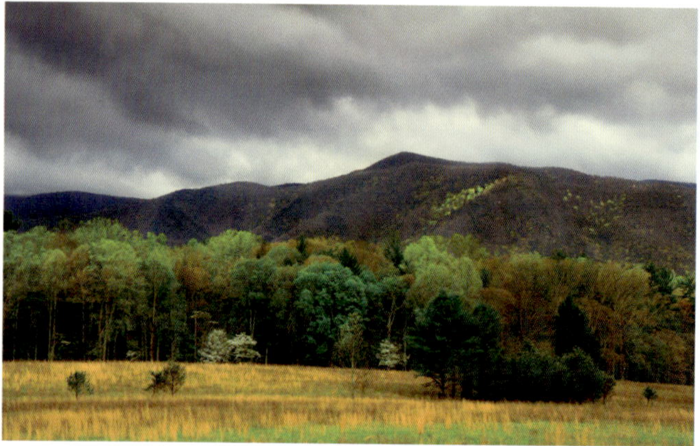

▲ Without the ND filter, the slowest possible exposure with the available light was 1/6 second. The clouds in this image have more definition and texture, whereas with the ND they are more fluid, showing the motion and drama of the sky.

FOCAL LENGTH: 70mm | ISO: 100 | APERTURE: f/22 | SHUTTER SPEED: 1/6 second

through the lens from two to eight stops. Singh-Ray also makes a Vari-Duo—a polarizer and variable ND filter in one.

The job of these colorless filters is to reduce the amount of light passing through the lens. A solid ND filter will slow down the shutter speed when you are at the maximum f-stop (i.e., f/22) and the lowest ISO setting (i.e., 100) of your lens and camera. Taking away stops of light allows for long exposures and creative opportunities. Slow shutter speeds change the appearance of moving subjects, such as waterfalls, ocean waves, or moving clouds, to a silky smooth blur. A tripod is an absolute must to keep the still subjects sharp and allow the moving parts to blur throughout the exposure. A cable release is also highly recommended when taking long exposures.

Note: These filters are very dark, making it difficult to see your composition through the viewfinder. You will need to set up your composition and focus before placing the ND filter over the lens, then set your exposure time.

GRADUATED NEUTRAL-DENSITY FILTERS

Graduated filters (also called *grads*) are clear on one end with the (gray) neutral density material on the opposite end. They can have a soft gradual fade to clear or a hard transition. Grads allow the landscape photographer to balance the contrast range by reducing the light in one half of the scene. When the dark part of the filter is positioned over the sky, for example, it will hold back the exposure to bring out the detail and prevent overexposure in that area. This effectively darkens the sky and balances the exposure with the foreground.

Using a grad filter can allow you to capture a better exposure in-camera and reduce post-processing time. Some folks may argue that you could just bracket several frames to capture a wide contrast range and combine the exposures in the digital darkroom. That is certainly an option if you don't have a graduated

ND filter. However, I prefer to the get the best-possible capture in the field.

Hard-transition filters should be used when there is a sharp and straight divide between light and dark in the scene. The ocean meeting the horizon at sunset is one instance in which using a hard-transition filter would make sense. Soft-transition filters are best used for scenes in which there is no clear edge between light and dark.

While round screw-in grads are available, I recommend using large rectangular filters, as they allow extra space to position the transition area precisely across the scene. These rectangular filters can be mounted in a special holder (Cokin makes a popular one) or hand-held in front of the lens. *(Note:* When hand-holding your filter, be careful to not have your hand in the frame or bump the camera!) To see the effect, look through the viewfinder and slowly move the filter across the front of the lens. Note that hard-edged graduated filters must be positioned precisely, but the soft-edge ones are more forgiving since the transition is gradual.

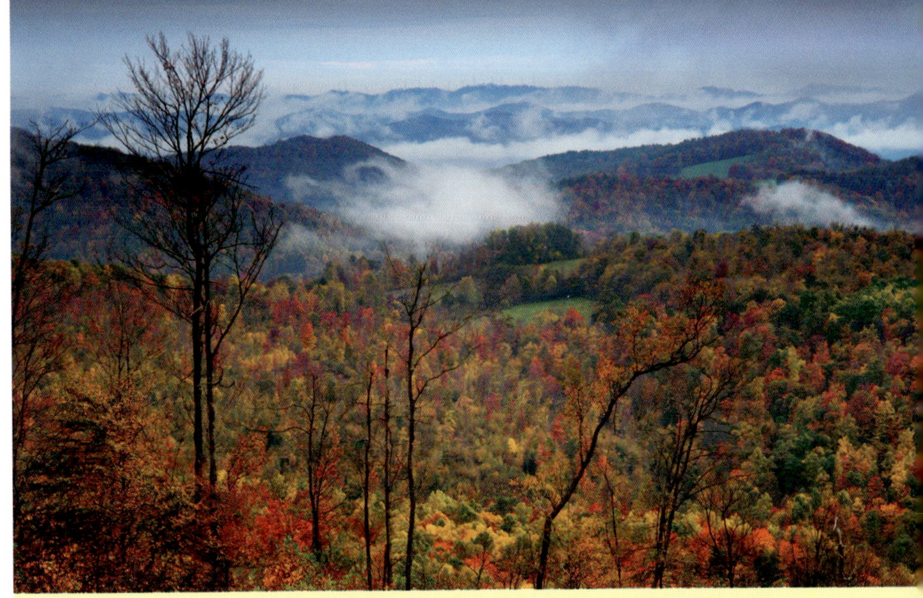

▲ To capture the best-possible image in the field, a graduated ND filter was placed over the sky to bring out detail and prevent overexposure.

FOCAL LENGTH: 170mm | ISO: 800 | APERTURE: f/14
SHUTTER SPEED: 1/60 second

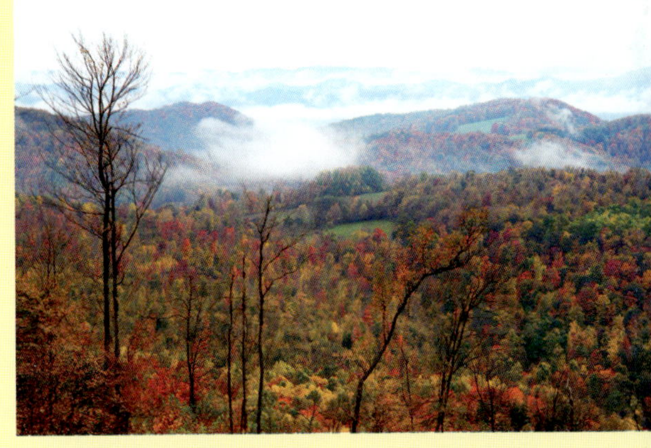

► Without the graduated filter the sky is overexposed and lacks detail and texture.

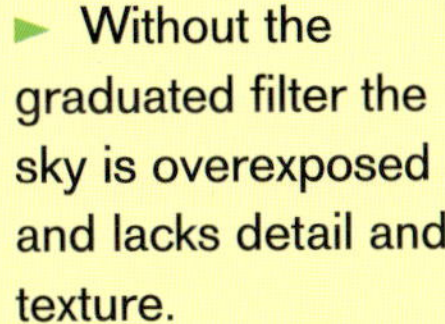

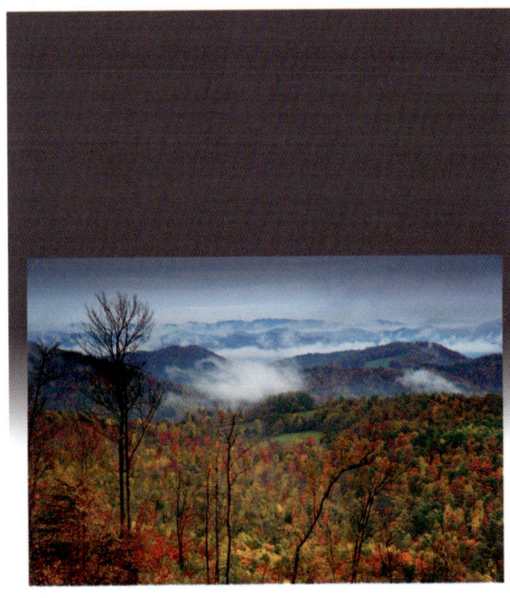

► A two-stop graduated filter was placed over the sky and distant mountain to hold back the exposure in the areas where the gray part of the filter is used.

11. THE DIGITAL DARKROOM

CAMERA RAW AND COLOR TEMPERATURE

The color of light is important in photography. To create the image we envision, we can improve the color rendition at the time of capture or creatively alter it if desired.

One of the great things about shooting digital RAW files is the flexibility and creativity

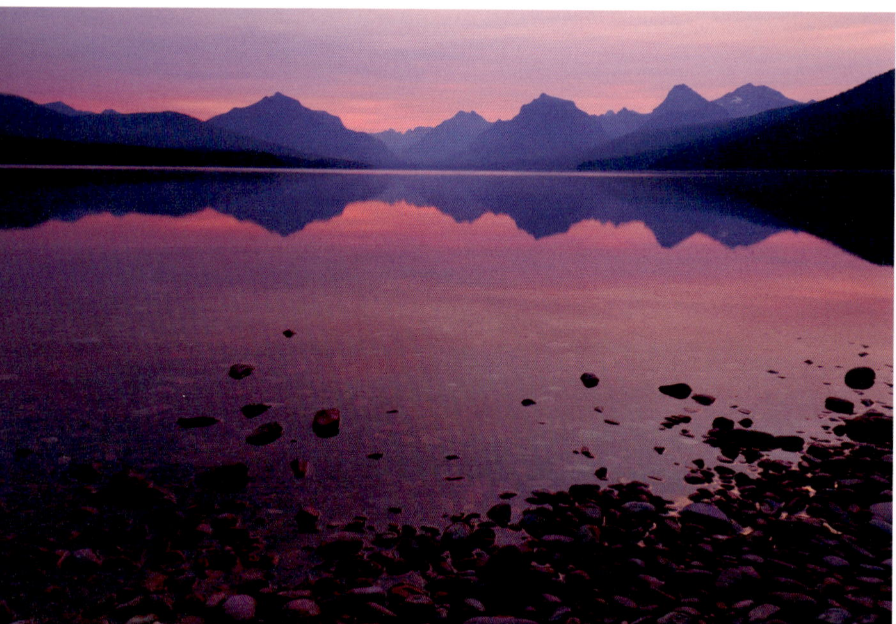

◄ Using the cloudy white balance setting in Adobe Camera Raw and adjusting the tint to +26 gave Lake McDonald a warm, pink tone.

▼ (left) Using the tungsten white balance setting in Camera Raw made the image appear blue and cool as if it were shot at twilight.

▼ (right) Here is Lake McDonald, shot using the daylight white balance setting. No color correction was applied.

FOCAL LENGTH: 28mm | ISO: 100 APERTURE: f/18 | SHUTTER SPEED: 2 seconds

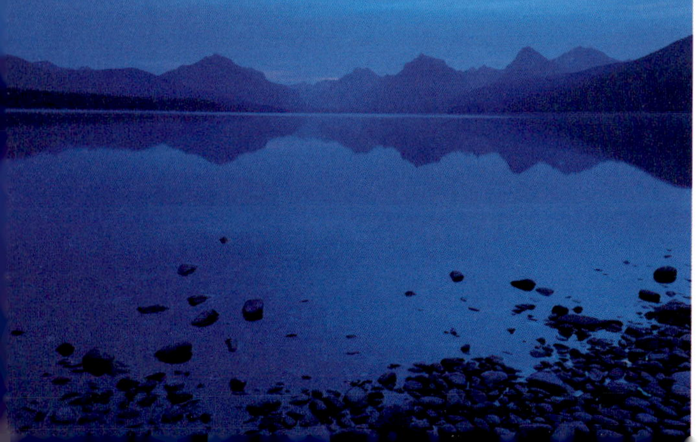

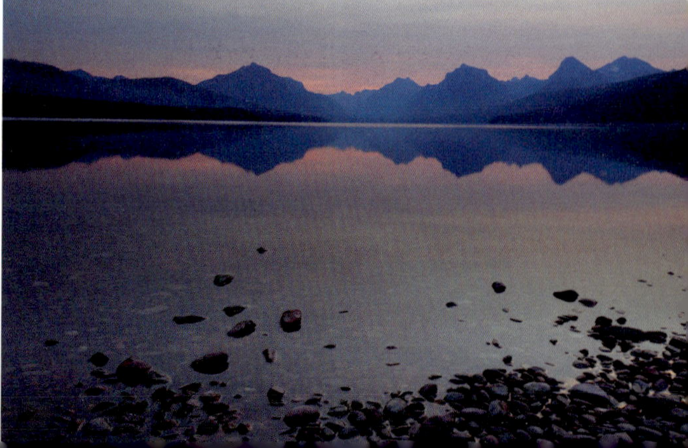

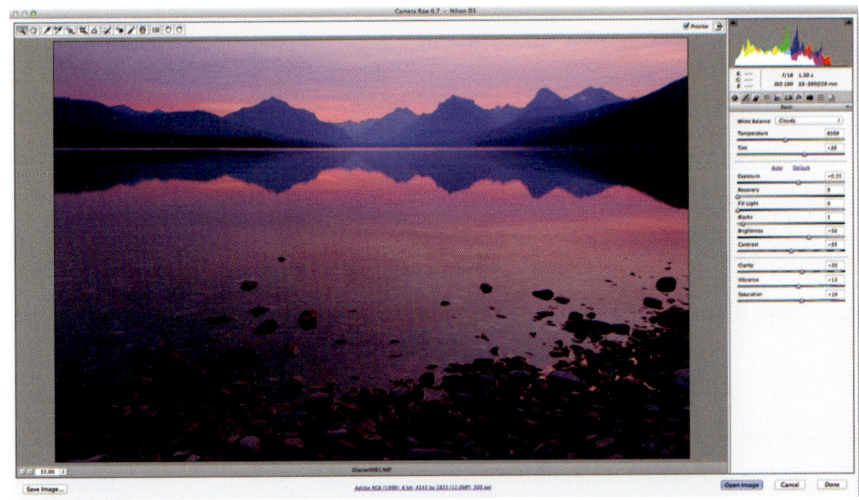

► Simply adjusting the sliders in Camera Raw altered the appearance of Lake McDonald.

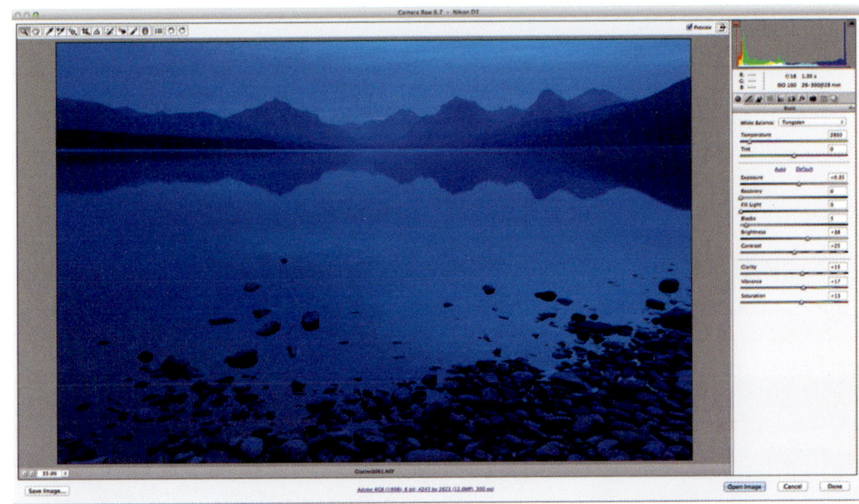

► A twilight version of Lake McDonald was created by selecting the tungsten white balance and making slight adjustments to the clarity, vibrance, and saturation settings.

we have to alter the image in the digital darkroom. Simply adjusting the color temperature slider in Adobe Camera Raw can significantly change the appearance of the image and affect the mood of the photograph, allowing for more than one interpretation of the same image.

> "When you photograph the landscape or other natural things you must endeavor to determine what is 'appropriate colour'—suitable for the mood or information you want your photograph to convey."[14]
>
> **Freeman Patterson**
>
> *Internationally recognized nature photographer and author*

The sunrise at Lake McDonald in Glacier National Park was not what I hoped on this morning. Shooting it with the white balance set to daylight applied no color correction, and the result lacked drama. However, a little post-processing modification of the color temperature setting enhanced the color and mood significantly.

I started by opening the image from Lake McDonald in Camera Raw. I changed the white balance from "as shot" to "cloudy." When

I did this, the color temperature moved from 5800K to 6500K, and the warm, pink tones were immediately revealed. Additionally, I set the tint slider to +26 to intensify the magenta and pink tones. The clarity was set at +20, the vibrance to +13, and the saturation to +19.

The second interpretation was made by selecting the tungsten (2850K) white balance preset with a 0 value for the tint. The clarity was set at +15, the vibrance to +17, and the saturation to +13. The result was a blue-toned image that looks as though it were taken at twilight.

Simply adjusting the color temperature in Camera Raw resulted in two new and different-feeling images. Although these images are not an accurate representation of the morning scene, it is amazing to be able to impart such profound changes in the color and mood of a scene in a few mouse clicks.

BLENDED EXPOSURES

Waterfalls are often full of contrast, as the white blur of water creates bright highlights compared to the darker surroundings. This contrast can make photographing waterfalls a challenge. To maximize the detail and color, soft light is ideal, but even then the contrast range may be too high to capture in a single image. Waterfalls often require bracketing and a post-processing technique called exposure blending to show the full tonal range of the scene. When capturing the images that will be blended in postproduction, it is critical to use a tripod so the images are identical except for the exposure (+ stops and - stops).

▼ A blended exposure of Cayuga Falls in Ricketts Glen State Park was created by manually "brushing" portions of two images together in Photoshop.

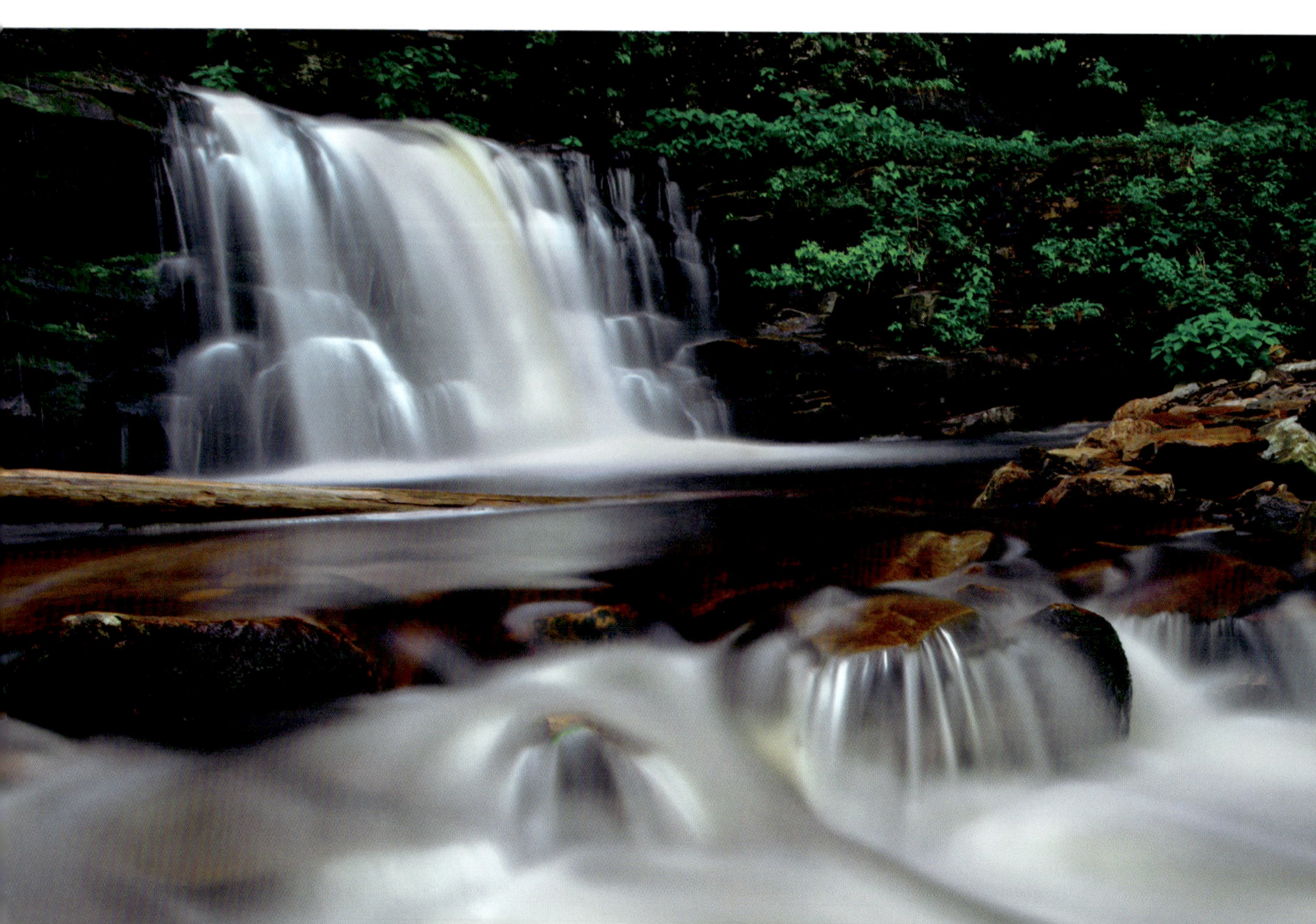

Similarly, strong flowing water is often several stops brighter than its surroundings. Bracketing two frames or more is often needed to record all of the tones without losing detail. These exposures are then blended in Photoshop using layers and layer masks to "brush" portions of the images together.

This is simply a basic overview of a blended exposure technique and how I create one. (Pick up a Photoshop guide if you need more instruction than presented in this overview.)

First, I start with the file that has the best exposure for the middle tones and use it as my base layer. Next, I copy and paste the dark exposure into the base file and add a layer mask to it. I fill the layer mask with black to "mask" or hide the dark exposure. Then I "paint" with a big, soft white brush onto the layer mask (not the image) in the areas I want to reveal from the dark exposure. The dark exposure is "blended" with the base exposure to fill in the hot spots, resulting in an image with a full tonal range. My example uses only two exposures, but the same technique can be applied with multiple exposures.

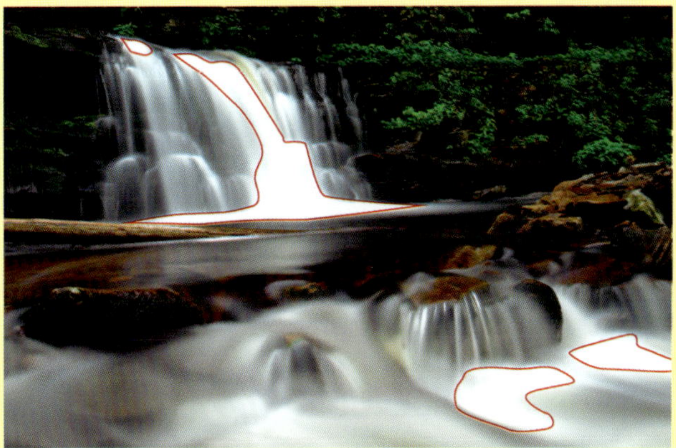

▲ This is the base exposure. There is a wide tonal range, but there are a few hot spots (outlined in red) that lack detail.

FOCAL LENGTH: 28mm | ISO: 160 | APERTURE: f/20 | SHUTTER SPEED: 15 seconds

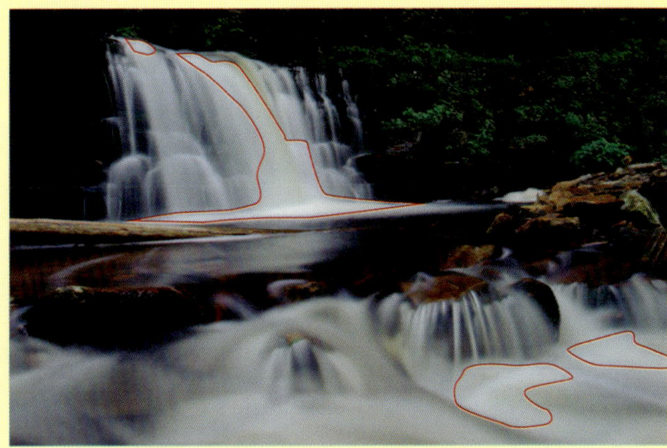

▲ In the dark exposure, there is detail in the brightest areas. Hand "brushing" sections of this image into the base layer will "add" the detail back to create a blended-exposure image.

FOCAL LENGTH: 28mm | ISO: 160 | APERTURE: f/20 | SHUTTER SPEED: 8 seconds

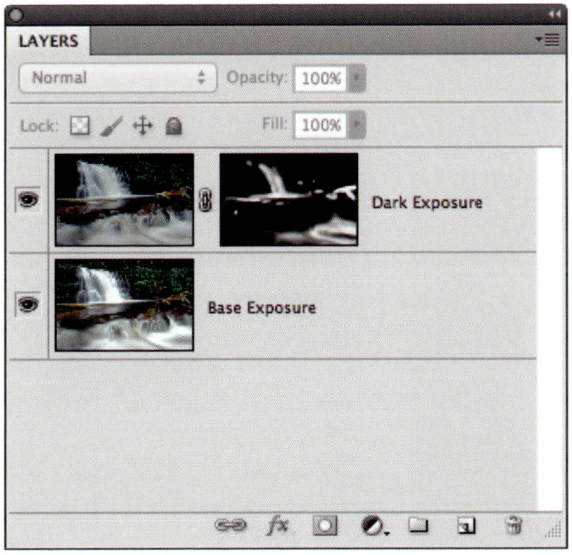

◄ A screen shot of the Photoshop Layers palette shows the base image with a second darker exposure that uses a layer mask over it to create the blended exposure.

HIGH DYNAMIC RANGE (HDR) IMAGING

The range in luminance between the lightest and darkest areas of a scene can be measured in stops of light. This contrast range is often referred to as *dynamic range* in photography. Digital cameras record about 7 to 9 stops, but the human eye can see roughly 13 to 14. We need to be aware of this when shooting high-contrast scenes. A popular method of preserving detail in the highlights and shadows is to create a high dynamic range (HDR) image.

A popular method of preserving detail in the highlights and shadows is to create an HDR image.

Dedicated HDR computer software, such as Photomatix, that "stacks" the bracketed exposures into one tone-mapped image makes HDR processing easy and fun.

Example 1. After a long and rough Jeep ride from Marble to Crystal Mill, Colorado, the light was bright, hard, and full of contrast. In my first exposure, the mill was very dark and the sky was too light. To compensate for this, I bracketed the exposures to capture detail in both the dark and light areas in a series of frames. To ensure that the scene was exactly the same in each image (save the exposure!), I used a tripod.

HDR works best with static subjects. In this scene, however, the aspen leaves were moving and, of course, the water was too. Due to the motion, the leaves were not perfectly aligned when the exposures were stacked together,

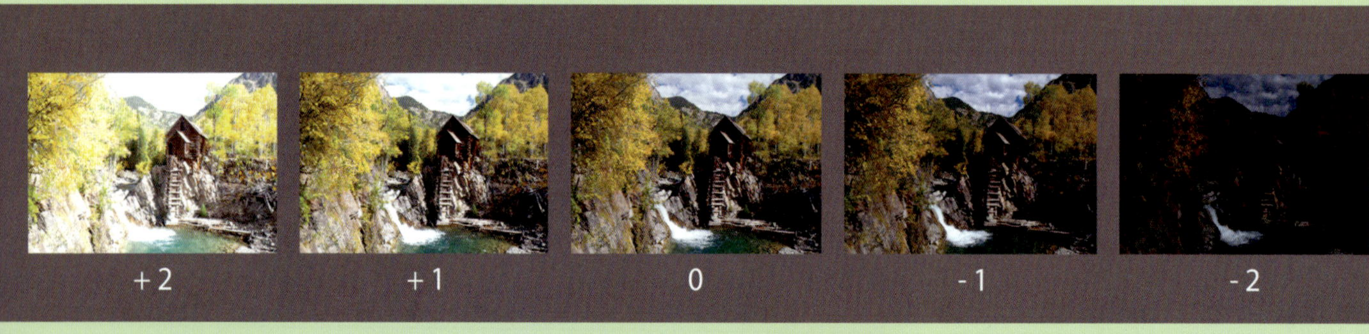

▲ A series of exposures was created by bracketing in one-stop increments to capture detail in the highlights and shadows.

FOCAL LENGTH: 35mm | ISO: 200
APERTURE: f/22 | SHUTTER SPEED: 1/3 second to 1/50 second

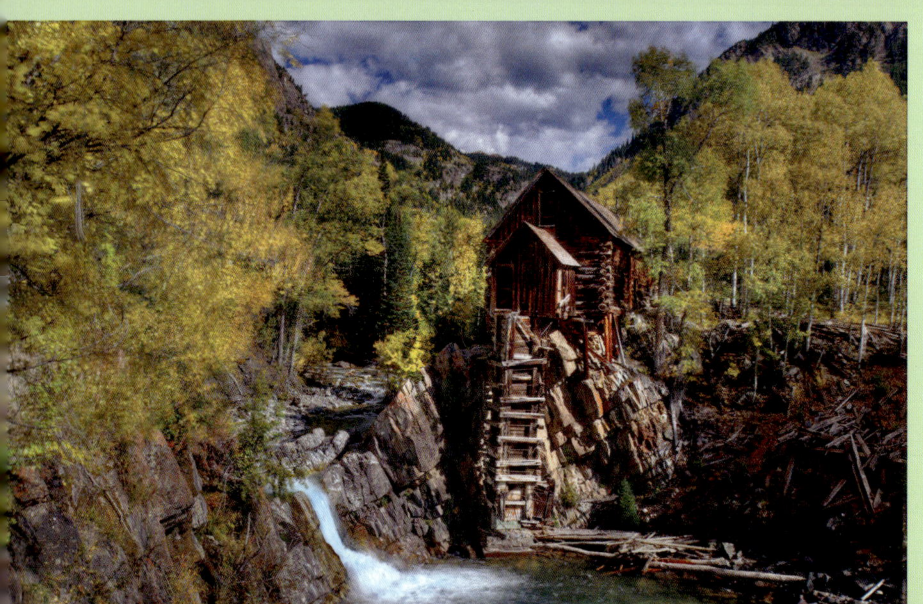

◄ Here, you see five exposures stacked together in the Photomatix HDR software. Notice the "ribbing" or ghosting effect in the leaves. This is due to the fact that the leaves were in slightly different positions in each image as a result of the wind.

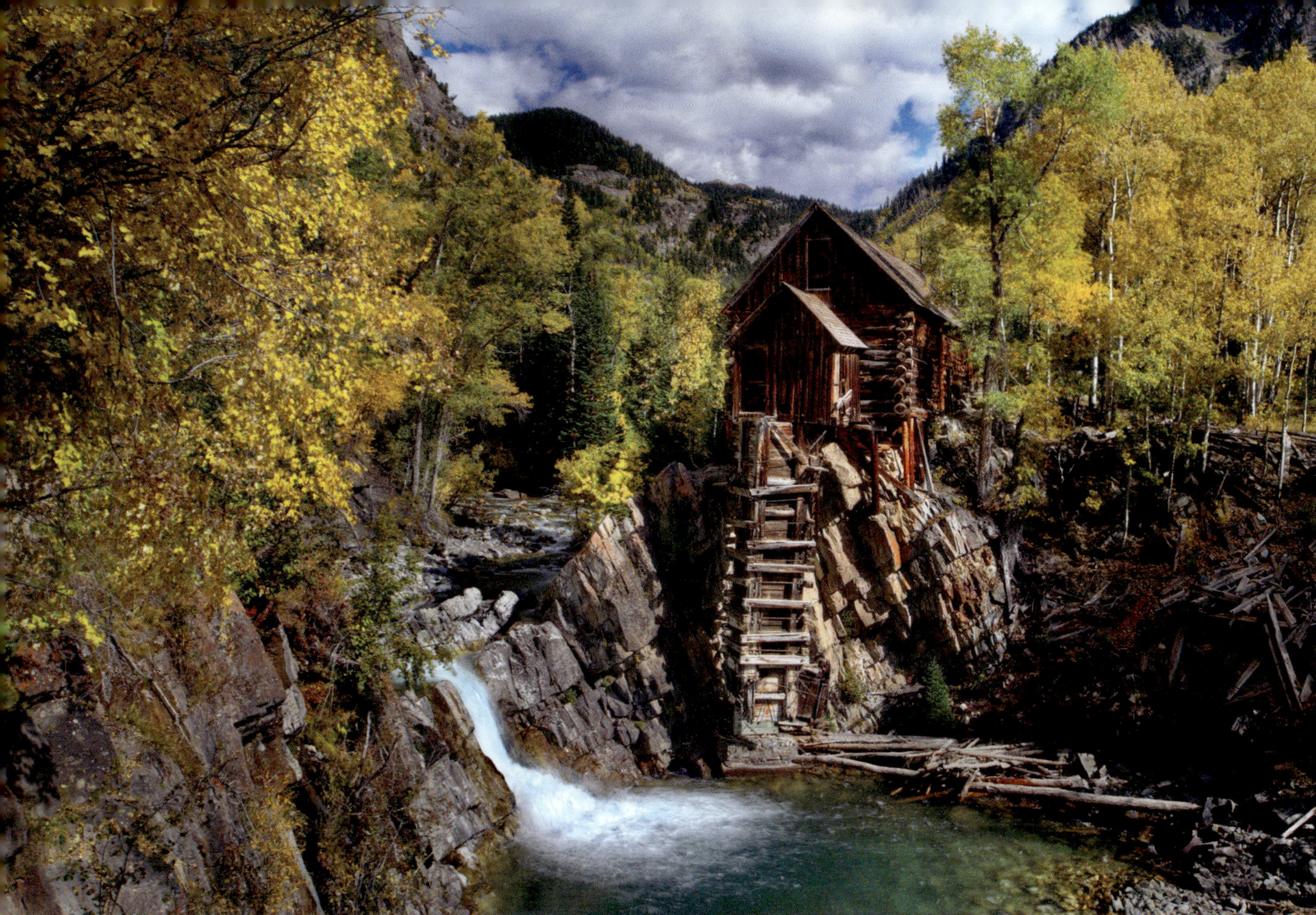

▲ The final image of the Crystal Mill is a combination of Photomatix HDR tone-mapping and exposure blending in Photoshop.

and a "ribbing" or ghosting effect is apparent. I could have frozen the blowing leaves by increasing my shutter speed, but the water would have appeared choppy. For this image, I liked the way the Photomatix software made the mill and rocks appear, but not the trees. My solution was to create a blended exposure, using a single frame of aspen trees and adding it to the tone-mapped HDR image in Photoshop.

Example 2. Let's look at another image made with HDR processing.

The contrast range of the scene along the Hidden Lake trail in Glacier National Park was very high, so I captured five exposures by bracketing (-2, -1, 0, +1, +2) in full-stop increments. Some of the frames lacked detail in the highlights or shadows, but it didn't matter because HDR combines all five exposures into one well-exposed image. For the best-possible results, one frame in the sequence must have all the highlight detail captured and another must have the shadow detail.

Creating HDR images offers a high level of creative options. As photographer Tony Sweet says, "It's all up to the maker. The important thing is that high dynamic range photography is a potent tool in our ongoing pursuit of higher levels of creative expression."[15] There are a variety of looks you can create, from

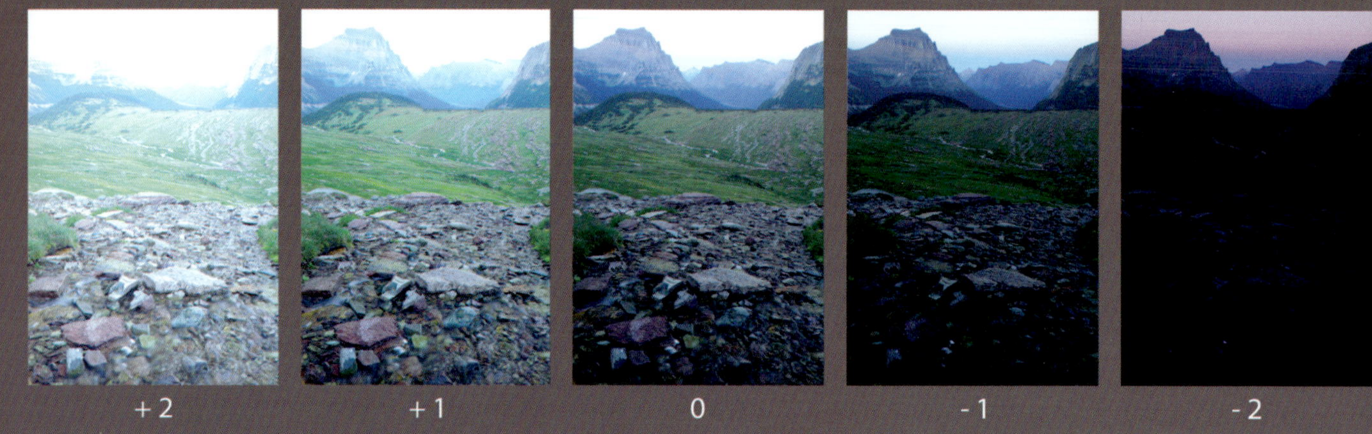

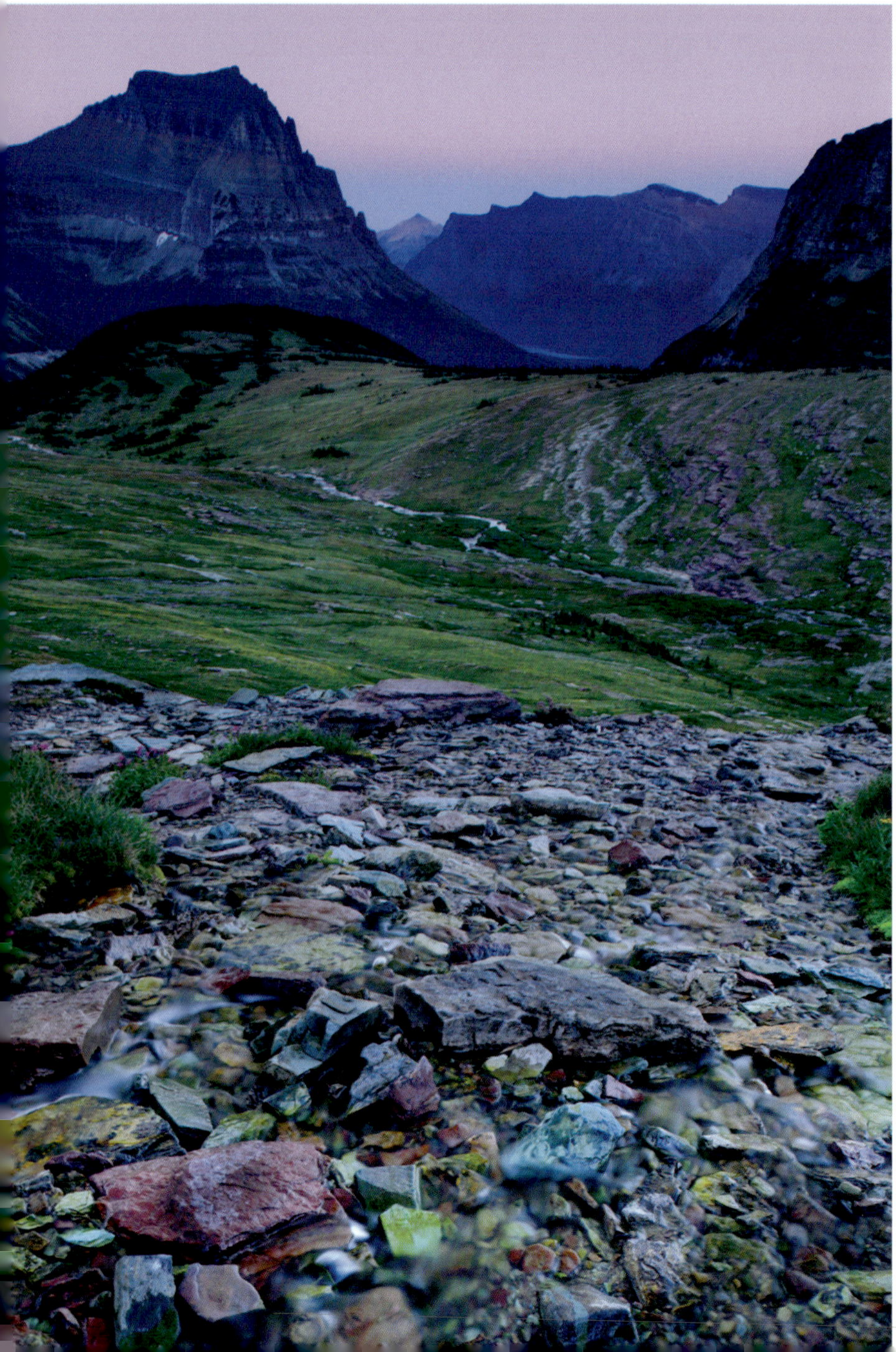

▲ Bracketing in one-stop increments for a series of five frames allowed me to capture the detail in the highlights and shadows that would be needed to produce an HDR image. Static subjects that align perfectly when stacked together ensure the best-possible results. Many cameras have a bracketing function that creates the various exposures. Please refer to your manual for the instructions. My camera allows me to bracket up to nine frames in .3, .7, or 1.0-stop increments.

◄ Tweaking a few adjustments in Photomatix Pro was an easy, creative way to create this HDR image from Glacier National Park in Montana.

surreal and grunge-like effects to photo-natural and anywhere in between, including black & white. There are plenty of choices and options in the HDR world, so go ahead and experiment.

There are several software programs that are dedicated to the HDR process. I prefer Photomatix Pro by HDR Soft. It's easy to use and offers several preset "looks" that can be selected with a click of the mouse and fine-tuned with the adjustment sliders.

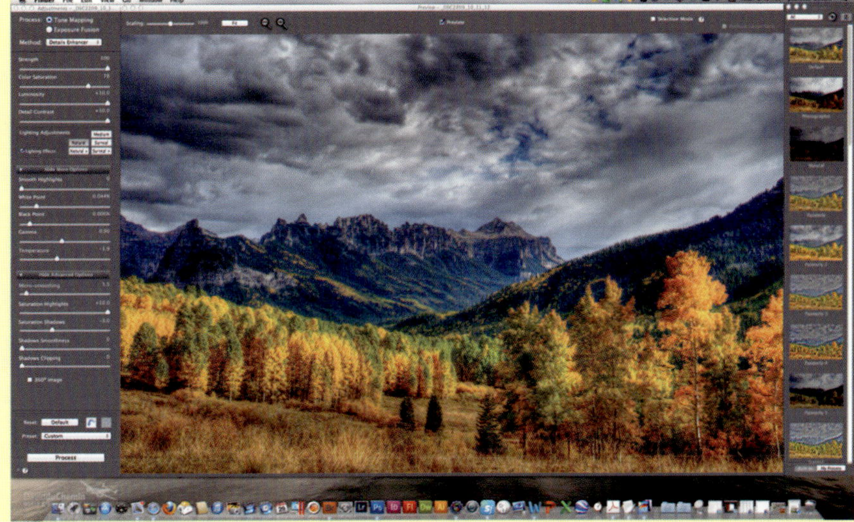

► The Photomatix Pro interface is easy to use with one-click presets on the right side and adjustment sliders on the left that allow for custom modifications.

▼ It is possible to create a variety of HDR looks from grunge to realistic. The Painterly 2 preset in Photomatix Pro was used to create this image from the Silver Jack Wilderness Area of Colorado.

FOCAL LENGTH: 48mm | ISO:200
APERTURE: f/18 | SHUTTER SPEED: 1/60 second

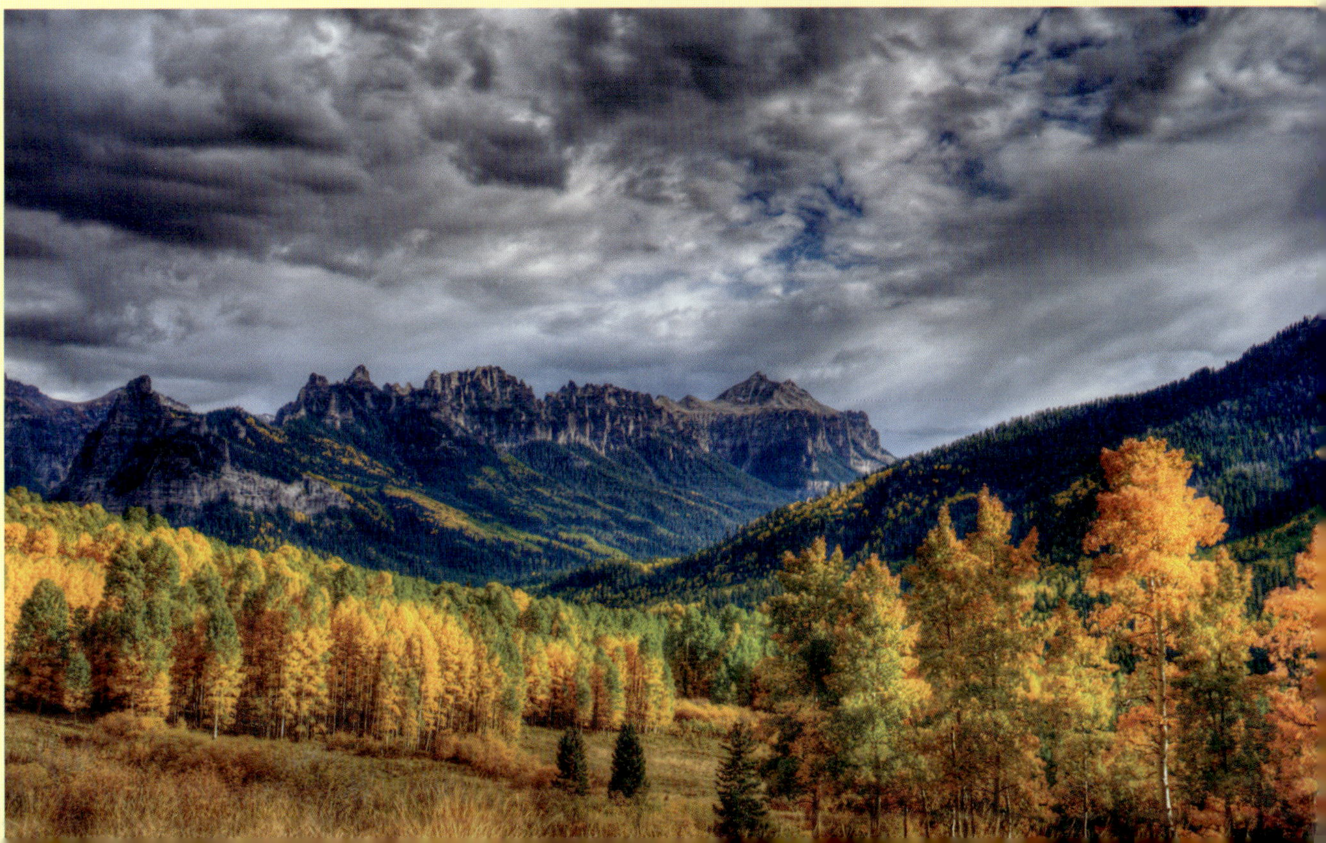

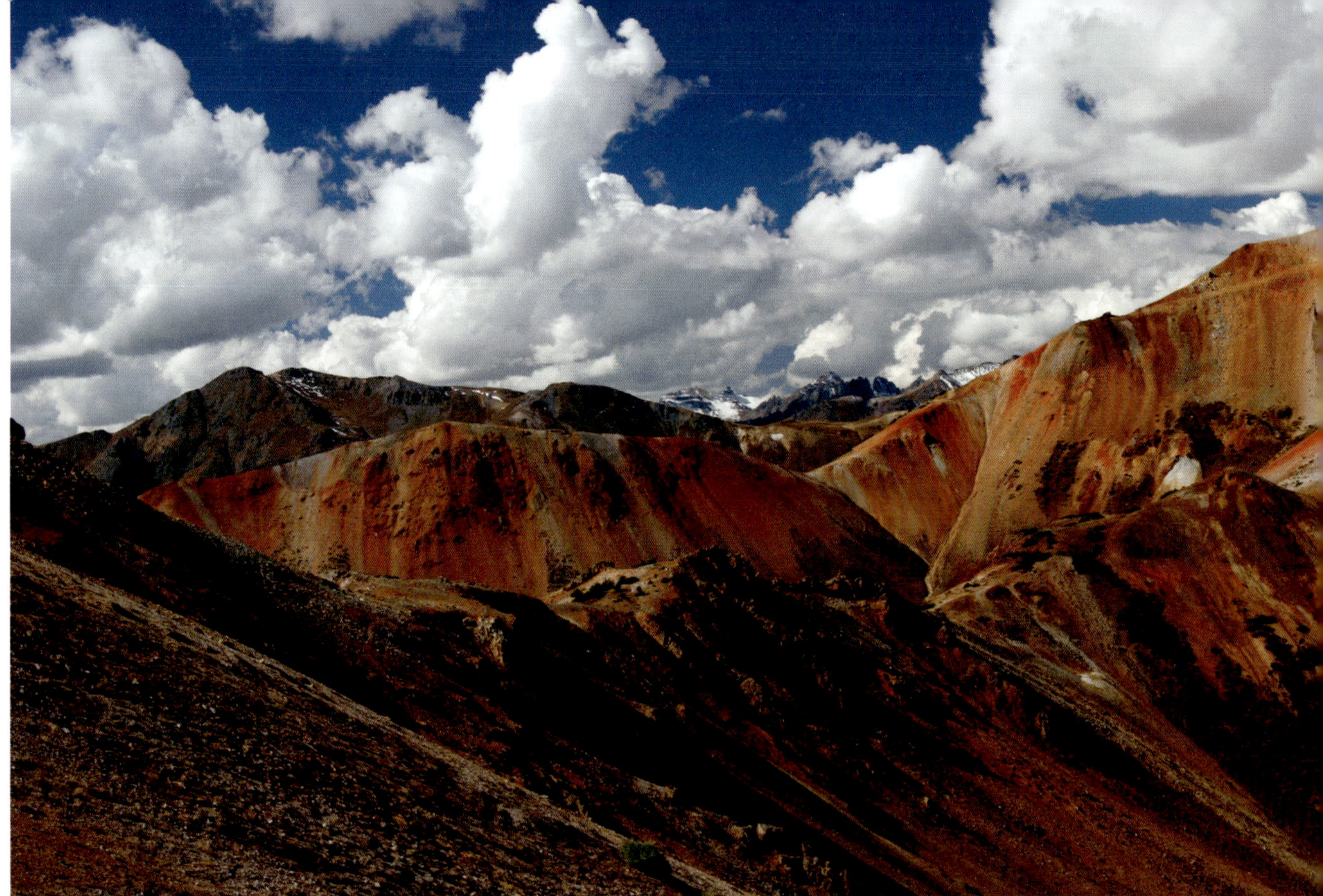

▲ This panoramic view of Red Mountain from Corkscrew Gulch Pass at 12,236 feet was created by merging three images together.

FOCAL LENGTH: 48mm | ISO: 200 | APERTURE: f/18 | SHUTTER SPEED: 1/40 second

PANORAMIC IMAGES

There is something about standing at the top of a mountain that lends itself to panoramics. I guess it is because once you're at the top of the mountain, you can't help but look all around and take in the view.

It is important that the ISO, shutter speed, f-stop, focus, and focal length are identical for each image.

The top of Red Mountain was a perfect place to capture images for a pano. I started by leveling my camera, which was mounted on a panning ballhead and tripod. *(Note:* There are several tripods that have built-in levels. If the model you use doesn't have one, you can purchase a hot-shoe bubble level, as I did, and attach it to your camera.) When creating panos, it is important that the ISO, shutter speed, f-stop, focus, and focal length are identical for each image. Using a polarizer is not recommended because the angle to the sun will change as you pan across the landscape and may result in uneven and patchy skies.

Starting on the far-left side for my first image, I gradually panned to the right, making sure there was a 30 percent overlap for each

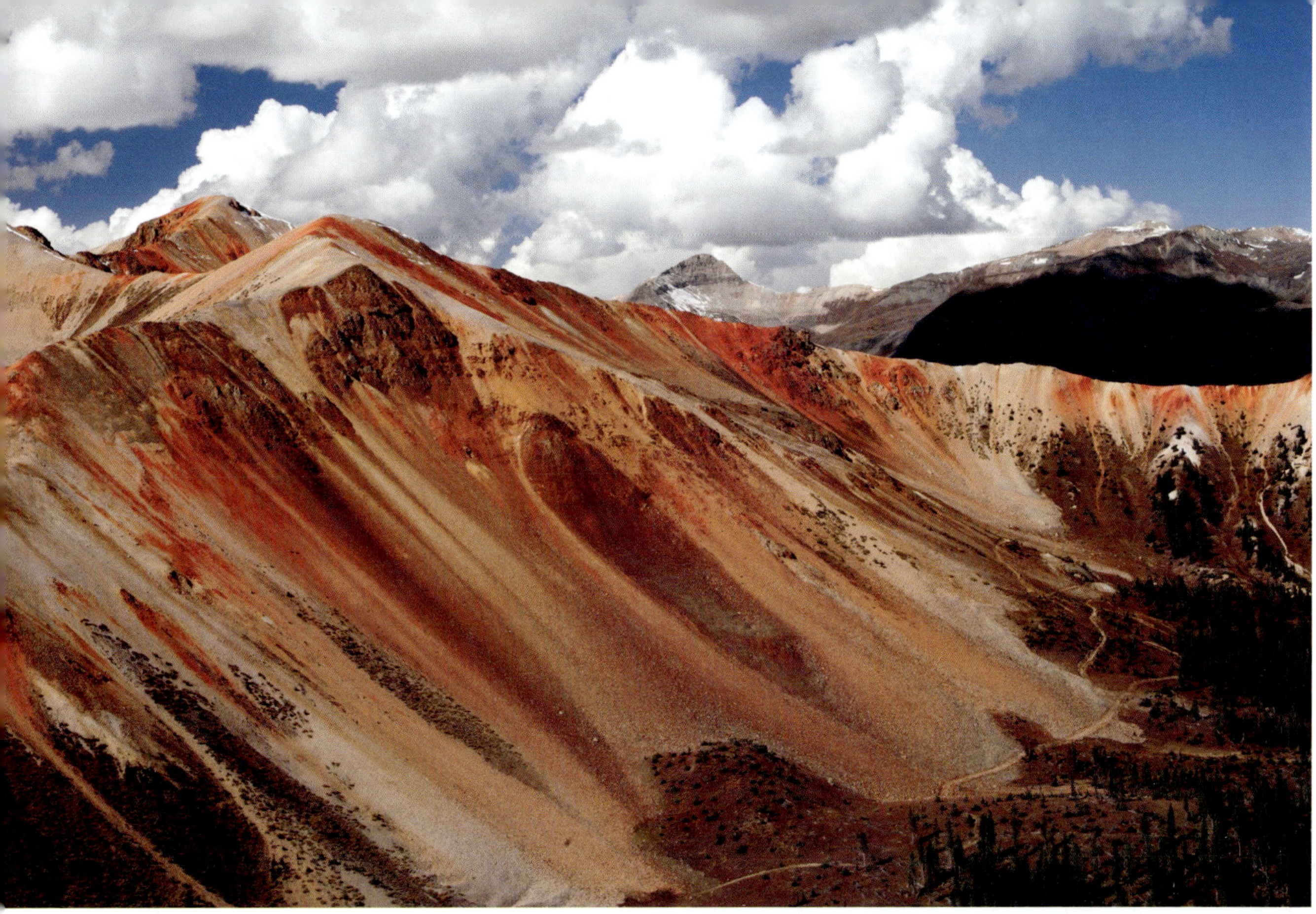

Using the Photomerge feature in Photoshop, three images were automatically stitched together to create one panoramic image. Always make sure to have at least a 30 percent overlap when capturing images for a pano.

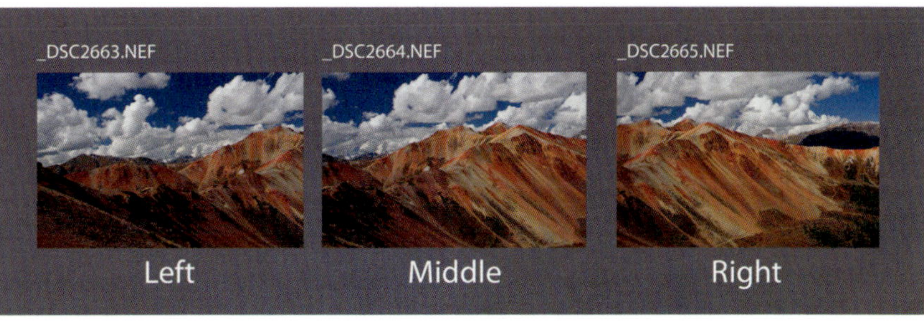

(left) This screen shot shows the three different images selected for automatic blending in the Photomerge window.

(right) The stitched layers were assembled in Photoshop with separate layers and layer masks. Once the images are flattened, they can be edited.

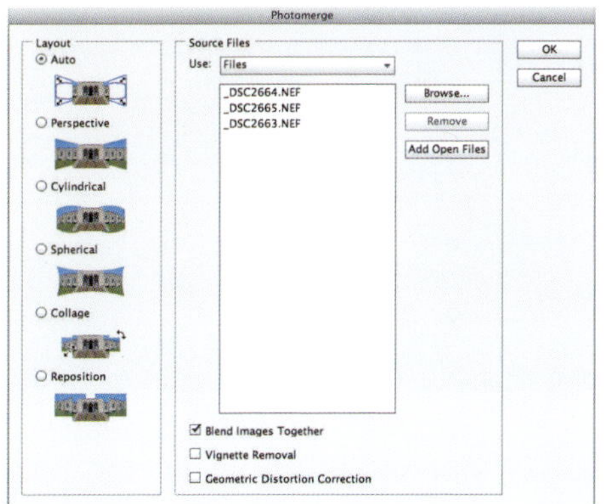

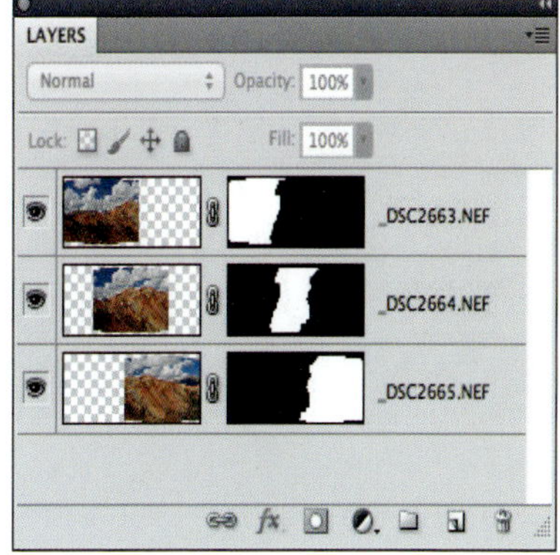

frame in the sequence. Stitching the frames together is a snap with the Photomerge function in Photoshop, as it automatically aligns the frames into one cohesive image. One of the easiest methods for creating a pano is to select the series of frames in Adobe Bridge, then go to Tools > Photoshop > Photomerge. When the images load, make sure Auto is selected in the Photomerge window, click OK, and sit back and watch the program create a seamless image. After the image is assembled in Photoshop, each image will have its own layer and layer mask. Simply flatten the image and edit as needed.

File Size. Panoramic images made from multiple frames will show a wider view with a higher resolution. Two images will be double the file size of a single cropped image. Shooting vertically requires more frames to span a given horizontal space, so the file sizes of panoramics "stitched" vertically are even larger still.

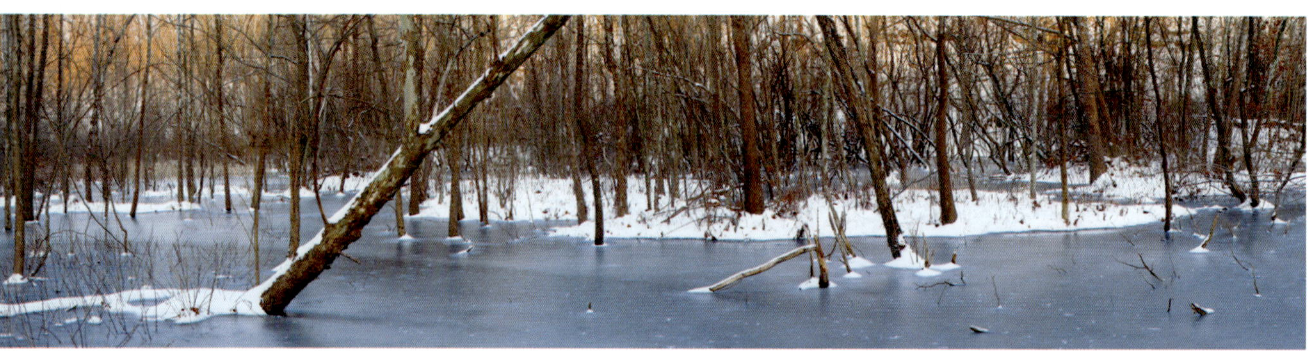

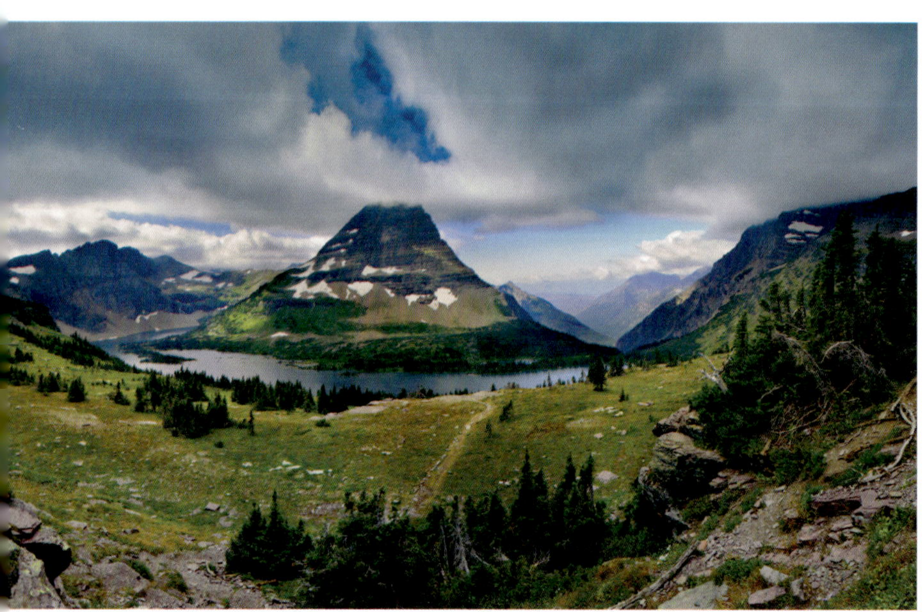

▲ Panoramics are not just for mountains. A sweeping view can be captured just about anywhere, including the icy swamps close to my house.

FOCAL LENGTH: 52mm | ISO: 250 | APERTURE: f/7.1 | SHUTTER SPEED: 1/60 second

◄ The panoramic view of Bearhat Mountain and Hidden Lake in Glacier National Park was created from five images stitched together with Photoshop's Photomerge.

FOCAL LENGTH: 24mm | ISO: 100 | APERTURE: f/22 | SHUTTER SPEED: 1/5 second

CONCLUSION

Photographing magic light is a challenging and rewarding experience. The thrill and reward of landscape photography is in capturing these moments. There are countless ways to create breathtaking images, whether it is at the edge of the day, just before a storm, or reflections in a flowing stream. Hopefully you will use some of the tools and techniques I have presented in this book to make the most of light and weather. I encourage you to see the light, harness it, and make it all your own for expressive and dynamic images.

NOTES

1. "Warm Light, Cold Light," *Outdoor Photographer,* last modified March 1, 2008, http://www.outdoorphotographer.com/how-to/shooting/warm-light-cold-light.html?start=2
2. David duChemin, *Ten* (Vancouver, B.C.: Craft & Vision, 2009), e-book, chap. 7
3. Galen Rowell, *Mountain Light* (Covelo, California: The Yolla Bolly Press, 1986), 4.
4. "Glacier: Through the Years in Glacier National Park", National Park Service, last modified January, 15, 2004, http://www.nps.gov/history/history/online_books/glac/appa.htm
5. David duChemin, *Photographically Speaking* (Berkeley, California: New Riders, 2012), 136.
6. Jack Dykinga, *Capture the Magic* (Santa Barbara, California: Rocky Nook, Inc., 2014), 6.
7. David Muench, *American Landscape* (New York, New York: Arrowood Press, 1997), 5.
8. Freeman Patterson, *Photography of Natural Things, 3rd Ed.* (Toronto, Ontario, Canada: Key Porter Books Limited, 2004), 50.
9. Galen Rowell, *Mountain Light* (Covelo, California: The Yolla Bolly Press, 1986), 58.
10. Tim Fitzharris, *National Audubon Society Guide to Landscape Photography* (Buffalo, New York: Firefly Books, 2007), 83.
11. "The Artist," Henri Carter-Bresson Foundation, accessed December 17, 2013, http://www.henricartierbresson.org/hcb/home_en.htm
12. Art Wolfe, *The New Art of Photographing Nature, Rev. Ed.* (New York, New York: Amphoto Books, Crown Publishing Group, 2013), 147.
13. Guy Tal, *Intimate Portraits of the Colorado Plateau* (Torrey, Utah: Guy Tal Books, 2011), e-book, page 8.
14. Freeman Patterson, *Photography of Natural Things, 3rd Ed.* (Toronto, Ontario, Canada: Key Porter Books Limited, 2004), 65.
15. Tony Sweet, *Prelude to Fine Art Photography: High Dynamic Range* (Mechanicsburg, Pennsylvania: Stackpole Books, 2011), ix.

INDEX

OTHER BOOKS FROM

Amherst Media®

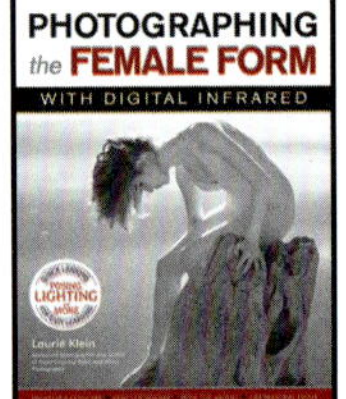

Photographing the Female Form with Digital Infrared

Laurie Klein shows you how to develop a concept, find locations, pose the model, and use natural light. *$27.95 list, 7.5x10, 128p, 180 color images, order no. 2021.*

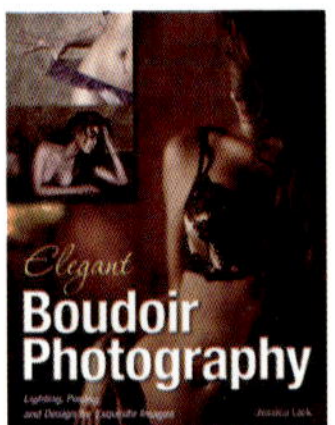

Elegant Boudoir Photography

Jessica Lark takes you through every step of the boudoir photography process, showing you how to work with clients and design images that are more engaging. *$27.95 list, 7.5x10, 128p, 230 color images, order no. 2014.*

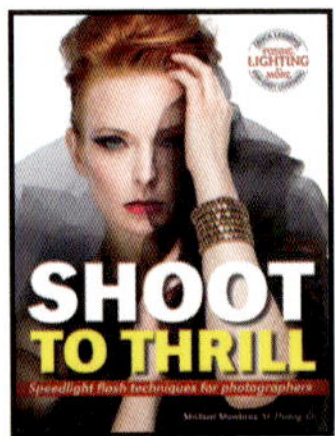

Shoot to Thrill

Acclaimed photographer Michael Mowbray shows how speedlights can rise to any photographic challenge—in the studio or on location. *$27.95 list, 7.5x10, 128p, 220 color images, order no. 2011.*

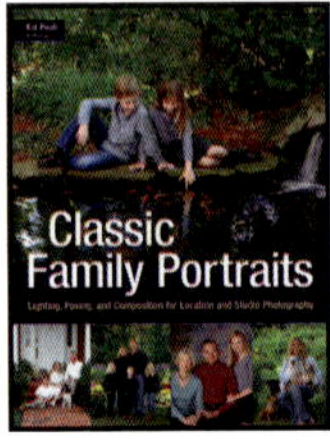

Classic Family Portraits

Ed Pedi walks you through the process of designing images that will stand the test of time. With these classic approaches, photos become instant heirlooms. *$27.95 list, 7.5x10, 128p, 180 color images, order no. 2010.*

Shaping Light

Glenn Rand and Tim Meyer explore the critical role of light modifiers in producing professional images of any subject, ensuring smart decisions at every turn. *$27.95 list, 7.5x10, 128p, 200 color images, order no. 2012.*

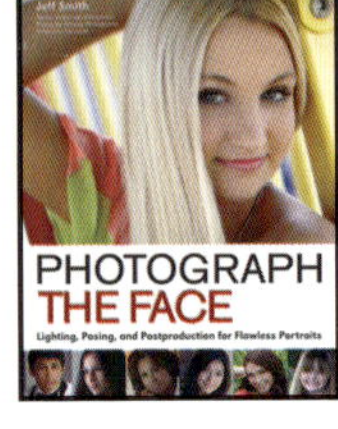

Photograph the Face

Acclaimed photographer and photo-educator Jeff Smith cuts to the core of great portraits, showing you how to make the subject's face look its very best. *$27.95 list, 7.5x10, 128p, 275 color images, order no. 2019.*

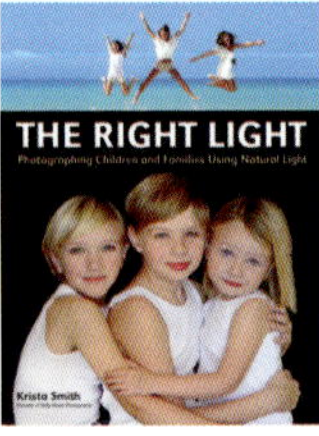

The Right Light

Working with couples, families, and kids, Krista Smith shows how using natural light can bring out the best in every subject—and result in highly marketable images. *$27.95 list, 7.5x10, 128p, 250 color images, order no. 2018.*

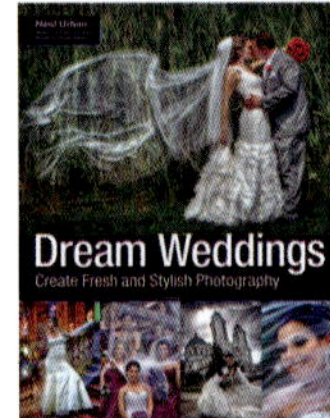

Dream Weddings

Celebrated wedding photographer Neal Urban shows you how to capture more powerful and dramatic images at every phase of the wedding photography process. *$27.95 list, 7.5x10, 128p, 190 color images, order no. 1996.*

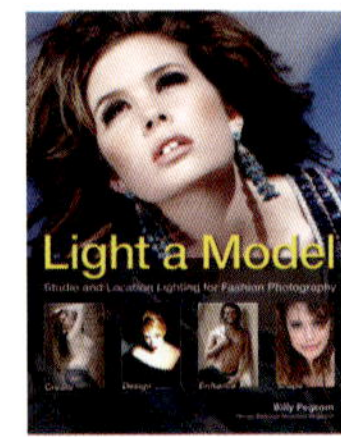
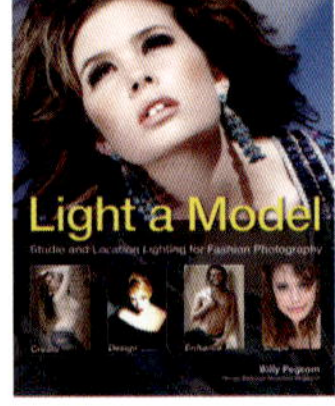

Light a Model

Billy Pegram shows you how to create edgy looks with lighting, helping you to create images of models (or other photo subjects) with a high-impact editorial style. *$27.95 list, 7.5x10, 128p, 190 color images, order no. 2016.*

MORE PHOTO BOOKS AVAILABLE

Amherst Media®
PO BOX 586
BUFFALO, NY 14226 USA

Individuals: If possible, purchase books from an Amherst Media retailer. To order directly, visit our web site, or call the toll-free number listed below to place your order. All major credit cards are accepted. *Dealers, distributors & colleges:* Write, call, or fax to place orders. For price information, contact Amherst Media or an Amherst Media sales representative. Net 30 days.

(800) 622-3278 or (716) 874-4450
Fax: (716) 874-4508

All prices, publication dates, and specifications are subject to change without notice. Prices are in U.S. dollars. Payment in U.S. funds only.

WWW.AMHERSTMEDIA.COM

FOR A COMPLETE LIST OF BOOKS AND ADDITIONAL INFORMATION